Greenhill Books

SAS Secret War

SAS Secret War
Operation Storm in the Middle East

MAJOR GENERAL TONY JEAPES CB OBE MC

Greenhill Books, London
Stackpole Books, Pennsylvania

Greenhill Books

SAS Secret War
Operation Storm in the Middle East

This edition first published 2005 by Greenhill Books
Lionel Leventhal Ltd, Park House
1 Russell Gardens, London NW11 9NN
and
Stackpole Books
5067 Ritter Road, Mechanicsburg, PA 17055, USA

SAS Secret War: Operation Storm in the Middle East was first published in 1980 as
SAS Operation Oman by William Kimber & Co. A revised edition was published
as *SAS Secret War* in 1996 by HarperCollins.

British Library Cataloguing-in Publication Data
Jeapes, Tony
SAS Secret War: Operation Storm in the Middle East
1. Jeapes, Tony
2. Great Britain. Army. Special Air Service Regiment, 22nd
3. Oman – History – Dhofar War, 1964–1976
I. Title
953.5'3

ISBN 1-85367-567-9

Library of Congress Cataloging-in Publication Data available

For more information on our books, please visit www.greenhillbooks.com,
email sales@greenhillbooks.com, or telephone us within the UK on 020 8458
6314. You can also write to us at the above London address.

Printed and bound in Great Britain by MPG Books Ltd, Bodmin, Cornwall

Nothing is here for tears, nothing to wail
Or knock the breast; no weakness, no contempt,
Dispraise or blame; nothing but well and fair,
And what may quiet us in a death so noble.

JOHN MILTON *Samson Agonistes*

CONTENTS

MAPS

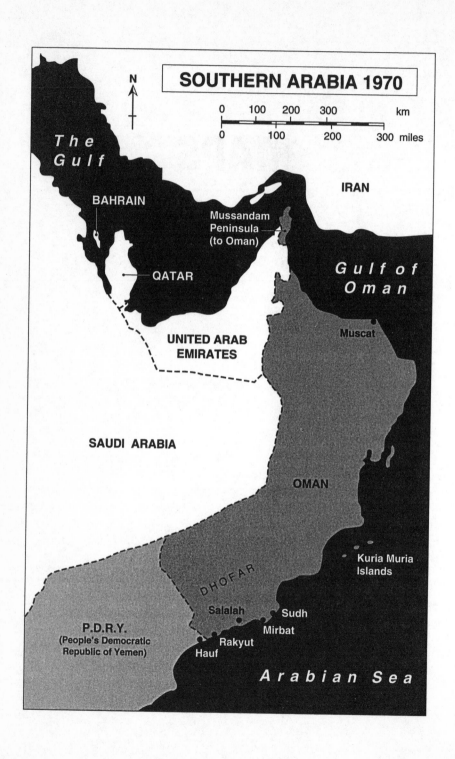

SOUTHERN ARABIA 1970

N

| 0 | 100 | 200 | 300 | km |

| 0 | 100 | 200 | 300 | miles |

The Gulf

BAHRAIN

Mussandam
Peninsula
(to Oman)

IRAN

Gulf of Oman

QATAR

Muscat

UNITED ARAB
EMIRATES

SAUDI ARABIA

OMAN

Kuria Muria
Islands

DHOFAR

Salalah   Sudh

Mirbat

P.D.R.Y.
(People's Democratic
Republic of Yemen)

Rakyut

Hauf

Arabian Sea

INTRODUCTION

The Dhofar War lasted ten years until 1976 and was probably the best conducted counter-insurgency campaign ever fought. It is still studied at the British Army Staff College as a model campaign, yet most people have never heard of it. The campaign took place under conditions of secrecy which today would probably be impossible to achieve. The Labour Government of the time was trying to disengage from Britain's residual colonial commitments, and to admit that some of its troops were engaged in the biggest campaign in which British troops had been involved since Korea would have been embarrassing. The previous ruler of Oman, Sultan Said Bin Taimur, had been autocratic and had not tolerated the press. The newly installed ruler, his son HM Sultan Qaboos, had come to the throne only one year before troops of the 22nd Special Air Service Regiment arrived in the theatre and had not yet carried out the reforms that he was later to put into effect. Press, radio and television commentators were just not allowed into the country. The campaign was conducted in a security blackout. For both the SAS and the British Government it was an ideal state of affairs.

The Dhofar War was a classic of its type, in which every principle of counter-insurgency operations built up over the previous fifty years in campaigns around the world by the British and other armies, often by trial and error, was employed. It was probably only the third campaign after Greece in the 1940s and Malaya in the 1950s and early 1960s to be won against a Communist armed insurrection. Also, it came at an important time after the defeat in Vietnam of the most powerful nation in the world when many people had become pessimistically resigned to the eventual victory of Communism. Perhaps the most important result of the Dhofar campaign was that it gave heart to democratic governments everywhere and exposed the 'historical inevitability' of victory for Communist -inspired revolutions as the myth it was.

This is the story of the part played in the war by the soldiers of 22 SAS. Their role was critical because they operated with the firqats, the bands of Dhofari ex-guerillas raised to fight for the Sultan and without whom the war could not have been won.

The 22nd SAS Regiment first came to the world's attention during the Prince's Gate siege of 1980 when they stormed the Iranian Embassy in London where a group of terrorists had taken hostages. Since then a flood of books on the Regiment has been produced, some of them accurate, some of them products of fertile and lurid imaginations which induce hoots of derision from the soldiers themselves. Until Prince's Gate, however, very little had been published about the SAS. Misunderstanding abounded, not only in the public mind, but in the minds of those who directed the Regiment's operations: the politicians and generals. This lack of knowledge had reached such a degree that it even affected the Regiment's employment. For example, for years it prevented the SAS from being deployed against the IRA in Northern Ireland because the Government considered their use to be too escalatory. And when members of the Regiment were first deployed, during my time in command, I was appalled by the lack of understanding of the Regiment's capabilities by those in high positions in the Province. The Regiment's insistence upon secrecy in all it did had become counter-productive.

Therefore, after I had handed over command of 22 SAS in 1977, I wrote the first draft of *SAS: Operation Oman*, as the book was then called. I did so while memory still served and facts could still be recovered, rather than leaving the account till later years, when things tend to be remembered as one wished them to be. It took three years to obtain security clearance from the Foreign and Commonwealth Office and the Ministry of Defence, and not until there was a change of government was permission given to publish the book in 1980. One of the conditions was that the names of all serving members of 22 SAS should be disguised. Many years have passed, but as some of these people are still in sensitive employment, and most ex-SAS prefer to remain anonymous anyway, I have not changed the names in this revised edition.

The Dhofar War began in the mid-1960s and ended in 1976. For most of the time, before 'arabisation' began towards the end of the war, all the senior command positions in the Sultan's Armed Forces were held by British officers. Many of the technical posts were filled by British servicemen, and Royal Engineers and Royal Artillerymen also played their part.

In scale the war was quite small: at most a division's worth of mainly Omani troops with Iranian and Jordanian allies and air and naval support on the one side; and about two thousand guerillas on the other. Casualties, too, were few and measured in hundreds rather than thousands. The aim was not to obliterate the enemy but to persuade them to join the Government side. It was first and last a war about people, a war in which both sides concentrated upon winning the support of the civilians of the Jebel Dhofar and which was won in the end by civil development. Military action was merely a means to that end.

Some may say I have not given enough credit to the Sultan's Armed Forces: if so it is not intentional. It was their war, with the SAS in the supporting role, but the SAF's story has been told elsewhere[1].

Though I was only one of many, my credentials for writing this book are perhaps as fair as most. I commanded the first full SAS squadron in Dhofar and raised the first of the firqats in 1971. I returned as SAS Commanding Officer in 1974 until the end of the war in 1976. Fortunately, during the period 1972-74, although there was plenty of fighting, the concept and strategy did not change. Indeed, my absence over those three years helped me to appreciate the enormous changes which took place in Dhofar during the campaign; from being a remote province of Oman garrisoned by a poorly equipped and overworked battalion, a country without roads or any modern amenities whatsoever, to a flourishing community, enjoying an explosion of building. Roads, hospitals, schools, mosques, farms: the landscape changed daily as civil progress moved hand-in-glove with military operations.

There are many people who played a key part in the campaign who are not even mentioned in this book: first, because too many names would merely serve to confuse, and second, because many of them would not want to be mentioned, particularly those in the intelligence world.

Every action was either witnessed by me or described to me personally by people who took part. Only in very minor details have I deviated deliberately and then only to make the story more easily understandable. Much of it came from my own diaries and I was surprised to find when I came to write the book how even a few months had dulled the memory and the sequence of events, although the events themselves were still burned into my mind. Actions I would have been prepared to swear took place in a certain order, on checking my diary I found took place differently. Yet, I was also surprised to find how vivid people's memories were, particularly at moments of drama or tragedy, when those who took part could remember the very words they had exchanged at the time. These I have tried to reproduce.

Being a personal story, albeit as far as I could make it a factual one, I have also tried to introduce some of the atmosphere of the campaign. Only after several chapters had been written, did I realise how we took for granted so many words outside the normal vocabulary. The campaign developed a patois of its own. This I have used as sparingly as possible and have added a glossary of those words whose meanings are not self-evident: for example, the SAS did not always talk of the firqats, they called them the firkins or the firks or even, in moments of stress, both. The SAS were seldom called the SAS; instead they were known as the Bat, from the initials of British Army Training Team or BATT, as the Government insisted they were called. Even at the end of the war when I had two Dhofaris to dinner in Hereford, they were surprised to find that I did not command the Bat Regiment, but the SAS. SAS meant nothing to them.

Similarly, I have tried to reproduce the SAS soldiers' way of speaking. 'Boss' is still more commonly used than 'Sir.' 'Sir' is used towards all officers. 'Boss' is a term reserved for their own and implies affection, as well as respect. In return, an SAS officer often uses a soldier's first name or nickname, a custom which has grown up over the years and comes from living together in small parties for weeks or sometimes months at a time. An SAS officer shares the same conditions and discomforts as his men: he has no batman. Indeed, if the radio operator is busy, it may be the officer who cooks him his meal or puts up his 'basha' (shelter). A relationship develops like that between a commanding officer and his officers in the rest of the Army. A commanding officer will invariably address his officers by their first names, whereas they would not dream of doing so in return. Such a relationship between officer and soldier could of course only exist among men of the highest quality who would not take advantage of it.

Despite some newspaper reports and popular fiction, the SAS are first second and last, soldiers. They volunteer from all over the Army and face a stiff physical and mental selection course. Those few who pass have to sacrifice rank to begin at the bottom of the scale as SAS troopers, no matter what rank they may hold in their parent units. At the time of the Dhofar War they also sacrificed pay, but thankfully this has now been remedied and the SAS soldier is rightly the highest paid soldier in the Army. Few very young men seem to have either the physical endurance or the mental maturity necessary to pass the selection course, so the average SAS soldier is in his mid- to late twenties when he joins, far removed in age and outlook from the eighteen and nineteen year- olds of normal units. I need hardly say that the privilege of serving with a squadron of such men is exceeded only by that of commanding a regiment of them, and it is to the soldiers of 22 SAS who gave their lives and health to ensure that the free world's oil continued to flow, and still does so, that this book is dedicated.

Notes
1 *We Won a War.* John Akehurst. Michael Russell Ltd.

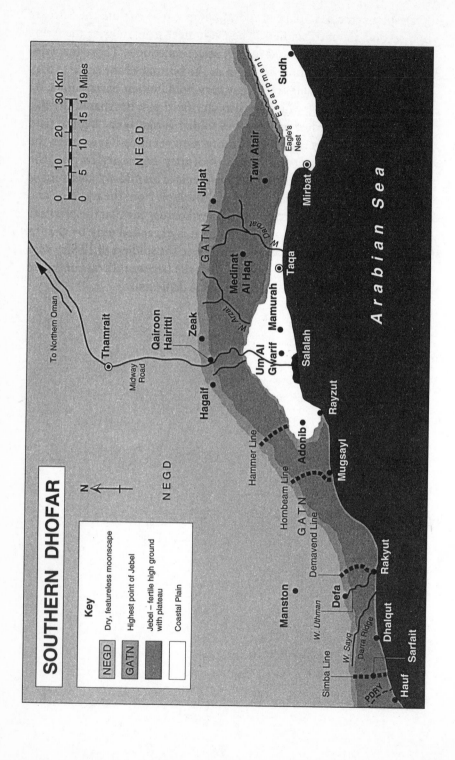

SOUTHERN DHOFAR

Key

NEGD — Dry, featureless moonscape

GATN — Highest point of Jebel

Jebel — fertile high ground with plateau

Coastal Plain

N

NEGD

NEGD

GATN

GATN

0   5   10   15   19 Miles
0   10   20   30 Km

To Northern Oman

Thamrait

Midway Road

Qairoon Hairitti

Zeak

Hagaif

Jibjat

Tawi Atair

Medinat Al Haq

Eagle's Nest

W. Darbat

Escarpment

Sudh

Mirbat

Taqa

Mamurah

W. Arzat

Um/Al Gwarif

Salalah

Rayzut

Arabian Sea

Adonib

Mugsayl

Hammer Line

Hornbeam Line

Demavend Line

Manston

Defa

W. Uthman

W. Sayq

Simba Line

Darra Ridge

Rakyut

Dhalqut

Hauf

Sarfait

PDRY

ONE

REBELLION

The hand on my shoulder shook me awake. I took the cardboard cup of coffee and, with bleary eyes, watched the retreating form of the bulky RAF quartermaster. Into my mind flashed an airline poster that had caught my eye back in England. It had shown a pretty air hostess with a dazzling smile, and read: 'For some people there is only one airline.' I reflected ruefully that for me it was the RAF.

I eased myself around in the uncomfortable parachute seat and looked out of the window. The sky was as blue as cobalt, without a cloud in sight. Below, a high-prowed Arab boom ploughed its way steadily north-eastwards through the sea of aquamarine towards Muscat, or possibly further still, into the Gulf and Bahrain or Abu Dhabi, leaving the furrow of its wake in a lance-straight line behind it.

In less than two hours the aircraft would land at Salalah, the capital of Dhofar. I shut my eyes and relaxed, trying to pull together in my mind what I knew about the place. It was quite a lot.

For a year previously I had known this day would come sooner or later. The Dhofar War was going so badly that it was only a matter of time before the SAS would find themselves there, and I had trained my squadron hard, without telling them why, to fight in mountain and bush. And I knew they were good. It was disappointing when the first SAS troop to be sent to Dhofar in 1970 had come from another squadron, but that did not matter now. At least it had meant that I spent Christmas at home with Jenny and the children. I would not see them again for several months.

I tried to recall how many hours I must have spent in that little isolation room in the Kremlin, the Regiment's ironic name for its headquarters, devouring all I could find on Dhofar, not just the military

17

reports but the journeys of Bertram Thomas, Wilfred Thesiger, Wendell Phillips, anyone who had visited Dhofar, and there were not many of them.

Dhofar was still a wild and unknown place. The final brief from Lieutenant Colonel Johnny Watts, the Commanding Officer, only two days ago, was still vivid in my memory. We had served together in Oman before in the Jebel Akhdar campaign of 1958–9 when he had been a squadron commander of the same squadron I was now commanding and I had been a troop commander in another squadron. It had been a short, sharp campaign. The Imam, the religious leader of the tribes of the Interior of Oman, called Ghalib Bin Ali, and his brother Talib had raised the Beni Hina tribe in revolt against the old sultan, Said Bin Taimur.

Britain has had a treaty of friendship with the Sultan of Muscat since 1798, when the sultan of the time granted the East India Company commercial rights and received in exchange the protection of the Royal Navy. Since Muscat was a sea-going nation with possessions in East Africa, Zanzibar, Socotra and Baluchistan, and piracy had become almost a way of life, the treaty did much to make the seas a safer place for trade. So it was natural for Said to ask Britain for help and, after a short campaign by his Armed Forces with help from a British regiment, the rebels fled to join the Beni Riyam tribe under their paramount sheikh, Suleiman Bin Himyar, on the great Green Mountain.

The Jebel Akhdar rose straight out of the desert to a height of seven thousand feet and there were only a certain number of routes up it. These were, of course, guarded, and it took a month of probing and skirmishing until an unguarded route was found. The SAS learnt to respect their enemy and some fierce little battles were fought, in which three SAS soldiers were killed and about twenty to thirty enemy. Then, after a feint squadron night attack in the north to draw the enemy's attention and reserves in that direction, the two squadrons of SAS climbed the jebel in one night from the south. It was a hard, long climb and only just accomplished. The leading troops dropped their bergen rucksacks and pushed on, carrying only their rifles and belt equipment to reach the crest just at first light. Had the squadrons been caught in the low ground still climbing up those bare slopes at dawn, it might have been a very different story. As it was, there was little opposition. My own troop accounted for four who tried to hold us up; one did a spectacular Hollywood-style death dive over a sheer cliff. Another troop killed the crew of a heavy machine-gun in a cave with hand grenades; but that was all. Once the squadrons had consolidated on top and had taken a parachute re-supply of water and ammunition, the rebels gave up and the three leaders fled for shelter to Saudi Arabia.

Yet that was a long time ago and a very different campaign. The enemy then were armed with weapons from the Second World War, or even old Boer War Martini-Henrys; this enemy were armed with the latest Chinese and Soviet bloc automatic weapons. That war had taken us six weeks to crack: this one, had we known it, was to take six years.

The tone of the aircraft's engines changed a fraction and I knew we had reached cruising height, leaving Masirah Island far behind. I reached into my bag and took out, once again, the brief I had written for myself. For the tenth time I opened it and began to read.

'Dhofar is the southern province of Oman, bordering on its north with Saudi Arabia and to the west with the People's Democratic Republic of Yemen (PDRY). Dhofar is separated from Northern Oman by a desert four hundred miles wide with the result that there are major differences of culture and social background between the two. Indeed the Dhofaris are not true Arabs at all. They are believed by some to have originated in Ethiopia, and their facial features certainly resemble Ethiopians or Somalis more than the true Arabs of the north. Like the Somalis too, Dhofaris take fierce pride in their herds of cattle; they build round houses of stone and straw which strongly resemble Somali manyattas; one even sees old men leaning on a staff, standing on one leg with the sole of the other foot resting against the inside of the knee, a typical Somali stance. Their language is called Jebeli, an unwritten language quite different from Arabic and said to owe its origins to Aramaic. Nonetheless, Dhofar is part of Oman, and Oman's northern tip dominates the Strait of Hormuz, through which sail tankers holding the major part of the Free World's oil. Clearly it would be disastrous if Oman should ever get a government hostile to the Free World.'

Although I had only set foot in Dhofar once before, and had not been allowed outside the wire perimeter of the RAF base just north of the province's capital at Salalah, I remembered leaning against the wire, staring, fascinated, at the distant dark green hills. I had seen then that it was a country of geographical extremes. Salalah itself rested on the sea, but a great fertile plain in the shape of a half moon, 25 miles long by, at its widest, seven miles deep stretched to the foothills of the jebel massif. It had been the granary of Arabia in days gone by and it was hard to believe now that its produce had helped to feed the British Army of Mesopotamia in the First World War. Now it was just a great bare dusty plain dotted with large bushes; each one all that remained to mark the site of a well in bygone days. From an aircraft even the edges of the old fields could be plainly seen, but under Sultan Said Bin Taimur agriculture had been not only discouraged but frequently banned, even to the extent of destroying wells. I read on:

> 'Inland from the Salalah Plain, parallel with the coast and stretching for a 150 miles down to the border with PDRY, runs the jebel massif and it too varies widely. As mountains go, it is not very high – 3000 feet at most – but it rises steeply from the plain to a plateau quite narrow in the east and west, but some nine miles wide in the centre. In the extreme east you find scant soil, mainly limestone rock formed into broken stony ground with little water or vegetation. However, as you move westwards, but still in the Eastern Area, so patches of red soil begin to appear and with it scrub and scraps of grass. In the centre of the Eastern Area the soil becomes richer and the plateau proper begins.'

The lushness of the plateau seemed totally incongruous in Arabia. It exists as a result of the rains caused by the south-west monsoon, the *khareef*, which covers the plateau with cloud and mist from June to September. In the Central Area you could easily think you were on Salisbury Plain. Grass grows thick and succulent, and great rolling downs stretch as far as the watershed to the north. Its bright green grass, in places four feet high, and its brilliant flowers of pink, white and yellow last for a month or two; gradually the colour dies away to the dried ochre the plateau assumes for most of the year. But there is always plenty of grass for the cattle or for thatching the Jebeli houses.

What made the jebel massif totally different from any British countryside, however, were the wadis which run down to the plain like great gashes and stretch for thousands of yards. They begin in the north as mere indentations, but quickly fall away into steep re-entrants and glens filled with thick bush. This bush provided excellent grazing for camels, but it would slow down a man to a snail's pace if he tried to move off the established paths. Suddenly the long-range, open warfare of the plateau would change to the tactics of the jungle, where visibility is down to a few yards and the first man to shoot usually wins:

'As the wadis run further southwards, they become deeper and wider until at the entrance to the plain they might be several hundred yards across, with great precipitous flanks rising sharply to the plateau. The wadi bottoms have formed natural routes for centuries. Generally speaking, they are best for north-south movement, but east-west finger wadis offer easy routes up to the plateau, across it and down to the next major wadi.'

But perhaps the most important feature of the wadis was that they contained the life-giving water. I had lived in the desert and I knew well the all-embracing importance of water, beside which anything else – gold, comfort, warmth, even food – is unimportant. Without water, you die.

I read on:

'The wadis contain clear, sweet pools set under rocks in shady glades or in natural waterholes often developed into tanks with cement and stones by the jebelis, or even in places in flowing streams.'

Some of these wadis, like the great Wadi Darbat, the Wadi Arzat or Wadi Nahiz, I knew from my reading were places of great beauty and peace, where you could sit in the cool shade and wash your soul listening to the sounds of the birds or watch the brightly coloured butterflies and dragonflies flitting among the deep grass and the shrubs, or pick and eat the fruit from the great fig trees. Delightful as all this appeared, however, it could not help the Jebeli herdsmen whose cattle had to spend the day grazing on the plateau and then spend up to several hours getting down to the water to drink, before returning to the high ground again to be shut away for the night:

'Life revolves around water. After the *khareef*, the small waterholes and dips in the rocks up on the plateau itself fill and the cattle can use these, but as the water dries up, the herdsmen have to move their families and herds down into the wadis, leaving their houses on the plateau to live in caves in the wadi sides. Then comes the period of the greatest misery, but at the same time that of greatest promise, as the *khareef* descends. Water begins to return to the waterholes, but the continual rain and mist and the swarms of mosquitoes make living wretched. The red soil turns into mud, and movement up or down hill becomes difficult at best and in many places impossibly dangerous. The Jebelis remain huddled in their caves growing thin from shortage of food, developing consumption from the damp and conjunctivitis from the continuous smoke of their fires, until at last the *khareef* begins to lift and they can move back to the plateau to enjoy the luxury the monsoon has brought, the time of fat, and the beginning of the whole cycle yet again.

'As you go further west towards the border with PDRY, the plateau disappears altogether and the jebel becomes a series of escarpments covered with grass and camel bush, running down to the sea. There is less vegetation in the wadis and the wadis themselves become more sheer and stark with huge precipices and few ways up or down.

'All along the top of the plateau at the highest point of the jebel runs the *gatn,* the watershed, an uninteresting flat-land of small rocks and bushes on the edge of the khareef mist and so still deriving some moisture from it. Being so flat, it makes for easy movement from one end of the jebel to the other, particularly for vehicles, and SAF already use a number of tracks along it. At intervals too, old airstrips are still just identifiable, some from past SAF operations, others used by civilian companies exploring for oil and minerals. Rumours of oil still circulate, but nothing has been announced officially.

'Beyond the *gatn* lies the *negd,* a dry, pastureless, featureless moon country of shingle and small rocks, split by boulder-strewn and sand-filled wadis, quite deep where they begin, although nothing like the great wadis of the jebel. They become shallower, with wide flat bottoms, as they run north until they run out into a great gravel plain where only a practised eye can tell, by the occasional stunted thorn scrub, that they are still wadis, and finally disappear into the sand sea of the Empty Quarter.'

Although apparently not very attractive to look at, I reflected, militarily the *negd* could be important. The boulders were too large and the ground too broken to allow vehicles to move freely across it, that is until it became the great gravel plain of farther north, but there were a number of good north-south routes already, and several more which could be developed with engineer effort. This meant that we could reach the jebel from the north across the open country which best suited our long -range weapons and where the adoo's (enemy's) local knowledge of paths and the lie of the land was less important. We could move with armour and artillery to support us and we could see what we were shooting at. On the other hand, of course, the adoo could see us too, but from less commanding positions than if we approached from the south.

The war was concerned, I knew, mainly with the jebel and *gatn* and spilt over only occasionally into the beginning of the *negd*, but should it spread further into the *negd* or into the desert itself, we were better equipped and trained than most to deal with it. The SAS Landrover was designed for desert warfare and at that time was probably the best vehicle in the world for such operations. My squadron had plenty of experience in the desert; indeed recently a troop had been the first ever to cross the great deserts of Iran, the Dasht-i-Kavir and the Dasht-i-Lut, from end to end.

But there would be no scope for using our Landrovers for some time. Loaded with a hundred gallons of petrol, they would simply turn into fireballs if they hit a mine, and the few roads that existed in Dhofar were all known to be mined. In any case, there were only two major roads. The coast road, which ran from one side of the plain to the other – from the port of Rayzut in the west to Mirbat in the east – was continually mined. Patrols cleared it regularly between Salalah and Rayzut, but east of Salalah it was not used at all. Convoys driving to Taqa, the first town east of Salalah, were either escorted by armoured cars across the open plain or, if the tide was right, along the beach.

The other road was the main graded but unmetalled road which joined Dhofar with Northern Oman. It began at Salalah and made its tortuous way up into the jebel and across the plateau due north of Salalah to the derelict oil exploration camp of Midway at Thamrait, 50 miles out in the negd; from here the road turned north-east towards Northern Oman. The part where it crossed the jebel had long been closed by the adoo.

I knew worryingly little about the adoo. But, then, nobody appeared to know very much. They were good fighters, that I certainly knew. They had cleared SAF off the jebel and it was over a year since SAF had spent more than 24 hours up there. The pattern of SAF operations seemed to be to move by night in up to a battalion's strength, on to the high ground, build sangars and wait for the enemy to attack. A long-range battle would ensue during the day, usually with few casualties on either side, and the SAF would withdraw at last light with honour satisfied.

I had plenty of evidence as to the adoo's fighting capability. They were brave men, not afraid to push home an attack if SAF made a blunder. They were skilful at using ground to provide covered approaches and their brown skins and dull clothing gave them natural camouflage. Whereas the SAF tended to stay in one place, the adoo were constantly moving, probing the SAF flanks, working around them to cut off their withdrawal, and using every dip and fold of the ground to advantage.

Whereas SAF, too, were still largely armed with the old .303 bolt-action British Enfield rifle and only just beginning to re-equip with automatic FNs, the hard-core adoo all had modern, fully automatic Soviet Kalashnikov assault rifles and machine guns, and even the soft-core had Simonov semi-automatics. Nor did their weapons stop at small arms. The Chinese 82-mm mortar, for instance, is not only very effective, but cleverly designed too. It will fire the bombs of the British 81-mm mortar besides its own, whereas Chinese bombs will not fit into the British barrel. The 60-mm mortar is smaller, but outranges by far its British equivalent. I read, too, that they were soon expected to take delivery of 75-mm and 82-mm recoilless guns, able to place a 6.5 kilogram shell 4.5 miles away.

Fortunately, not even these could reach Salalah town from the safety of the jebel, or worse, the airfield of RAF Salalah with its parked Strikemaster fighters, transport planes and helicopters:

'The adoo move out from the cover of their hills by night on to the plain until they are within range, fire off some shells or bombs and then scurry off back into the shelter of the jebel before the SAF artillery can range in on them. The adoo patrol will come out one night and set up the heavy base plate position, covering the plate itself with sand. The next night they return with the barrel and bipod and the exact amount of bombs to be fired. They fire them off, dismantle the mortar, kick sand over the baseplate, which can be used another night, and flee. By the time the SAF shells are bursting around the firing position the crew are well into the shelter of the jebel. Feeling very pleased with a good night's work no doubt. And well they might.'

I had already developed a sneaking respect for the adoo and the more I read of the old sultan's reign, the more that respect began to develop into sympathy. Sultan Said Bin Taimur must have been a remarkable man. On the one hand, he clearly inspired respect and even love amongst his advisers and those close to him, and on the other hand, he kept his country in the Middle Ages by his parsimony and feudal system of government. He would have argued that he did not have the money to spend, but even when oil was finally discovered in Oman, he still refused to spend it until he had the money in hand. He appears to have distrusted totally any form of advanced budgeting. Those who knew him say he was well-meaning, but, well-meaning or not, the facts are that in Dhofar, as in the rest of his kingdom, there were no schools, no hospitals, no roads, and no developed water resources of any kind. Even attempts at self-help were frustrated. When a group of villagers concentrated their finances to buy a tractor, they were forbidden to do so. 'It would make others restless,' said Said:

'Like highlanders all over the world, the Dhofaris are an independently minded people and many of the young men, seeing no future in Dhofar, left the country to seek their fortunes abroad. Most went to Saudi Arabia, Kuwait, Qatar and Bahrain, where they saw for the first time the advantages money can provide, not only in terms of material goods, but in health and education. Others joined the Trucial Oman Scouts or the armies of the Gulf States, where they quickly earned reputations as first-rate soldiers and where they gained military experience which was to stand them in good stead on the Jebel Dhofar. Yet others went across the border into PDRY to attend the schools in Al Ghayda and Hauf.

'In 1962 the flag of rebellion was raised. It seems to have been a small enough rebellion to begin with: an oil exploration truck was mined in the *negd*, a few sniping shots were taken at long range at SAF patrols, but the SAF, at this stage only one battalion in Dhofar, could go where they wanted anywhere on the jebel and most of the rebels' time was spent on the run. Nonetheless, gradually they persuaded more people to join them and they built up a medley of

25

old weapons to arm themselves with.

'A favourite pastime was to blow up the well at Ayn Arzat, which supplied water to the Sultan's gardens at Mamurah along a long concrete channel. Said took great pride in his gardens and sent troops up the Midway Road on punitive raids, presumably because the Midway Road was the easiest way up on to the jebel.'

The tribes there can have had nothing to do with blowing up Ayn Arzat, I reflected, as that was in a totally different tribal area. I could see it all so clearly – the mistake which has happened so often in revolutionary wars the world over – angry troops unable to get to grips with wily guerillas, venting their frustration on the civilian population. There would be no question of atrocities, but you can antagonise people without committing atrocities, simply by making life unnecessarily uncomfortable and by punishing them for things they have not done:

'These punitive operations had the predictable result of recruiting still more Dhofaris to the rebels' cause until a political party was formed, calling itself the Dhofar Liberation Front. It appears to have been a party motivated by high ideals and mainly pledged to bringing modernisation to Dhofar. Its slogan was 'Dhofar for the Dhofaris', not an unreasonable motto on the face of it. In tone, although opposing sultanic rule, it was conservative, maintaining the tribal structure and encouraging the traditional religion.

'Meanwhile, however, over the border in PDRY, a political party was developing with very different aims, the People's Front for the Liberation of the Occupied Arabian Gulf (PFLOAG).(Later, after Britain's total military withdrawal from the Gulf they were to drop the Occupied Arabian part and change their name to the People's Front for the Liberation of Oman (PFLO)).

'PFLOAG is strongly Communist and received heavy backing from the Chinese and, later, Soviet consulates in Aden in the form of arms, money and training. Soon PFLOAG made overtures to the DLF and suggested that the two should join together against the common enemy. The DLF were, to begin with, lukewarm about the suggestion. They had no time for those who said there was no God, but finally, seduced by the money and the superior weapons PFLOAG could offer, they agreed. The result was a foregone conclusion. The DLF traditionalists were no match for the highly organised, energetic and well-motivated Communists. Within a short time, cells were established throughout the jebel, discussion groups and Communist propaganda indoctrinated the minds of the Jebelis and the Communists took over control. The next phase was to break down the tribal structure by fear, persuasion and coercion. Tribal elders and sheikhs were killed, often with extreme cruelty. In the west, five elderly sheikhs were pushed over a cliff 450 feet high. At Dhalqut the sheikh and his sons were stood against the wall of their house and machine-gunned. Children were forcibly removed from their parents to be sent to school in PDRY, and young men were sent to China and Russia for training in guerilla warfare. By 1970, PFLOAG controlled the entire jebel. Today, the Sultan's sway holds only in Salalah and, to a lesser degree, in the coastal towns of Taqa and Mirbat, which the adoo tolerate as sources of re-supply for food and equipment and even as rest centres for their fighters from the jebel.'

I put down the brief, eased my cramped buttocks, then sat back and forced my mind to concentrate upon what other facts I knew.

Some say that, with the coming of oil Sultan Bin Taimur would have eventually got around to modernising the country. Perhaps, but he was not allowed the time. Waiting in the wings was the man who was to liberate his country and lead it out of the Middle Ages into the 20th century.

I could not find the exact date Sultan Said Bin Taimur married his second wife, but it was late in 1939 or early 1940. The marriage had a stormy start in that it nearly did not take place at all. The lovely young Mizoon was the daughter of Sheikh Ahmed Ali of the powerful Bait Ma'asheni tribe of eastern Dhofar. The Bait Ma'asheni did not think the marriage settlement was enough, so they seized the Sultan's betrothed and carried her away up into the jebel. A tribe from the Central Area, the Bait Tabook, who had no love for the Ma'asheni anyway, gave chase, caught up with the Ma'asheni raiding party and forced them to return with the girl to Salalah. The wedding took place with the usual rejoicing and, on 18th November 1940, Mizoon gave birth to Said's only son, Qaboos.

Said found the cool breezes of Salalah, the shade of the groves of coconut palms and the greenery of his gardens particularly attractive after the glaring heat of Muscat and, as his reign progressed, spent more and more time in his palace on the Salalah waterfront. The palace was built more for defence than for luxury, with the high windowless walls and reinforced gates of a fortress. They were prudent precautions. Said's brother, Sayyid Fahr, now the Deputy Minister of Defence (the Sultan is the Minister) later recalled to me vividly his recollections as a boy, as the brothers gazed awe-struck from the walls at crowds of milling Dhofari tribesmen, most stripped to the waist, wearing only their futas, a sort of kilt dyed with indigo, stamping their feet, shouting, dancing to the beat of drums till their bodies shone with sweat, waving their swords in the air, all to express their pleasure or displeasure at one or other of his father's, the Sultan's directives. It must have been a terrifying display and no doubt made a great impression on Said's young mind. And the happy times, too, when he rode for miles along the coast on his camel, never once leaving the shade of the great groves of palms. Perhaps incidents like these make it easier to understand Said's distrust of the mountain men when he himself came to the throne, having seized power from his father.

Qaboos was well educated, as befitted the son of a sultan, first in Salalah by an old Arab scholar, who is still an adviser to him in moral matters, and later privately in Britain. Any sultan who hoped to control the heterogeneous warrior tribes of Oman, particularly Dhofar, had to be a warrior himself, so Qaboos was sent to the Royal Military Academy Sandhurst and was then commissioned into a British regiment, the Cameronians, as a second lieutenant. Finally, he was sent on a grand tour of Britain, sitting on city councils, watching committees at work, visiting industry and familiarising himself with all the administrative paraphernalia of a modern state. Having completed his military training and rounded off his education, Qaboos returned to Oman ready to take up the reins of responsibility as heir apparent

He was immediately committed to virtual house arrest in Salalah. He was surrounded with servants and with the comforts befitting his rank, but was totally forbidden to take any part in affairs of State. His mail in and out was censored. He had become too westernised, declared Said, and his mind was too full of dangerous liberal ideals. He was to be given intensive instruction in the Koran. No doubt Said also remembered how he had overthrown his own father and he was taking no chances with this able and popular prince.

For seven years, in an extraordinary example of filial duty, the frustrated, bored Qaboos accepted his lot. But it was an impossible situation and eventually, exasperated by the decline in his country's standard of living, which was elementary at the best of times, the total lack of any form of material or social progress, and his father's reluctance to spend, or even to plan to spend his developing oil revenues, Qaboos decided to act.

Said dropped his guard. Qaboos's isolation was not complete enough and on 23rd July 1970, aided by the young Sheikh Baraik Bin Hamood, he deposed his father in a palace *coup d'état*. It was meant to be bloodless and in the event nobody was killed, but Sultan Said was not a man to give in easily. Although deserted by most of his followers, he put up a last desperate stand with his Mauser automatic pistol. Bullets cracked and whined down the dark corridors of the palace. Baraik, trying to run from one doorway to another was hit in the thigh, but Said had exhausted his magazine and fumbling to reload it – no doubt unsteadily and in a state of shock – he finished the argument by shooting himself through the foot.

From then on he took it calmly enough. He signed the declaration of abdication and, after some medical treatment, was flown to London by jet airliner, where he lived in great comfort provided by his son until he died in 1972. It is said that whenever anyone mentioned Oman to him, he roared with laughter.

Within days Qaboos had announced his first plans for the development of Oman and, as expected, they were greeted with delight and relief. People danced in the streets, bonfires lit the dingy alleyways of Salalah until well into the night and everyone who was anyone gave a feast. A general amnesty was declared and a number of the older members of the DLF came down off the jebel to take advantage of it. But it had little effect on the hard-core. They wanted to see proof first.

However, the atmosphere on the jebel had changed. By now the high-handed arrogant behaviour of the Communists and the atrocities they had committed had antagonised many people. Fathers were forced to offer their daughters to the young fighters as their duty to the Front. Old men had their noses cut off and were blinded by red hot knives for refusing to deny their God. Suspicions that PFLOAG was attempting to take over the DLF altogether began to deepen until on 12th September, when the counter-revolution took place. PFLOAG ordered the disarming of the DLF, but, although surrounded, the hard-core members of the old DLF in the Eastern Area refused to co-operate. A battle took place, and 24 of the best fighters in the East, led by the second-in-command of the Eastern Area, Salim Mubarak, came off the jebel and surrendered to the Sultan.

★ ★ ★

It was quite evident that Qaboos had seized power in the nick of time, but the question was whether or not he would be allowed time for his plans to mature. Two things were clear: first, that the answer to the insurgency lay in civil development, and second, that the answer had to be found by the Omanis themselves. Vietnam had shown that there is no future for a foreign army of intervention in a national revolutionary war. Nonetheless, the new Sultan needed all the friends he had. His army was losing the war. It needed expanding, re-equipping and re-training if it was to turn the tide on the enemy. It was with this in mind that Lieutenant Colonel Watts and his operations officer had been sent to Oman to see what help was needed. How could SAF be helped to help themselves? Until the jebel had been at least partially cleared of enemy, any plans for civil development could not even begin.

The first encouraging point for Watts was that the commander of the Sultan's Armed Forces (CSAF), Brigadier John Graham, was well aware of his troops' deficiencies and was doing all he could to increase his force's strength, procure modern weapons for them and train them properly. He asked for a training team straight away to prepare the next battalion from the north to go to Dhofar, in tactics and fighting in bush country. In Dhofar itself, Commander Dhofar then a lieutenant colonel, also offered Watts every assistance. But there was a marked attitude of mind amongst many of the junior officers in Dhofar which the SAS had seen before in other places.

The battalion in Dhofar had had a hard time. They were restricted in where they could go, they had been driven off the jebel, they were surrounded by mines, they were taking casualties, and the enemy offered no tangible target, nothing on which the SAF could bring their weaponry to bear. Yet above them was the massive jebel, glowering down on them, dominating them 24 hours a day, 365 days a year. There were enemy eyes up there 'watching every move you made'. There seemed no respite from it.

SAS soldiers called it 'jebelitis' but jebel-phobia, fear of the jebel, would be more accurate. They had seen the same sense of defeatism in the Jebel Akhdar campaign. Then they had been told stories by old soldiers on the plain, which in the event proved to be absolutely wrong, that the jebel was unclimbable by Europeans, the top covered in a veritable paradise of fruit and vegetables, and you could wander through leafy glades plucking limes as you went. The SAS proved that the jebel certainly was not unclimbable and that, although there was fruit on the top, it was nothing like the description.

Now the stories were different, but the phobia was the same. Time and again the SAS were told that movement on the jebel during the monsoon was impossible. Even the cleated soles of British Army boots could find no grip. It was impossible to stand up on the slippery rocks and fluid mud, let alone walk.

If the war was to be won, SAF must get back up the jebel and stay up there, monsoon or no monsoon. The problem was, how? The population on the jebel were actively hostile, so that even if SAF managed to establish a position, they would be surrounded by enemy territory. A war in Dhofar had to be won with the help of Dhofaris, but as far as the jebelis were concerned SAF was an army of occupation. Most of its officers were British, either seconded from the British Army or 'on contract'. It would be quite wrong, however, to equate contract officers with the mercenaries, who had achieved such notoriety in Zaire and Angola. Most of the Sultan's officers were ex-regular British commissioned or non-commissioned officers serving in a properly disciplined force. Their duties were identical to the seconded officers, the only difference being that they were paid by the Sultan, not by the British Government.

There were a few Arab and Baluch officers also, but the rank and file were almost entirely Baluch or Northern Omani Arab. For years a close relationship existed between Baluchistan and Oman, indeed part of Baluchistan had until quite recently belonged to Oman. As the British knew well, Baluchis were hardy and brave and made fine soldiers. They took to discipline more easily than many Arabs and, being a long way from home, were less inclined to go absent without leave. In turn, the wages they could get in the service of the Sultan were far greater than at home and, after their service was finished, they could return as reasonably well-off men. It was a convenient arrangement for both sides, but since most Baluchis could not speak Arabic, let alone Jebeli, they could not even converse with the people of Dhofar. Northern Omanis were considered better, but nonetheless foreigners still, whereas the British, although mostly respected, were the most foreign of all; even their skins were the wrong colour. The Arab considers himself to be a white man; Europeans are said to be red. Somehow the fighting men of Dhofar had to be recruited to fight for the Sultan. Salim Mubarak's 20 men would be a start, but many more than that would be needed.

Life was going to be much better under the new Sultan than under his father or any form of government the Communists were likely to produce. People had only to look at the shambles the Communists had made of PDRY since the British left Aden and the Hadramaut to see that. But somehow the people had to be told the truth of what was already beginning to happen for their benefit, and what was planned in the future for them. Somehow the stream of lies and abuse being broadcast from Radio Aden had to be countered. In short, there was a need to broadcast to the people information on the progress of civil development. An aggressive information service was necessary.

However, it was one thing to tell the people what was about to happen; they would want to be shown too. Salalah was no problem. Already roads and buildings were being planned and contractors were bringing in their plant and equipment in preparation. The first school had begun, a hospital was opening, the promise of progress was there for all to see. But at Taqa and Mirbat there was nothing, and it would not be until SAF were firmly secure on the jebel that any civil development could even begin on the jebel itself, There had to be some way to persuade the people that they would be better off under the new regime, rather than the old.

Two things these people valued before all else; their health and the health of their animals. The SAS could do little about the latter from their own resources, but they were the ideal unit for the former. In general war, the SAS operate far behind the enemy lines, well out of range of the Army's medical system, so they have to be medically self-reliant. And since they operate often in very small patrols, they have a large number of men highly trained in medical aid, far more and to a much higher standard than any other unit in the British Army.

Watts had finished his assessment. He recommended that the SAS contribution to the campaign, codenamed Operation Storm by the Ministry of Defence, should be on 'five fronts':

1. An intelligence cell
2. An information team
3. A medical officer supported by SAS medics

4. A veterinary officer

5. When possible, the raising of Dhofari soldiers to fight for the Sultan.

It was stressed, however, that these were stop-gap measures to plug holes until the Omani Government could provide its own people to do these tasks. The short-term aim was to bring immediate relief to the people. The medium-term aim was to train Omanis to take over these measures and then to hand over to them. The long-term solution, however, was in the hands of the Omani Government: to better the lot of the Dhofari people by the development of resources and the construction of roads, wells, schools, clinics, mosques – everything that goes to make up a modern state. Military operations must simply be a means to that end.

TWO

THE FIRQAT SALAHADIN

I stumbled off the aircraft steps on to the tarmac and looked up quickly to see if I was behind an engine exhaust, but the heat continued. I was in Arabia. My eyes watered against the glare as I made out a tall, athletic figure wearing the SAS beige beret and striding towards me. Captain Tony Shaw's deep tan made me feel I had crawled out from under a stone.

We exchanged news and made small talk while we waited for my luggage. The Andover was a unique aircraft in that it sank to its knees, like a camel, to unload. The rear door gaped open; I hauled my bergen off the platform, slung it into the Landrover, and we set off along the dirt track to the SAF camp at Um Al Gwarif where the SAS base was set up. On the way, Shaw pointed out various pieces of empty desert where experimental farms, the Taylor Woodrow Towel construction company's complex, and so on, were planned to go, the first seeds of civil development.

The base at Um Al Gwarif was much like any other SAS base throughout the world. The only buildings were reserved for important matters: the operations room, the armoury and the radio room, with a tall radio mast erected alongside, but everything else was tented. An SAS base requires the same number of men to man it, whether there are two patrols in the field as now, or 20. The 19 men, who were all at this stage the SAS were allowed to have in Dhofar, made an inefficient little unit. It was too top heavy, but it could not be helped. Shaw led me to a comfortable tent, eight feet long by six wide, equipped with table, chair and a camp bed. A thick layer of fine sand covered everything The north wind, the *shimaal*, had started early. I shook the bed free of sand, dumped my bergen on it and walked over to the operations room where

Shaw was waiting.

There was not much to show. The BATT camp stood to one side of the Dhofar resident battalion's hutted camp, its battalion headquarters in an old white washed Beau Geste fort. It was cool and dark within its thick walls. We quickly paid our respects to the battalion hierarchy and walked the hundred yards back to the BATT camp.

Shaw waved at four or five tired-looking vehicles scattered about. 'This is the MT park,' he said. A pair of legs protruded from under one truck and I squatted on my haunches alongside them.

'What d'ye reckon?' I asked the legs.

'Load of crap. Bloody thing's clapped out.'

A model military report, I reflected, succinct and to the point. As we walked back Shaw pointed out the funk-holes in case of shelling and explained the stand-to procedure if we were attacked by night. Two huge 5.5-inch guns stood a hundred yards away.

'They shell the mouths of the wadis with those by day and night,' he said. 'You never know when they're going to go off. Keeps the adoo on their toes – and us short of sleep.'

As we talked through the rest of the day and well into the night I realized how much Shaw had achieved with his few men. He had two four-man civil action teams at Taqa and Mirbat, each with its own clinic, and who were paid regular visits from the BATT medical officer. The vet also visited regularly so that he was seen, but he pointed out to me that his treatment was just a drop in the ocean. What was needed was a thorough review of the problem, the diseases prevalent among the animals, the resources on the jebel, the possibilities of introducing different strains to improve the native stock, et cetera. There might be some come-back, he added; for example, foot-and-mouth disease and brucellosis were endemic to jebeli cattle, but over the centuries they had developed an immunity. Perhaps a serum could be developed from them. He understood the reason for having to be seen giving injections to goats and cattle, but his greater contribution by far was in the experimental farms he had in mind and which he was already explaining to the Director of Civil Development, another Briton, in Salalah.

The intelligence cell, run by Warrant Officer Birrell, was at last beginning to get information, mainly from those ex-members of the DLF now living in Salalah, and from the many influential men, usually sheikhs, who had fled from the jebel after the Communist take-over.

But, although Birrell with his excellent Arabic was adept at discovering information, the credit for producing intelligence from it – that is, information achieved by deduction which would be of practical value to the Government forces – lay with the collators, two young Intelligence Corps NCOs who worked over their files well into the night and every night trying to tie up this snippet of information with that. Even so, it took them three months to crack the problem and to be able to put together the adoo organisation and outline command structure; and it was to be many more months before the details were known.

★   ★   ★

The information services, too, were getting off the ground, run by Corporal John Lane. Lane was, and is, an extraordinary man. He was an average SAS corporal, but at information services he was brilliant, and was later employed by the Sultanate as a civilian consultant. A quiet, courteous and unassuming man, his fertile mind saw through the problem and what was needed; he patiently developed his contacts in the various Omani Government departments, suggested what should be done, and arranged the delivery of the equipment they would need in the shape of printing presses and broadcasting equipment from Britain. It was not long before he had to be told to drop the rank of corporal and call himself 'Mister'. Senior British and Omani Government officials would listen with more respect to what an obvious expert in his subject called Mr Lane had to say, than to Corporal Lane. Such is prejudice.

The whole subject of information services is one bedevilled by emotive phrases and misunderstandings. Sometimes called 'psychological operations', it smacks of brain washing, with Goebbels-like propaganda, lies and sinister grey figures flitting about the alleyways of government. But it does not have to be like that, and in Dhofar it was not.

The aims and the reasoning behind it all were very simple. The first aim was to bring the truth to the people of Dhofar, whether they were on the jebel fighting, or just civilians, both on the jebel and plain, about Government actions and plans. A government must always tell the truth. Just one lie, once it is found out (and it will be eventually) will invalidate everything else that has been said and that will be said in the future. It had been decided very early on in the campaign that there would be no black propaganda, that is material purporting to come from the other side, or even grey. This campaign would be fought 'white' to contrast ever more strongly with the vituperation and hatred vomited forth every day from Radio Aden. It would take time, but once it was realised that Radio Dhofar always told the truth, Radio Aden's propaganda would be totally discredited. And so in the end it was.

The trouble was that Radio Dhofar was then only a small transmitter hastily installed in an old shack, instead of the palatial and powerful radio station of today, and it could not cover the entire jebel. Then, too, there was little point in having a transmitter if few people could listen to it, and though there were plenty on the plain, there were very few radio receivers on the jebel. So, with the aim of getting the news to every jebeli family, several hundred cheap Japanese transistor sets were bought by Lane and distributed free to the Jebelis when they came down to the plain to trade. The idea was good, but in practice it was not a success. The adoo pickets on the routes back up took the transistor sets away and either smashed them if the commissar was looking or pocketed them if he was not. It was found to be far better to put the sets on sale cheaply in the souk. It is one thing to take away something which had been given free by the Government and so is, in a sense, Government property, but if you really wish to arouse an avaricious Jebeli's ire, try taking away from him something which is his by purchase. The adoo tried it and so made themselves unpopular, and enough sets got through for the jebel 'jungle-drum' news system to do the rest.

For centuries, word of mouth had been the only news system on the jebel and it had become refined into an extremely efficient one. News travelled from mouth to mouth at an almost unbelievable pace, all the more extraordinary because it took a little while when Arabs met before the news was reached. An Arab did not rush up saying. 'Hey, have you heard the news?', as in the western world. It was all done far more graciously. A typical meeting might go:

'Peace be with you. How are you?'

'And with you be peace. How are you?'

'I am well. How are you?'

'Thanks be to God. I am well. All is well. How are you?'

'By the grace of God, I am well. Welcome to the hearth.'

'Thanks be to God.'

These greetings would be exchanged for some little time before one asks the other,

'What is the news?'

'No news. By the grace of God. Never.'

He pauses.

'But ...'

Radio alone, however, was not enough. The news had to be brought to the people by every means possible. A weekly newspaper was started, and proved popular, but perhaps the simplest and most effective means was the use of notice boards. These were large boards in glass frames set up at every gate through the perimeter wire which surrounded the towns, where packs were inspected for mines and weapons coming in and for suspicious amounts of food and medical supplies going out. A queue of people always stood at these gates waiting to be checked through. What better way to pass the time than by looking at the Government notice board with its latest news, pictures, leaflets and photographs? Besides Salalah, boards were also set up at Taqa and Mirbat, again at places where people gathered.

The second aim of information services was to encourage our own troops and to discourage the enemy's by the simple means of emphasising our successes and minimising our defeats. The impression had to be created in the minds of all three parties – enemy troops, own troops and civilians, that the Government was going to win. Successes became yet more proof of Government invincibility, disasters merely temporary set-backs in the overall inevitable outcome.

So it was quite a simple matter to show that development had at last come to Dhofar and that the people would be far better off under Sultan Qaboos than under his father. But people do not fight only for bread. Dhofar needed a 'cause' and fortunately the Communists had given the Government one on a plate. Dhofar, like all Oman, is a strongly Muslim country, and has been so for centuries. The young Communist teenage fighters, fresh from the Lenin school at Hauf, and indoctrinated with all the fervour of the newly converted, were adamant in their denial of God, or in permission to worship or even mention God. The phrase '*Al hamdu l'Illah*', by the grace of God, is probably the most used phrase in Arabia. Even this was denied to the Dhofari supporters of PFLOAG. Praying was totally forbidden.

The adoo were divided into two groups: the hard-core full-time fighters of the People's Liberation Army, and the soft-core militia. The hard-core had been trained either in PDRY or abroad in Communist countries. The militia were just tribesmen given weapons but who lived in their own tribal environments. The militia were strongly Muslim and prayed regularly – when there was no hard-core present. Many of the hard-core, too, we knew were very unhappy about their enforced lapse from their religion and its moralities. Even the hardest had only been under Communist domination for, say, ten to twelve years by the end of the war, so a seventeen year-old in 1971 had spent not more than three or four years under Communist thrall. The Jesuits were reputed to have a saying: 'Give me a child to the age of seven and he is mine for the rest of his life.' On the same principle, even in the minds of the hardest hard-core Communist there must remain the seeds of Islam from his childhood. This was where the wedge would be driven, between Islam and Communism. We would try to remove the soft-core first and then drive the wedge into the hard-core itself.

This policy set the tone for the attitude taken towards enemy prisoners (SEPs, short for Surrendered Enemy Personnel), although the word 'surrender' must never be used, for the only fault in the adoo was that they did not know the truth. An SEP had to be treated with honour and his 'return' was treated with joy. The fatted calf must be killed for the errant son who had seen the folly of his ways. Similarly, the killing of an adoo was no grounds for satisfaction, even though he was doing his best to kill you. The BATT soldiers were instructed to show regret at the waste of a life. After all, his brother might well be in your BATT's firqat.

SEPs were not interrogated. They were merely invited to sit down in a tent, given tea and a cigarette and asked questions. They would be initially hostile and suspicious but they gradually relaxed, and if there were still doubts, after a night or two spent talking with their tribesmen in the family atmosphere of the firqat, most of them were happy to tell all they knew.

Persuading a man to join you is far cheaper than killing him. Words are far, far less expensive than bullets, let alone shells and bombs. Then, too, by killing him you merely deprive the enemy of one soldier. If he is persuaded to join the Government forces the enemy again become one less, but the Government forces become one more, a gain of plus two. So the use of information services is not only a humane weapon of modern warfare but a singularly cost-effective one.

★　★　★

The next two or three days were busy ones spent visiting all those people who were principals in the development of the province or in the prosecution of the war. It was on the second day that Salim Mubarak came to see me. He was a man of medium height, lean from his years on the jebel, dressed in a plain long dark blue gown stretching to his ankles, with long sleeves, the neck buttoned but without a collar, a leather belt about his waist, and a blue and white shamag tied tightly around his head. On his feet he wore leather sandals and on his wrist a gold watch. I took him to the marquee, where he could be comfortable and called for tea and biscuits – Army tea, strong and with plenty of milk and sugar as the Dhofaris like it. We studied each other. I do not know what he thought of me, but I liked what I saw. He had a lean hard face with the long nose, high cheekbones and fine features of his race. His chin was firm and his mouth tight, the jaw of a man used to command. A small, neatly trimmed moustache completed the military appearance; but it was his eyes which impressed me most. They were large eyes, but alive with a frankness and sparkle in them unusual in an Arab, who likes to sum you up carefully at first meeting. They were the eyes of a man of intelligence and quick wits, but the eyes too of a far-sighted man, a man with a mission. They could also become, I decided silently, the eyes of a fanatic. Here was a man I would very much rather have on my side than against me.

He had been the second-in-command of the entire Eastern Area, he explained, and as such knew it like the palm of his hand, but he had a good working knowledge too of the Central and Western Areas and could lead a firqat right across the jebel. Yes, he could raise a firqat, he said, if I could provide the weapons and training for his men in modern tactics and new weapons. He spoke with confidence and purpose as he unfolded his ideas. He did not underestimate the enemy, but once they knew the truth, he was sure that many more would come and join him. No, there was no need for tribal firqats. If the Communists could break down the tribal traditions and tribal isolation by forming units from several tribes, so could the Government. His eyes glowed. There would be one firqat which would grow until it was a thousand strong and it would sweep the jebel from end to end. He made an expansive gesture with his arm.

'What will you call this firqat?' I asked.

'The Firqat Salahadin,' he replied. 'After the great Muslim warrior who fought the infidels.'

'The Franks,' I said, using the Arabic term for Europeans.

We exchanged grins. He nodded.

'But this time, the Communists.'

We talked for a long time. The discussion ranged from the strictly practical problems of how his firqat should be armed to his reminiscing about his life on the jebel and the evils of the old days. He said that he had never feared the SAF soldier, but he did fear the SAF artillery, and above all, the jets.

I was naively surprised and impressed by the speed with which he understood the reasoning behind information services, not yet knowing that in the coming months I was to learn more from him than I could teach. He wanted maximum publicity, he said, once the firqat was formed. He would design me a badge for use on all Government leaflets and stressed the need for his firqat members to be allowed to talk on Radio Dhofar. Nothing would impress the adoo more than hearing the voices of their former comrades urging them to join them.

It was not far to Taqa by air, although it took half a day's journey by land under armoured car escort and a company of infantry. I do not say 'by road' as the roads were impassable because of mines. Movement by land had to be across country. We flew high out of small arms range and along the coast to avoid heavy machine-guns dug into the jebel face. The helicopter landed under the walls of the old fort, and Shaw and I climbed out on to the sandy and rock-strewn landing strip.

The dusty figures of two BATT men came forward to greet us. Both wore olive green shorts and shirts, had their belt order on and carried Armalite rifles. They looked enviably sunburned and fit, but also tired and in need of a good meal. The BATT house was not far away, they explained, and we set off, automatically moving into single file, spaced out five yards apart, walking steadily at that ground-devouring lope developed by the SAS soldier.

The BATT house was recognisable from some distance by the information board standing outside and by the Sultanate's flag hanging limply in the mid-day sun from its home-made flag mast on one corner of the roof. The house stood on the side of a small square opposite a much larger house flanked on one side by coconut palms. This was clearly the *wali*'s house, although there was no wali in residence at the time. A small child scuttled from one house to another on the side of the square. Otherwise nothing moved.

We pushed open the carved wooden door and stood in an entrance like that of an old English coaching inn, with a high roof and rooms on either side. A sun-bleached courtyard of sand surrounded by tall walls lay beyond. The house must have belonged to a man of substance. We were led across the courtyard into a room where two figures, dressed in tattered shorts and flip-flops, stood over an Army stove, burning with that roaring hiss that only Army stoves seem to have.

'Brew up, boss,' one said, and handed me a tin mug, the lip edged with black masking tape to protect the lips. Two long benches flanked the table, obviously a do-it-yourself job, and I sat down with the others who were busily slitting open their mail. For several minutes the occasional remark or the crunch of an oatmeal biscuit was the only sound.

The mail read, life could return to normal. The BATT commander's fair hair and bright grey eyes looked even fairer against the mahogany of his tan. Although he was from another squadron, I knew him well as a man bursting with energy and life. He spoke with the same animation.

'Bleeding terrible place this, sir. Locals won't say a word to you more'n they have to. There's no wali, y'see, so they come to us for everything, but they're frightened to open up. Still, we got 'em to help with the wire, and some of the *askars* are guarding the gate. Now, they're a good lot, mostly *shaibas* and kids, but a cheerful mob, know what I mean, though what they have got to be cheerful about I don't know. Fancy being stuck in this place for the rest of your natural, without your families or anything. You staying the night? Great. The form is, we separate at stand-to and Johnny and Phil here go up to the fort to spend the night there; Doug and I stay down here by the radio.'

'Fine,' I nodded. 'What about intelligence?' I asked. 'Any problems?'

'Hard to come by. Locals don't like talking at all. There's a funny attitude in this town,' he wrinkled his nose, 'but I can't put my finger on it. Most of the info we get comes from Doug's medical rounds.'

Corporal Doug Steadman sat opposite me. His red hair hung down over his ears and his blue eyes observed me steadily as he held his mug to his lips with both hands. A piece of parachute cord was looped round his neck, grey with age and sweat, with his two personal morphine syrettes and identity discs attached to it covered in black tape. At the bottom of the loop a wristwatch tapped against his chest.

'Doug's opened a clinic just inside the door there for men and boys. That's open every morning from eight to twelve. Then, in the afternoon, he goes visiting the really sick who can't get here, and sees the women in the evening. There's no point in visiting them earlier because if they can even move they will be sent out to work, so they don't get back till evening. The men won't let the women come to the clinic at all. What we need is a female medic here really. That's an idea, boss, how about

WRAC, one per four-man patrol?' There was a chorus of approval. 'Seriously, they only used to let Doug near them when they were at death's door, but it's got much better over the last couple of months. They call him now when the women are really ill, but they still won't always let him touch them. Tell the boss about your brilliant diagnosis last week, Doug.'

The other three sat grinning from ear to ear as Steadman looked down at his cup, smiling the weary smile of someone who has had his leg pulled for a long time.

'Well, it was like this.' He had a calm strong voice with just a suggestion of West Country. 'This old bloke came to me one night in a high old dudgeon. Said his wife was sick. So I went to see her. She was lying in this little room, all dark except for one candle burning in the corner. She was quite an old woman, I could see that from her face and hands, but I couldn't see her shape or anything, just a bundle of clothes, lying there. He said she had stomach-ache. Her temperature and pulse were OK, so it was not appendicitis. I thought she was probably constipated; there's a lot of that here – they don't drink enough. Anyway I gave her some vitamins and iron tablets – all the women need them because the men take all the good food– and gave her a dose of senna pod for constipation. I thought I would go back and see her in the morning, by daylight, like.'

It was obvious from the looks of delight from the others that he was coming to the crunch line.

'What happened?'

'Well, nothing really. The old boy turned up with a goat next morning as a present for the birth of a fine son.'

★　★　★

It was 4 o'clock when Steadman, the patrol Arabist, and I set off on the rounds visiting the sick. As the afternoon wore on and as he became immersed in his task, Steadman lost some of his reserve and began to talk more freely about his work.

The people of Taqa had never had any medical help, he explained, so that their reaction to any drugs at all was near miraculous. A disease, which in Britain would require a course of antibiotics, would be cured within days. A single aspirin would drop a man's temperature overnight. The numbers of people who attended his clinic had dropped dramatically over the four months he had been there, he told me, as their bodies responded to the drugs and treatments denied to them under

Sultan Said Bin Taimur.

'Teeth and eyes are the worst,' he went on. 'It's pathetic. You get the little kids coming in with teeth rotten to the gums. You show them how to clean them, but they think it's all a huge joke. They might do it for a day, but they forget after that. It's all this Allah's will business, you see. Man's fate is predetermined. If their teeth fall out, it is the will of Allah, and if they don't, it is *Allah kareem,* God is merciful.'

'It's the same with their eyes,' he continued as we trudged on. 'You saw the piles of rotting sardines on the beach. They use them as fodder for the camels in the *negd.* You can smell them from here, so you can imagine what the place is like for flies. You try to explain that they must keep the flies away from their eyes, but you can't expect them to change centuries old ways overnight. Here we are, we'll go in here.'

We ducked through a low door and went into a large, white-washed room. The ceiling was high with blackened round beams supporting rush matting which, in turn, supported about four inches of earth, and on top of that would be a layer of hardened lime. It was cool and pleasant inside.

An old man rose from a cushion placed against the wall. We went through the usual lengthy greetings as courtesy demanded, but declined his offer of tea and moved through a door into a smaller room lit only by an opening high up in one wall. A boy in his late teens lay wrapped in blankets. His eyes were shut and his face was grey.

'This one has malaria,' said Steadman and began to ask the old man questions about his son. I examined the boy's ashen face carefully. Across his forehead a piece of transparent tape held a little white pill in place. Steadman saw me looking at it and smiled.

'Psychological. We're still fighting this sort of thing.' He rolled back the boy's shirt to reveal an ugly brown scar across his chest three inches long and half an inch wide.

'*Wazim*, it's called – branding. There's a man who practises it in the town. They still don't trust the white man's medicine and they usually hedge their bets by calling on him and me, one after the other. They do it to their kids, cattle, camels, the lot. In fact I'm treating a camel at the moment. One of my most successful treatments,' he grinned. 'They'd burned this camel on the rear leg and it had gone bad. The flies had got into it and the maggots had eaten the flesh to the bone. I've been packing the wound with tetracycline gauze swabs and it is coming on a treat now.'

We said farewell to the old man and Steadman promised to return at the same time tomorrow.

'There's one more old boy I want to see and then we'll go back to the house for a brew. Yes,' he went on, 'this *wazim* business has got to stop. I'm going to recommend to the bloke from your squadron who takes over from me that we go hard-line and refuse to treat anyone who has been recently branded. Then they will see that someone treated with medicine gets better and someone treated by *wazim* doesn't. At the moment the *wazim* bloke claims our miraculous recoveries for himself. Wicked old bastard,' he muttered. 'Though I suppose he's not really wicked. Doesn't know any better, does he?'

We walked down a narrow alley and into a single-roomed hut at the end of it. An ancient man sat huddled in rags on a stool. Two women were with him. One, a pretty young girl in a yellow and red dress, a grand-daughter I supposed, gave a shy smile and edged past us out of the door; the other, a wizened old woman, dressed all in black, remained sitting or squatting, impossible to see which in the poor light, at the feet of the old man. She eyed us suspiciously from her one good eye, as if we were *jinns* about to whisk her husband away, and shrieked at him unintelligibly.

The ancient could not see us, but smiled in welcome. 'The old boy is near blind and near deaf,' Steadman said, 'but I think I can cure him – in one eye anyway. He can already see something.'

He held his fingers in front of the ancient's face.

'How many today?' he shouted.

'Four, thanks be to God,' the old man cried and seized the soldier's hand in both of his.

'And how are your ears?' the soldier shouted again.

'Better, thanks be to God.'

'He's still as deaf as a post, but it's only wax, I'm pretty sure. His ears were stopped up like tar. I'm working on him every night with hydrogen peroxide. He couldn't hear a sound when I started on him a fortnight ago.'

'So the blind see and the deaf hear,' I murmured.

His teeth showed white in the gloom. 'Yeah, well. He didn't have anti-biotics, did He?'

We walked slowly back through the town, the big gentle man loping alongside me, his rifle in one hand, his medical pack in the other. It was cooler now and people were appearing to go about their business. I gave several a friendly 'Peace be with you' or wished them 'Good evening' and received a courteous enough reply, but I knew what the patrol commander meant. There was no warmth in the replies. Taqa was not a happy town. There could be only one reason: the adoo were still present in it.

★   ★   ★

Shaw and I said our farewells next day to the Taqa BATT and climbed aboard the helicopter, again bound for Mirbat, where it had been arranged that we would meet Salim Mubarak and the man he wanted as his second-in-command, Mohammed Said of the Bait Gatun. Mohammed Said had an impressive military reputation amongst the adoo, both as a fighter and as a leader, but I was interested in Salim's choice of a Bait Gatun as his number two. Of course, it could be that he was choosing this man on his merits as a commander of men; on the other hand, since there was an Arabic saying, 'The best way across a square is via three sides', there may have been something more to it. The Bait Gatun tribe were the hardest of the hard-core. Their tribal area lay in the great Wadi Nahiz, which runs parallel to the Midway Road in the Central Area, and so they had been at the receiving end of many of Said Bin Taimur's punitive operations. The Bait Gatun were also numerically a small tribe, but they owned the beautiful and fertile Wadi Nahiz and no doubt they had had to fight hard to keep out other envious tribes. The Bait Gatun were hard men, and I knew that we could say that we were winning only when, one day, we had the Bait Gatun fighting for the Government. In the event, it was not until 1975 that a Bait Gatun firqat could be formed and not until 1976 that the last important leader of the enemy, 'came over' in the Eastern Area, another Bait Gatun.

Was Salim playing for high stakes, I wondered, hoping to attract the hard-core with his Bait Gatun second-in-command, or did he think that his own commanding position would be better established if he had someone from a minor tribe as his number two? But there was little point in speculating. I could certainly not ask him and he would certainly not tell me.

One man might be able to give me a clue though. I had met him briefly in Salalah, another Bait Gatun called Said Bin Gheer. At first sight Bin Gheer appeared to be the worst example of the type of Arab British soldiers had met in Egypt and which did much to sour the image of Arabs held by many Britons in the 1950s and 1960s. He was a newspaper caricature: fat, swarthy, his face covered with sweat, his hair

46

flattened with grease. His appearance put many British officers off, and I was warned against him by a number of SAF officers. He was treacherous, I was told, he had been an adoo, he was only out for his own ends: he was not to be trusted.

He had indeed been an adoo, one of the very first, but he had been wounded early on and had 'come over' in the time of Said Bin Taimur. If there had been anything treacherous about him, Said Bin Taimur of all men, would have discovered it. He had taken part himself in actions against his own tribesmen. If any man had a cause to be loyal, I resolved, it was Said Bin Gheer.

He had struck me as a very shrewd man, despite his amiable banter, and he had intelligent eyes. He had gone to Kuwait in his youth, where he had learned good English and had become rich. Paradoxically, instead of earning him respect for his enterprise, as he had earned mine, it did him no good at all in Dhofar. The tribal elders considered him a dangerous parvenu, the young men considered him a merchant, rather than a soldier, which was the only respectable profession for a man, and the British officers of SAF considered him 'too clever by half'. Even in our short talk together he had revealed a remarkable and mature understanding of the undercurrents on the jebel. Of course he was out for his own and his tribe's ends; who was not? But, provided one took account of that, he was a shrewd and wise counsellor. Said Bin Gheer was to prove even more valuable than I hoped.

The helicopter droned on. Below, the hairpin bend where the road crossed the Wadi Ghazir lay still cratered where the adoo had destroyed it. Ahead stretched the steep jebel wall, climbable only in certain places, until it reached the highest point, a tangle of great rocks and boulders at the top of an almost sheer wall that rose straight out of the desert nearly 4000 feet high. I checked the map but the feature had no name. It was clearer now and I could see that it would make a strong defensive position. Provided the defenders could be supplied with water, it was impregnable. The rocks threw off a grey-pinkish colour in the sun and a line from school days Macaulay flashed into my mind, 'Like an eagle's nest, hangs on the crest of purple Appenine.' If Point 1250 did not have a resident eagle, it should have.

The Bay of Mirbat with its blue sea and silver sand looked more like something in a tourist brochure than a theatre of war. The town itself grew larger as the helicopter descended; green smoke began to billow out from a point on the beach and a tiny figure stood with arms outstretched guiding us in. A strange rapid rhythmic tapping began to sound in my ears. It was not coming through the earphones and I glanced at the door in case a piece of seat belt or webbing had caught in the slipstream outside. My heart leapt as I realized what it was. 'That's fire!' I blurted out even as the pilot threw the aircraft into a stomach-churning manoeuvre to the right and downwards.

He levelled out just above the sea and my heartbeat returned to normal as common sense took over. We were two thousand yards out from the coast. Some adoo had just been trying it out; his chances of a hit were almost zero.

Mirbat was a more impressive town altogether. It was bigger, there were more houses than in Taqa, and the houses were better looked after. In place of the few fishing boats at Taqa, a small fleet was drawn up on the beach and a boom from the Trucial Coast lay a hundred yards out. A group of men, stripped to the waist, were offloading rush sacks full of dates from her into a small boat before ferrying them ashore. Dynamism would be too strong a word, but at least the place felt alive after the apathy of Taqa. The story from the BATT was much the same. The BATT commander was in effect town governor, but he was concerned that without local knowledge he was not making the correct decisions. The sooner a wali was appointed the better.

Salim and Mohammed Said were waiting for me in the BATT house. They had come down the previous day and planned to return to Salalah by boom. But first, Salim said, he had work to do. Both here and in Taqa the adoo still had a cell of supporters who organised food and medical supplies for the adoo. From time to time, they even hid fighters who came into the town disguised as herdsmen or who brought in camels loaded with wood from the jebel which the townsmen needed for fuel. Mohammed Said and he wanted to find out the names of these people.

'Will you be safe?' I asked.

Salim smiled. 'We have many friends in this town.'

Before Shaw and I left, all four of us walked over to the southern part of the town to a large clear area, and I discussed with Salim the advantages of training his firqat in Mirbat. There would be administrative problems, but no insuperable ones provided we used foresight, and the Government boom for re-supply. And the advantages were many: the firqat would be out of the reach of prying eyes and unnecessary visitors; the area had all that was needed in the way of ranges and training areas; and, most important, the men would have nowhere to go. They could not be attracted to the delights of Salalah and would be forced to concentrate on the training.

Salim was not happy, I could see that, but he agreed to think about it. Mohammed Said had said very little. He was an impressive man, taller and broader than Salim, but he had the same military appearance. His features were not as fine as Salim's, but his bearing held confidence and authority. He smoked heavily, watching everything that went on through shrewd eyes, and patiently bided his time. Mohammed Said wanted to see action, not words, before he committed himself.

It was a week later when I returned from Muscat. There were advantages in travelling by slow aircraft, De Havilland Caribou one way and Short Skyvan on the return trip. Today you fly BAC 111, but the long day it took to fly from Salalah to Muscat brought home to me the huge expanse of desert which separates them and which accounts for the cultural and ethnic differences between the Northern Omani and Dhofari.

No love was lost between the two. It was the traditional hostility you meet all over the world between mountain men and plains men; the latter, for their advantages of communications and trade have a higher standard of living and a more developed culture; the former for their hard life in the wild terrain of the hills, become a hardier race and are attracted to the flocks, herds and general loot to be had by raiding the plains men. So, an enmity develops over the centuries which lasts for generations. The Northern Omani had a saying, 'If your path is blocked by a snake and a Dhofari, kill the Dhofari first', and on the few occasions Dhofaris went to the North, they were treated with the contemptuous respect reserved for someone culturally inferior but physically dangerous.

The tribes of Dhofar and the Highland clans of Scotland in the 17th and 18th centuries would have had much in common with their interminable clan wars and the impossibility of getting any two clans, or even any two Highlanders, to agree for very long. Like the Dhofaris, many Highlanders fought on the side of the Government and like the Dhofaris too, they were eventually defeated, not by their lack of courage or fighting ability, which could never be doubted, but by superior organisation, administration and fire-power.

The whole atmosphere in the two provinces, Dhofar and Muscat, was very different. In Dhofar I slept in my sleeping bag on a camp bed in a tent, with the 5.5s shattering the night as they shelled the wadi mouths. In the North I slept peacefully between sheets in a comfortable bed in an air-conditioned room at Headquarters SAF, Bait Al Falaj. The headquarters was again in an old fort, but much bigger and more impressive than the one at Um Al Gwarif. As I walked through the gate, the Baluch sentry stamped to attention. He did not know whether I was a field officer who is entitled to a 'present arms', or a captain who only gets a butt salute, so he stayed at attention, sensible man. I should have done the same. I walked past the two burnished bronze cannons on their wooden carriages and into the coolness of the Fort. A short flight of stairs led up to a balcony overlooking a courtyard surrounded by the offices of the Commander and his staff.

Brigadier John Graham was the last officer of that rank to be Commander Sultan's Armed Forces. Thereafter the post became a major-general's appointment. I was shown into his office and an athletic, fair-haired man rose to greet me, the red tabs on his collar standing out against his light khaki drill uniform. After a small Arab boy had brought in two cups of coffee, Graham began to question me closely about the situation in Dhofar. I told him how well the first four of the five recommended 'fronts' were doing, with the limited number of men we were allowed, and then began to unfold my ideas on the formation of the firqat and how it should be used, not as guides, but as a fighting formation. He listened carefully, punctuating my monologue with little grunts of agreement or with quick questions to clarify any vagueness. I stressed that these men would be under his command and I was thinking in terms of a thousand. They would need to be armed with the modern *Fabrique Nationale* rifles just becoming available to the SAF if we were to attract the right men, not with the old-fashioned .303 Enfields. These were not askars: they would be properly trained by us, properly equipped and properly supported. Graham appreciated the implications immediately.

'What do you mean by properly supported?' he asked sharply. 'Are you going to train them in GPMGs and mortars? What if they turn against us and turn their weapons over to the adoo? What about radio? As I understand it, many of these people don't even speak Arabic, let alone English. How are they going to communicate with the artillery and SOAF?'

'We'll have to do all that ourselves, sir,' I said. 'Which brings me on to the question of numbers. We can't possibly raise the Firqat Salahadin with the numbers I have. Before I left Salalah there was a rumour that the Bait Kathir also want to raise a firqat, so they'll need another troop to run them. I must have the whole squadron out.'

We talked a little longer whilst he fired several more seemingly hostile questions at me and I was beginning to doubt my chances of persuading him, when he brightened.

'Don't worry. I was being the Devil's Advocate. I like it, I like it.' He mused to himself for a while then he turned to me again.

'I must see the Consul, and so must you. Come around to my house for drinks tonight and we'll talk some more. Then I want you to write me out your concept in detail and let me have it by tomorrow morning.'

The main hurdle was over. If CSAF had wanted no part of it that would have been the end of the whole matter; but as I talked with his staff, it became clear that it was easier said than done. They could let me have 110 FN rifles, no more, and a similar number of sets of uniform, but that was all. SAF were desperately short of equipment and were about to embark on a major expansion programme. They were sorry, but they would need what little they had for themselves.

I was early for my appointment at the consulate that afternoon. I had to stoop to get through the small door set into its great brass-studded gates before I found myself in a courtyard flanked by buildings, the main entrance on my right. Straight ahead lay the sea and I walked quickly across the courtyard to a low wall, which looked down on to the pebble beach, and drank in the view. To the left, across the sparkling sea of sapphire stood the great Portuguese-built Fort Mirani, with its cannon still protruding from its emplacements. Below the fort, several booms lay gracefully at anchor, and further to the right, a Royal Navy frigate lay closer to the great rocks on which were painted in crude white letters the names of ships which had visited Muscat over the last hundred years. Further to the right towered Fort Jelali, which was still used as a jail. It looked a grim place, but at least now it was visited every day by a British medical officer. I turned and walked back across the courtyard and through the large doors flanked by two small brass mortars into the consulate. A cool English girl with a cool English voice smiled helpfully across her desk at me through a wrought-iron grille.

The consul could not have been nicer. The tea was delightful. It all seemed very far removed from the war in Dhofar where the province was virtually under siege and the Communists were poised to descend upon Salalah, but here was where the power lay. This was the man I had to convince.

I did not have to work very hard; CSAF had prepared the ground thoroughly. Indeed, the consul was often ahead of me. The concept made absolute sense, he said, but in turn he had to convince his superiors. Nonetheless, he was sanguine about getting the rest of the squadron, and promised to pass the news the moment he had an answer from London one way or the other. He cannot have let the grass grow under his feet, for only two days later Shaw met me as I climbed off the Skyvan.

'Three bits of news you'll like,' he grinned. 'Your advance party are all here as planned but your complete squadron arrives on 14th February. Second, Salim Mubarak is getting married this afternoon and we are both invited. And third, the Bait Kathir want to raise a firqat.'

This was news indeed for the Bait Kathir were one of the largest tribes on the jebel.

★   ★   ★

The wedding took place in Salalah and it was a gay affair. Salim greeted me with open arms as we slipped off our sandals and entered the large white washed room where the feast was to be held. For a second I thought he was going to embrace me, a greeting normally reserved for members of his own tribe, but perhaps because there was ten inches difference in our height he merely seized my hand and led me to the top of the room.

We had taken no part in the procession which accompanied the groom. Our white faces would have been too obvious and I was not sure that as Christians we would have been wanted. Perhaps I was wrong because Salim chided me good-naturedly about our absence. Already the walls were lined with men reclining against the brightly covered cushions packed with hard straw on the floor. The last three or four on either side rose politely as our small party was ushered to the place of honour at the head of the room. We went through the pantomime of declining the best seat and finally settled ourselves against the cushions, taking care to tuck the soles of our feet out of sight.

Salim was marrying a girl in the Bait Ma'asheni. It was a clever move and I doubt love had any part in it. He himself came from a minor sub-tribe and a marriage with a Bait Ma'asheni would both ally him with a powerful tribe, and, because of Sultan Qaboos's mother, align him firmly with the Sultan. I never saw his wife, but they said she was very pretty. The poor girl was not to be a wife for long.

Salim was an excellent host. Relaxed, smiling, confident, he took the banter directed at a prospective bridegroom and threw it back easily, causing laughter all round the room. My Arabic was not good enough to follow the jests, but it did not need Birrell to translate for me to understand the gist of them. They were universal. Salim was splendidly dressed, still in a dark-blue robe but with gold edging to it and a gold embroidered shamag. A white woollen shawl was wrapped about his waist and for the first and only time I saw him carrying in his waist band the ornate curved Omani knife, the *khunja* in its L-shaped sheath worn in the middle of the body. He looked magnificent. However, he had not forgotten business, even on this day.

'*Taweel*,' he lowered his voice so that only the few of us could hear, but he continued to smile. 'What is the news from your visit to Muscat?'

Taweel, tall one, was an inevitable nickname… I suppose in English it would be equivalent to 'Lofty'. I continued the charade and smiled broadly back.

'All the news is good,' I whispered. 'We will get the automatic rifles for your firqat, but the *geysh* are short of equipment. We will have to buy it in Salalah. By the way, I have a present for you.'

I felt under my shirt and produced a brand new Smith and Wesson .357 magnum, fully loaded. The pistol gleamed blue-black in my hand, accentuating the whiteness of its ivory handle.

'It is too big,' he said. 'I want one smaller, an automatic.'

I was staggered. It was a beautiful and expensive pistol which I had gone to much trouble to get for him. I had thought he would be delighted with it, or if not, would have had the courtesy to pretend to be.

'Well, take it now,' I said lamely, 'and I will give you more ammunition for it tomorrow. I will see if I can get an automatic, but it will not be easy.'

★ ★ ★

It was my first experience of that Dhofari forthrightness which in the early days was to cause some friction between BATT and the firqats. In due course BATT came to understand the Dhofari attitude, and the firqats came to realise that BATT were not a God-given goldmine to be exploited at every opportunity, but in the early days there were misunderstandings. It took BATT some time to understand that no such sentiment as gratitude exists in the average Dhofari's character. Since all things come from God anyway, and the giver is merely doing the will of God, he cannot help himself, so what is the point of being grateful to him? Similarly, the logic runs, if God wishes you to have something, he will give it to you; if he does not, he will not give it to you, so there is no point in beating about the bush; go in and ask for it.

Allied with this philosophy is that of equality among individuals. The Dhofari tribal system, for all its faults, is possibly one of the finest examples of true democracy known to man. Similarly, it provides care and attention for the old and weak better than any Welfare State. Tribal leaders are elected on merit because of their personal virtues. Heredity and class are meaningless; and even when elected, the leader is by no means paramount; he must consult on almost everything he does and all major decisions are arrived at collectively after every man who wishes to do so has had his say. Now, a sociologist may find this admirable, but it is no way to run an army. It took the SAS some time to understand this and many SAF officers never understood it. A disciplined tribal unit is a contradiction in terms. Discipline, in the military sense that it is understood by a regular army, cannot possibly be achieved when everyone in the army thinks he has just as much right to decide what is to be done as his leaders, and if he dislikes their decision feels free to take no part in the outcome.

The only way to achieve discipline was to break down the tribal structure. Salim knew this and it was why he insisted on a multi-tribal firqat, the Firqat Salahadin; and it was one of the reasons, no doubt, why the adoo concentrated so hard on destroying tribalism.

It had a frustrating effect on the SAS, because every firqat member who wanted anything came directly to the BATT. No matter whether the BATT were eating or in the middle of a discussion, the door of their hut would open and in would come a firqatman. He would come to the point immediately: 'I want a ... After five hundred '*Ureed...*' the SAS men came to dread the word.

In the early days it was hard. BATT had to try to build up the trust of the firqats and this could only be done by personal contact and immense patience. Any firqatman who wanted anything had to be listened to. Later, when the trust between BATT and firqat had been forged by fire, the SAS were able to obtain some measure of privacy by insisting that every request was put through the firqat leaders, and would deal with no one else.

★   ★   ★

The wedding breakfast was brought in on large round brass dishes by servants and placed on the floor before the seated men around the room. We eased forward into a kneeling position and huddled around the dish of rice and goat meat, topped with the goat's head. The meat was well spiced and we tucked into the food with a will. I reached into the hot rice with my right hand and kneaded a handful into a ball stuck together by the goat's grease poured over the rice beforehand. I flicked it into my mouth and tore a piece of meat apart with my fingers. It was juicy and tender and I thrust it into the centre of the mound where the rice kept hottest. The man to my left seized the head and began to strip off the meat that still remained on it. He placed the pieces on the rice and smiled as he politely put a particularly choice morsel in front of me.

After each man had eaten his fill he sat back, but was careful to leave plenty still on the dishes, since they were to be taken out to the less important guests in another room. Servants now brought in tinned fruit, a great delicacy, and *halwa*, a sweet Omani fudge.

Salim did not appear to have eaten anything. Throughout the main meal and sweetmeats he walked about the room encouraging his guests to eat well and from time to time disappeared, presumably to visit the other guests.

It was not until after the guests had washed their hands with soap while a servant poured water over them from a jug, and had returned to their places for coffee, that he came back and sat down alongside me. We talked generalities until I smelt the fragrance of frankincense. There is an Arabic saying 'After the incense, do not tarry'. It was time to leave amongst many protestations of friendship and wishes for a long and happy marriage.

Alas, it was not to be.

★　★　★

The next few days were busy ones. The Civil Action Teams from my own squadron were despatched by boom to Taqa and Mirbat, and Shaw and his men returned to England.

It was time I called on the Wali of Dhofar, Sheikh Baraik Bin Hamood, in his house within the town walls, opposite the fort-palace on the Salalah sea front. I pushed my way through the crowd of supplicants that filled the entrance and the stairwell, each with his own private reason to see the Wali, and climbed the stairs.

At the top I was shown into an office furnished in the Western style with desks and chairs. I was keen to meet this man who had played a major part in the *coup d'état*. He rose with a slight smile. He was tall for an Arab and well-built, but with a fine-boned Arab face and knowing eyes. A simple white gown showed off to best effect the dark leather belt covered with intricate silver thread-work around his waist. The handle of his *khunja* was of plain wood and ivory, but the sheath, set between two silver embossed whorls, was superbly worked. He was a man of taste.

My Arabic was not good enough to use before someone of his quality and he, I knew, spoke English but did not like to use it formally, so I apologised and asked for his interpreter, a Sudanese whose English and Arabic were fluent. I told Baraik everything I had done and seen and emphasised that BATT's aim was to hand over to Omanis as soon as it was possible. I told him of the impressions of the BATTs in Taqa and Mirbat and of the need for two *naib walis* to be found for the towns. In return, he explained to me the problems of finding men of calibre who would agree to serve in the towns, but he felt that now there were BATTs there, and particularly since the Firqat Salahadin had begun to train in Mirbat, it would give the confidence needed. We had much to talk about on paying and equipping the firqat and their administration generally, but finally I rose to go. Baraik beckoned me to sit down and told the Sudanese to bring in coffee. He spoke in his usual gentle voice which I never, in all the time I knew him, heard him raise. I was to see errant firqatmen go pale before this same quiet voice. The coffee boy entered and handed both of us a small handle-less cup which he filled with black Arabic coffee. A clove of cardamom gave it a refreshing bite. I drank the polite two or three cups, the first of many I drank in that office, and then shook the cup gently to show that I had had enough. As I rose to my feet I mentioned the possibility of the Bait Kathir raising a firqat. Baraik smiled a knowing smile more to himself than to me.

'Perhaps,' he said gently.

THREE

FIRST STEPS IN COUNTER REVOLUTION

The Bait Kathir were a powerful tribe. They were split into two broad factions and, between them, probably controlled more ground than any other tribe in Dhofar. In the north they dominated virtually the whole of the barren wilderness of the *negd* apart from some areas held by the Mahra. For centuries the camel-mounted Bait Kathir had used the speed of their camels and their knowledge of the few water-holes in the negd to raid other, more affluent tribes before disappearing into the safety of their own desert. Unlike the Jebelis, the northern Bait Kathir had no flocks or herds, other than a few underfed goats; they lived by the camel alone.

The tribe's southern faction lived in the extreme west of the Salalah plain, a barren area and not dissimilar to the *negd*. Even the foothills of the jebel where they grazed their goats were barren in comparison with the Central and Eastern Areas, and the plateau had all but disappeared by the time it reached their part of the jebel. They also used camels, but were more pastoral than their northern cousins and owned large flocks of goats. To make it easier to distinguish between the two factions, these were called the Al Kathir.

To complicate matters further, the leader of the northern faction was Sheikh Musalim Bin Nufl and the leader of the southern faction Sheikh Musalim Bin Tufl, but their names were the only similar thing about them. Nufl was built quite unlike the people he represented, the under-nourished, light-boned camel men of the *negd*. He was a portly man, impressive to look at, with a well-groomed beard, but he was much slower mentally than his mercurial cousin Bin Tufl. Tufl was a thin, hard man with a strong determined jaw covered by a wispy grey beard. He habitually wore rimless steel glasses and his lined face reflected the adventure and hardship he had endured as a raider of note in his youth. It was Bin Tufl who had been Wilfred Thesiger's guide during his epic journey from Dhofar into the Empty Quarter in 1946–47.

The Bait Kathir met in a Kathiri sheikh's house in Salalah. A second Intelligence Corps interviewer had arrived a few days before, Warrant Officer Steve Raven, a square-framed voluble Welshman, and the two of us bent to enter the narrow room where the meeting was to be held. It was night and candles placed in niches along the walls flickered in the draught as we entered. To my surprise, the men on either side of the room were sitting on chairs and two more chairs stood at the head of the room for Raven and me. A smoke-encrusted hurricane lamp spluttered feebly at their feet. Tufl's men were ranged on one side of the room and Nufl's on the other. As I advanced up the aisle, I looked down at the faces of the men. The shadows from the candles' light accentuated the sharpness of their features and threw into angular relief their hook noses, lean jaws and pointed beards. Many of them were without shamags and their unkempt woolly hair stretched down to their shoulders. Their wolf eyes studied us as we sat down, and several moments of mute appraisal passed before anyone spoke. Then Bin Nufl began a long monologue.

It gave me time to look at them further. By God, these are raiders all right, I thought. What a band of pirates! Thesiger said that in his day the Bait Kathir were particularly avaricious. This lot looked as if they were motivated entirely by the promise of pillage and loot, with a little rape thrown in for good measure. By their appearance things did not seem to have changed very much.

Nufl spent the first five minutes being obsequious and I smiled regally at the inflated compliments. Tufl, not to be outdone, spent another five minutes offering his. I thanked him too. The next five minutes were spent by Nufl expressing loyalty to the Sultan and the following five by Tufl. At last the question was put. Would BATT train a firqat formed from the Bait Kathir? I asked why they would not join the Salahadin. No, they would only fight amongst other Bait Kathir, they did not trust other tribes. I suspected the truth was that the Bait Kathir had preyed on the other tribes for too long and were worried about a bullet in the back for revenge. In any case, added Tufl, the Salahadin were to train at Mirbat (that secret had not lasted long) and the Bait Kathir's area was in the north and west. He would not get any volunteers to go to Mirbat.

Now we were beginning to come to the point. How many men, I asked, could they provide between them for BATT to train? This began a long discussion between everyone in the room about who could produce how many men. At last Bin Nufl spoke.

'Eighteen,' he said.

'Thirteen,' said Bin Tufl.

Eighteen and thirteen: thirty-one. Not many, but enough for a start, I said. No, no, both hastened to tell me, I had misunderstood. Between thirteen and eighteen in total. I was incredulous.

'Do you mean that the great Bait Kathir tribe can only produce this pitiful number?' I asked. 'And who would command?'

'I will,' said Nufl.

'No, I will,' said Tufl.

'You are both far too old,' I said. 'You are famous warriors whose deeds will always be of great renown, but the firqat must have a young commander, a fighting man of stature and independence.' (Independence from you two old schemers.)

'I know just the man,' said Nufl.

'I know a better one,' said Tufl.

The discussion meandered on, the two of them concentrating more on scoring points off each other than in producing anything constructive. We were getting nowhere. I stood up.

'I want you to get all your fighting men together and let me look at them. I shall expect to meet them here in say, ten days. Good night. Go in the grace of God.'

'Go in the grace of the Merciful,' they muttered.

★ ★ ★

John Lane was waiting back in the operations room with the good news that 14 more SEPs had come in that evening and were being interviewed in the marquee by Birrell and Raven. He next showed me the badge he had designed with Salim's advice for the Firqat Salahadin in the green, red and white of the Omani national colours, the top in the traditional Islamic onion shape to reflect the firqat's religious significance. Finally he gave me a short list of three slogans.

As Salim Mubarak had suggested when we first met, a national slogan was needed to unite the people in the national cause. I had been impressed during my time in Kenya by President Kenyatta's political use of the national slogan '*Harambee*' – 'Pull Together', and had asked Lane to come up with something similar. He had, as always, done it with imagination and thoroughness. He had asked his Dhofari assistants for some suggestions so that they should have a natural ring about them, a cardinal principle in information services, and he had obtained the Wali's agreement. The Wali's favourite, which was also Lane's and, as it turned out, mine, was 'Islam Is Our Way, Freedom is Our Aim'. It did not have the impact of *Harambee,* but it linked Freedom, Islam and the Government, the triplex I wanted. The slogan was adopted and used at the end of every day's broadcasting on Radio Dhofar and it was incorporated whenever possible into pamphlets and leaflets. Years later I was assured by a Dhofari that it was an old Dhofari saying whose origins were lost in antiquity.

★ ★ ★

The BATT commander was an adviser. It was a curious and often frustrating position to be in because he could advise but he had no executive authority; he had to persuade the man with power to issue the order. The advantage, however, was that whilst a person in an appointment of authority had defined limits to his work and tended to concentrate his mind upon the problems facing him within those limits, an adviser could look across the board and identify problems from outside which an insider, because of his many other worries, might not always see.

Administrative work to organise the infrastructure for a counterrevolutionary war took up a lot of my time. Consultations had to be held and papers written to put together committees, under the Wali's chairmanship, on development and on civil affairs, neither of which existed. Many people were working separately towards the same ends, but nobody seemed really sure about what those ends were. Papers had to be written suggesting the status of prisoners of war, scales for firqat pay compared with SAF, the policy on rewards for enemy arms and ammunition; a myriad of details to be resolved if the campaign was to be set on a successful footing.

★ ★ ★

It was time to get the Firqat Salahadin to Mirbat, where the seven SAS men had set up camp ready to receive them. The tents had been prepared, the necessary stores, ammunition and rations had been sent down by boom, and the instructors had had time to look at their training areas, prepare their training aids and rehearse their lessons in Arabic.

But first the firqat had to be brought together and motivated. The scene was carefully set and the 32 men, who had been checked and agreed by Wali Baraik and Salim Mubarak, presented themselves at Um

Al Gwarif. They were a motley band. Most of them wore civilian shirts and *futas*. Some had sandals, but many were bare-footed. Most wore a *shamag* of some sort, many the red-and-white one worn by soldiers throughout the Middle East, but several too, were bare-headed. Nearly all carried the bolt action .303 rifles they had been given when they handed in their Communist weapons and most wore the traditional leather belt studded with coloured rivets and filled with bullets.

They sat down in a semi-circle before the marquee which held the cups of sweet tea and biscuits for later. I began my pep-talk, praising them and their courage in resisting the Communist tyrant, pointing out the problems which lay ahead, and ended by telling them that they were like the figs from which a great tree would one day grow. Finally, with a flourish, I produced a gleaming black FN rifle from its white poly-styrene packing case and held it before me.

'You will all receive a rifle like this at Mirbat,' I said. 'It is the rifle used by most armies of the free countries. Not even the geysh is equipped yet with it.'

'Is it fully automatic?' asked one.

'No.'

'It is too heavy,' said another.

'Can we not have Kalashnikovs?' asked a third.

I tried to convince them of the superiority of the FN, but it was no use; they wanted Kalashnikovs. They were lighter, shorter, easier to carry and they fired fully automatic. I agreed that if they killed an adoo with a Kalashnikov they could carry it, but of course they would not get the reward for it. At this, most feigned disinterest, saying they were not fighting for money, but I could see that the news of rewards for captured enemy weapons had not been disagreeable, nonetheless.

The following evening the firqat met once more for a last meal together in a house in Salalah before sailing to Mirbat next morning. They were all in good spirits and several made short speeches about the need to kill the Communists. They were a fierce, impressive little band. Most had had some form of military training somewhere or other and Salim Mubarak was the undisputed leader. I could not help comparing them with the wild men of the Bait Kathir.

★ ★ ★

The first casualty happened much sooner than I had expected. SAS soldiers are fighting men: you do not train tigers and expect them to sing like canaries. BATT had to get some SAS soldiers on to the jebel as

61

fighters or morale would have suffered. Besides, BATT needed to learn all they could from the SAF and the only way to do that was to accompany them on operations.

I had taken three other SAS men on a company ambush a few days before, when the adoo were reported to have a camel convoy moving along the foot of the jebel that night. We took two bren guns, each fitted with an image-intensifying sight like a large telescope (inevitably nicknamed 'shuftiscope'), which enabled the gunner to see out to several hundred yards by night. The SAF were not yet equipped with them. Nothing came of this patrol but it was instructional nonetheless. The SAS were impressed by the lightness of the SAF equipment and by the speed at which the plimsoll-clad soldiers moved at night, but dawn found the company on a forward slope dominated by high ground within small arms range. Had the adoo had even half a dozen men up there, the SAS and many SAF soldiers would have been dead men. It was a thoughtful patrol which returned.

Another SAS patrol had gone out with the Northern Frontier Regiment on the north of the jebel. A GPMG, which again SAF were not yet equipped with, was carried by Trooper Alex Glennie, a tough, square, 30-year-old Edinburgh Scot. He was with the reserve platoon of a company which had carried out the usual SAF operation of moving by night into a defensive position and, as dawn broke, the adoo began to snipe them and move around their flanks. After some minutes probing fire, the adoo must have thought they had found a weakness in the reserve platoon for they began to push home an attack. Glennie opened fire with a long burst from his GPMG. Abruptly all shooting stopped and, for perhaps half a minute, there was total silence as both sides considered this new weapon – the SAF soldiers with awe and the adoo no doubt with concern – but they were brave men and began the attack again. A group of four or five men began to skirmish up a shallow wadi towards Glennie, moving up in short dashes from rock to rock whilst a light machine-gunner to a flank kept the SAF heads down. Glennie waited until he saw a man skip behind a small rock then opened up on him, chopping the rock to pieces and killing the man behind it. Another adoo tried to move forward and Glennie cut him down as well. Then, as he was aiming at a third, a shattering shock numbed his arm.

I had briefed the Commanding Officer about security over any BATT casualties, but when a radio message reached Um Al Gwarif that Glennie had fallen over a tent peg and broken his arm, I took it at face value; accidents happen. He would be arriving by helicopter at the airfield in 20 minutes. I took the medical officer with me and drove up to the airfield, calling on the Field Surgical Team on the way to borrow their ambulance Landrover. A broken arm was not very serious, but the medical officer said he wanted the ambulance just in case.

The helicopter landed close to the ambulance and one glance was enough. Glennie's ashen face, the 'M' for morphine written in ink on his forehead followed by the time '0920', and the heavily bloodstained arm with little bits of bone sticking to his shirt told their story. Carefully we lifted him on to a stretcher in the back of the Landrover. One side of the canvas ripped from end to end. Cursing, we lifted him off on to the second stretcher: it ripped too, but fortunately only from the waist down, so that the top half still offered him support. Despite the morphine, he was still wide awake but not once did he groan, and on the drive to the Field Surgical Team made self-deprecating jokes and apologised for causing me embarrassment. He apologised to me!

I sat on the steps of the FST in the sun under the curious gaze of the local people until the head surgeon came out to say that, although it was a serious wound, he was confident he could save the arm. Then I returned to Um Al Gwarif to think. Watts's last words before I left Hereford were still crystal clear in my mind. I could still see his stocky, swarthy figure as he paced up and down his office, the words pouring from him in a torrent, taking great drags from his cigarette to marshal his thoughts for a moment, before he embarked on another tirade. Finally, he had paused and ran his fingers through his long black hair, then turned his dark eyes on me.

'And don't go thinking it will be easy, Tony, because it won't.' He stabbed his forefinger at me in emphasis. 'And whatever you do, you must not (stab) have (stab) casualties. Got it? Because if you do, that will be it – finished. We will be withdrawn. So, for God's sake don't take chances.'

No casualties: that had been the order. But you cannot go to war without casualties. There had to be a first sooner or later, but I must admit I had hoped for a bit later than this. We had only been in the theatre for a month, and had not even started the proper fighting yet. I carefully composed three radio messages: one to the Ministry of Defence, one to HQ SAS in London and the third to Watts: then waited for the brickbats. They did not come. Typically the first message came from Watts, a comforting and congratulatory one for Glennie and a reassurance to me that he would square matters in London.

★ ★ ★

By mid-February the training of the Firqat Salahadin at Mirbat was going well. They had a whole SAS troop to train them, separate from the SAS Civil Action Team, although obviously the two lived together and helped each other in every way. Captain Ian Cheshire, the troop commander, was a dour, angry Lowland Scot in his mid-twenties and a typical rebel-without-a-cause, but I knew him as an efficient, imaginative and hard-working leader of men. If anyone could mould the Salahadin into a fighting unit in the short time we had, it was he.

The helicopter – and at this time there was only one flying in Dhofar, a far cry from the fleet that was to come – was unserviceable, so I decided to go to Mirbat by sea. The boom sailed that night and as she chugged out of Rayzut harbour I sat with the British captain and drank a relaxing brandy before retiring. It was a clear cold night on deck and I snuggled up in my sleeping bag under the stars, lulled by the rhythmic chug of the boat's engine and the hissing of the sea along its sides.

I awoke to find my sleeping bag soaked with dew; it was no incentive to get up and I did not. It was the beginning of a delightfully idle and refreshing day. I had become more tired than I realized from the long hours of discussions, meetings and visits, the late nights writing in my tent, and the incessant wrangling with the Bait Kathir. Now there was nothing to do but lie in the sun or watch the dolphins streaking alongside the boat or flashing across its bows.

The sun was setting as I climbed over the side of the boom into a Gemini rubber boat. The SAS cox'n put the powerful Johnson engine into gear and the boat planed its way the short distance to the shore where Cheshire was waiting with Salim Mubarak and Mohammed Said.

I should have foreseen that in the absence of a *naib* wali, Salim considered himself the town governor. His hospitality was, as always, excellent and that night he and the firqat killed a goat and entertained BATT to a meal, so it was not until next day that Cheshire and I could talk together. We walked out to look at the training.

'How's it going?' I asked.

'Very well. There've been one or two hiccups, but nothing serious. They admired our olive green uniform and tried to buy it off the blokes, so we got some green dye from the souk and suggested they dye their khaki in it. Trouble is, it was an Indian dye, a sort of fluorescent green, used for saris, I imagine. Anyway, they came on parade next morning looking like a bunch of demon kings. We tried to keep straight faces, but someone gave way and we all burst out laughing. God, they were furious,' he grinned. 'You know how sensitive they are. They threw their rifles down and rushed into the sea to wash it off. In fact, it's dried quite well, as you can see, a sort of German field grey. Anyway, anything will be better on the jebel than the sandy khaki stuff the SAF wear: it stands out a mile.'

'What about the FNs?'

'They still don't really like them. Many of them are small men as you know, and the FN is too heavy for them. They keep harping on about the Kalashnikov, so we got hold of one and made them fire it at a hundred yards fully automatic; then we made them shoot an FN semi-automatic and compared the hits. They're good shots and most had all 20 shots on target with the FN, but they'd be lucky to get more than five with the Kalashnikov, so I think we've probably cured them of wanting to fire fully automatic the whole time.'

We stood watching the firqat training for some time without speaking. At last Cheshire raised an eyebrow at me. 'Decided yet where we're going to blood them?'

'Yes, Sudh,' I answered.

★　★　★

When a unit is being 'blooded' for the first time, it has to be successful or their confidence may be irretrievably destroyed. Sudh would suit well, I had decided. It was a small town on the coast 20 miles east of Mirbat. It had been abandoned by the SAF some 18 months previously and was now controlled by an adoo band, 50 strong and led by a famous adoo leader nicknamed Qartoob. Intelligence had it that the 50 were seldom in the town itself, but that the two headlands which guarded Sudh Bay were always picketed. It was not a hard target; it was as far east as adoo sway extended and on the coast far from the jebel so the adoo could not move reinforcements to it quickly. If disaster fell, we could always fight our way back along the coast to Mirbat; and it agreed with all the principles I had studied of counter-guerilla warfare: to begin in the soft areas and gradually expand into the harder ones.

That night I called a 'Chinese Parliament' to get the men's ideas about Sudh. A 'Chinese Parliament' is a peculiarly SAS institution. The Regiment recruits from the rest of the Army and volunteers come from all Arms and Services to undergo a rigorous selection course. The average age of those who pass the course is around 26 or 27, at which age most men are non-commissioned officers in their own units.

However, although he may be a very good artillery sergeant, for example, a successful volunteer will know nothing about SAS operations when he joins. He will therefore be given the lowest rank of trooper in the SAS, although he may hold a rank several places higher in his own unit. Consequently, an SAS troop consists mainly of ex-non-commissioned officers of considerable and varied experience. At a Chinese Parliament, a troop, or sometimes even a squadron, comes together to discuss a problem. Anyone can suggest anything he likes. His idea is kicked around and usually discarded, or it may lead to another. The commander will often have thought of most of them anyway, but occasionally a gem will crop up which he had not considered, and therefore quite probably the enemy will not have considered it either. Security was not endangered in discussing the target this far ahead; all SAS soldiers are trained to keep their mouths shut. Nothing startling came out of this particular Parliament, but the two options, to approach by land or sea, were given a thorough airing and helped me to make up my mind.

Next day, before I left, Salim asked for a word with Birrell and myself. We went for a walk along the beach where he told me of the follow-up to an unpleasant incident the day before, when someone had thrown a stone at one of the members of the CAT. Salim had been incensed when he heard about it and had traced the miscreant, the son-in-law of a well-known adoo leader. Salim told me that he intended to do nothing about it yet, because that afternoon he intended to arrest the four members of the PFLOAG town directorate whom he had now identified, and no doubt they would implicate this man in more serious crimes. He went on to say that he had men in Taqa who had identified the town directorate there too.

But I must clear this with the *Siasi* I argued. Intelligence may already know these people and want to keep them in position a little longer, although privately I doubted it. No, he said, the two groups must be cleared out by the Firqat Salahadin before the two *naib walis* were installed in three days' time. He twisted his lip disparagingly in the soldier's distrust of the politician.

I had to return to Salalah and could not stay for the arrests, but Cheshire later told me what had happened. The four were arrested that afternoon and, by the evening, had implicated another 25 townsmen. Salim let it be known that he held the names of all those who had helped the adoo in any way, but provided they were prepared to come in and sign a confession and to renounce the adoo in public next morning, they would not be arrested. If they chose not to, of course they would be sent to Salalah for trial. Then he let the town stew overnight.

The next morning at ten o'clock he sent the firqat around the town to round up all the inhabitants and bring them to the town square where, one by one, forty of them stood on a dais and denounced the Front. The whole thing took more than four hours. Cheshire said that the attitude of the people changed overnight. The surliness had totally disappeared. The town had at last declared openly for the Sultan.

Next day Mohammed Said did the same in Taqa.

★　★　★

I returned to Salalah the way I had come, by boom. During my absence there had been several developments. The Bait Kathir had sorted out the inter-faction dispute, and all the fighting men they could muster, which were not many, had declared for Sheikh Musalim Bin Tufl. They wanted to train at Adonib, a flat piece of nothing on the western edge of the Salalah Plain. Bin Nufl had retired in dignified distaste to the north and was talking of forming a firqat to be mounted on camels patrolling the *negd*.

This was good news, but better was to follow. An important adoo leader had walked in to Taqa to say that a complete adoo firqat, formed mainly of Mahra, had deserted the adoo. They were moving northwards to avoid the adoo main forces, who controlled the southern routes off the jebel, and intended to keep walking out into the *negd* until they were safe. They would need water and food.

This was another important development. The Mahra were, and are, more of a nation than a tribe. They controlled most of the Hadramaut in PDRY and most of Western Dhofar, but a small group of Mahra had fought their way along the *gatn* in the past and had established themselves in the north-eastern part of jebel Dhofar, where the adoo firqat were now walking out. Provided this was handled properly, it could only be a matter of time before the whole eastern tribe came over to us, and, looking ahead in the long term, they had cousins in the west.

The final cream on the cake was that an ex-adoo mine-layer, Sheikh Ali Bin Mahad, had come in and was telling all he knew about re-supply routes and stores caves. Most of his information concerned the Central Area, but at last we had a man of influence who knew the names of the adoo leaders in the Centre and who could describe the dissensions which existed between them and the effect our information services were having upon them, above all, the effect on them of the news of the formation of loyal firqats. He was providing invaluable information, also, on the adoo's organisation, tactics and re-supply system: how they moved, how far, where they lay up, what routes they preferred – all good contact intelligence which would help SAF to interrupt the adoo's re-supply chain. Birrell and Raven were working round the clock on information and were quietly jubilant at the week's progress.

It was Raven who introduced the idea of the Flying Finger. Ali Bin Mahad was one of the few Dhofaris who could understand a map. Most Dhofaris would draw a series of straight lines at right angles to each other to represent wadis, which were in fact anything but straight, and at any angle but right angles. The distance between wadis meant nothing to them. They could only say that such-and-such a wadi was third on the left up the Wadi Darbat or whatever. How far up it, or in what direction it ran meant nothing to them. Ali Bin Mahad was different and he picked up the skill quickly. Ali and Raven spent hours poring over a large-scale map trying to pin-point the exact location of the caves and baits where adoo stores were held. Their task was complicated further by the difference between the Arabic names shown on the map and the quite different Jebeli names they were called by most Dhofaris. One felt sympathy for the unfortunate British cartographer who had had to do his best to put into the English alphabet the curious grunts, clicks and hisses of the Jebeli language, but the results were often unrecognisable.

In despair, one day Raven took Ali up in a helicopter and asked him to point out the positions on the ground. Ali picked up the idea in an instant and was able to draw the exact locations, using what he saw from the aircraft of the ground's lay, the shape of the hills, and the curves in the wadis to produce identifiable diagrams of the places he was describing.

The next step was to hit them. Ali, Raven and a Strikemaster pilot would fly in a helicopter together. Ali would point out the exact position of a cave which contained the cache or adoo unit, Raven would translate and the pilot note it on his map and, more important, identify it in his mind. Then he would return in his jet to strike it with cannon, rockets or bombs as the target required.

The method proved so accurate that Ali, and later others, were able to indicate a single *bait* being used as an arms or ammunition store. The *bait* would be destroyed in one pass without any others being touched. Frequently the blaze of exploding ammunition could be seen all night from Um Al Gwarif.

A *bait* or cave, or even sometimes a large tree, known to be used by the adoo as a meeting place required more subtlety. Each adoo group had a rallying or meeting place to which they would go if they heard warning shots, but which they also used for pre-arranged meetings and meals. The group dispersed at night to sentry positions or to separate *baits* to sleep, and came together soon after first light for breakfast at the meeting place. So the Strikemaster pilot would identify his target, but would delay his strike for several days in case the helicopter had caused the adoo to change their habits temporarily. Then one morning, without warning, the meeting place would be struck. It was a hit-or-miss affair, but news soon came off the jebel that the adoo feared the Flying Finger more than anything else the SAF could do at that time.

★ ★ ★

Musalim Qaraitas was a Mahra in the Firqat Salahadin. He had deserted from the same adoo firqat which was now trying to walk out and he was asked if he would be prepared to take a message to the adoo leader. He would be delighted, he said, for he knew the man like a brother. Raven dropped him off in the *negd* by helicopter within easy walking distance of the *gatn* with food, water and a rifle, and arranged a rendezvous at a particular wadi junction two days later.

Qaraitas had been given a smoke grenade and a sarbe radio, but now as Raven and I peered down at the rendezvous through the windows of the helicopter, we saw no sign of any smoke. I checked the map with the ground to see that we were at the right wadi junction. There was no doubt about it.

'Any sound from the sarbe?' I asked the pilot.

'Not a thing.'

Two Strikemasters streaked past and below us, then pulled up into the sky in a noisy show of force.

'Well, there's nothing for it. You had better put us down, then push off into the *negd* and sit there till we call you.'

The helicopter put its nose down and fell out of the sky in a dizzy spiral. The ground spun rapidly before us and we came in to land on a small flat plateau top in a whirlwind of flying sand and small stones. Raven and I leapt out and tugged at the bags of food and the heavy jerrycans of water. We turned our backs to the stinging sand as the aircraft took off, then stood up thankfully as the wind and noise receded.

We were on a small flat hill of baked earth, some hundred yards long and fifty across, and covered with small black angular stones. There was no sign of life and the only sound came from jet engines high up in the sky. I took out the sarbe from my belt and let the wire aerial spring into position.

'Hallo, Red Leader, this is Tiger Nine, radio check, over.'

'Red Leader, OK over.'

'Tiger Nine, OK out.'

Well, that was a relief at any rate. I walked across to where Raven was standing on the lip of the plateau with a good view of the wadi 150 feet below. It was wide here – a good 200 yards across. Round stones ranging in size from pebbles to the size of footballs, and all bleached white by the sun, formed the wadi bed. Together, we lugged the heavy loads down the path into it. There was nothing to do then, but wait. Raven sat on the jerrycans, his white shirt and shamag plain for all to see, unarmed, whilst I took cover behind an outcrop in some shadow 50 yards behind, checked my rifle sights and waited.

It was not long before a file of men came into view around the wadi bend 200 yards away. They were moving slowly for Dhofaris. Most of them appeared to be unarmed and I recognised Qaraitas' black *futa*. He was still carrying the Kalashnikov and wore the Chinese ammunition belt we had given him.

Raven walked forward to meet them and there was a lot of hand-shaking and talk I could not hear. I counted 24 of them, but they appeared too genuinely pleased for this to be a trap. I lowered my rifle and walked forward out of the shadow to meet them. They were all desperately thin and undernourished and pathetically grateful for the little we had provided. Although they had just walked 32 miles in the sun without water, they still sipped carefully from the mugs as they were handed around, and I wondered what British troops would have done in the same circumstances. Qaraitas was in high spirits, grinning from ear to ear.

They still had a long walk ahead, but they were out of range of the adoo now. After a pause of 20 minutes, the weary little group moved off northwards once more, most of them giving a tired little smile or wave as they passed.

It had all gone very smoothly. Nonetheless it was not until they were out of small arms range that I called the helicopter in. I flew to Mirbat reflecting contentedly that it looked as if we had the beginnings of a third firqat.

FOUR
SUDH

23rd February 1971

The boom sailed from Mirbat at 1400 hours with two SAS troops and the Firqat Salahadin embarked in her. She had not come into Mirbat Bay, but had loaded the hundred men from a secluded beach a thousand yards south of the town. Nonetheless it was probable that she had been seen, but that had been anticipated. Rumours had been deliberately spread for some days before that the firqat were about to mount an operation on to the jebel north of Salalah, and to help the deception the boom sailed off in a south-westerly direction until she was out of sight of land, then turned eastwards on to her proper heading.

It was a tight squeeze aboard. The two Geminis used to ferry the troops from the shore were stowed on the deck and reduced the available space still further, until the firqat and SAS were so mixed together that it was not always easy to distinguish between the brown sunburned SAS men and the Dhofaris. The whole boat radiated an atmosphere of controlled excitement combined with a tense confidence: men stripped and re-oiled their weapons, magazines were emptied and re-loaded, radio sets checked. But at last, after an hour, the activity lessened and the mass of men settled down and tried to sleep.

It was almost dark as the big boom eased her way into Qinqari Bay, 4000 yards south-west of Sudh and hidden from it by the Jebel Qinqari, the only feature of any size for miles. I had decided to approach the town from the northern, landward side. The adoo appeared to be expecting an attack from the sea and if, somehow, the news of the Firqat Salahadin's departure from Mirbat by boom had reached the adoo, they would strengthen their guard on the headlands that protected Sudh beach. By attacking from the landward side after a sea move I reckoned

71

that with luck we could be in the town before we even had to begin to fight.

The boom did not approach too close. The noise of marine diesels carries a long way across water, particularly at night. Her anchor splashed gently, her engine stopped, and she lay rocking quietly a thousand yards off shore. It seemed very still. All eyes peered through the darkness, trying to make out the shore line as the first of the Geminis was lowered over the side.

It was a pitch-black night. I leant a shuftiscope on the gunwale and switched it on. The high-pitched, normally inaudible hum sounded loud in the silence. The coast became clearly visible with small white breakers showing up brightly. Large breakers revealed some clumps of rock, too, between us and the shore, but I could see no sign of life. Cheshire appeared at my elbow and I passed him the 'scope for a final look. He peered through it for a few seconds, then passed it back.

'Looks good,' he said. 'See you later.'

He swung over the side and dropped into one of the two boats bobbing in the slight swell, both filled with SAS men. Cheshire commanded the squadron's amphibious troop and night landings were their bread and butter. I wanted that beach properly checked and secured before the firqat, most of whom had never been in a boat in their lives, were ferried ashore. The noise as the 40 horsepower Johnsons roared into life made me wince for a moment before they throttled back to a throbbing bubble. The two craft nosed away from the boom and headed for the beach.

I watched them through the shuftiscope and passed directions to keep them in line with the landing point and out of the way of the rocks to the man standing alongside me with the radio. Captain Peter Farran was the second troop commander and he and Cheshire were as alike as chalk and cheese. Whereas Cheshire was dark, angry and Celtic, Farran was a big, fair-haired Rhodesian. Whereas Cheshire went from cool to boiling point and back again, Farran was permanently just off the simmer. Cheshire would glower when I gave him something to do he did not like; Farran just looked at me without expression, betraying his annoyance only by a tightening of the jaw muscles. If they had both come to a deep wadi filled with thorns, Cheshire would have climbed down into it, fought his way across and climbed up the other side to emerge sweating, bleeding and triumphant. Farran would have sat down, lit his long curving Meerschaum pipe, thought about it – and built a bridge.

I swung the 'scope away from the boats for a few seconds to scan the beach for a final check – and stiffened.

'Hold it. There's a light at the right hand edge of the beach. Let me talk to Ian direct.'

Could it be adoo? It made absolutely no sense. They could not know we were coming in here. Why, I had not even told the firqat where we were going until they were all aboard, let alone where we were going to land.

Cheshire's voice was calm. He would go and find out. A minute later, his whispered voice came over the radio again.

'The beach is secure and the light was the fire of a couple of fishermen. They're frightened out of their wits. Better get some firqs here to talk to them.'

I felt a flood of relief. The tricky part, the landing, was going to be all right.

Twenty minutes later the whole force was ashore. The two fishermen were related to one of the firqat and volunteered to guide us on the overland march to Sudh. The long line set off in single file keeping to the wadi shadows and by 0100 hours had reached our lying-up position in the main Wadi Sudh, a thousand yards north of the town where we were to wait until nearer dawn. The moon had risen fully now and it bathed the wadi in silver light, revealing in the shadows of the wadi sides the huddled mounds of men trying to sleep. The only sound was the whispered relief of sentries. I wrapped my shamag around my neck, pulled my anorak hood over my head, undid my belt order, and tried to sleep, but it was too cold to do more than doze fitfully.

At 0530 hours the huddles unfolded and cramped men stood up to stretch their stiff joints before they re-formed into their groups. A last few whispered orders and the force set off once more towards Sudh, this time in three groups. Two firqat groups moved along the high ground either side of the wadi, whilst the main body of firqat and SAS kept to the wadi bed. By 0600 all these groups were in position a hundred yards short of the town. At 0630, when the tops of the first houses became visible, a small reconnaissance group of ten firqat moved cautiously down the wadi and slipped into the town.

A minute passed, then two shots echoed loudly in the dawn stillness. Here we go, I thought, and waited for the return fire. Silence. A figure materialised out of the dawn mist and spoke briefly to Salim. Salim turned around to me.

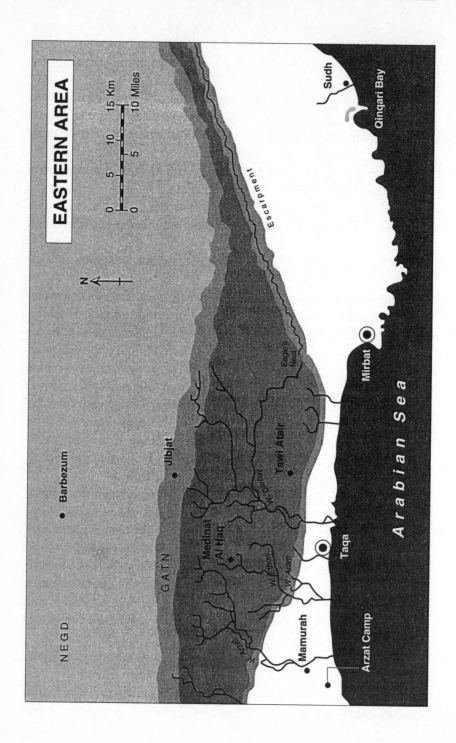

'He says there are no adoo in the town. One man had to be warned to halt, that was all. We will go in. *Al hamdul'Illah.*'

The town was soon secured. Mixed SAS and firqat pickets climbed up to the high ground which dominates the town, and began to build sangars. The command group set up its headquarters in the fort in the centre of town, and patrols were sent down to the adoo's picket position on the headlands, but found them empty. The town was very quiet. Nothing moved. I followed Salim into the fort and up the dark stone steps on to the roof, where Mohammed Ali Isa, the firqat sergeant major, produced the Sultanate's flag and hoisted it on a pole to hang limply in the windless air.

With the simple flag-raising ceremony over, Salim walked to the edge of the battlement and began to shout. He spoke in Arabic and Jebeli, and his voice echoed around the 50 or so houses that made up the town. For half an hour he harangued the silent town telling them of the Firqat Salahadin, the evils of the Communists and the promises of the new Sultan. He emphasised that this was not just a visit. More soldiers would arrive tomorrow and they would not go away again – this time they were here to stay. Sudh was once again free of the Communists. Finally, he announced that all able-bodied men were to report to the wali's house at ten o'clock that morning.

It had been a *tour de force* and I congratulated him as I handed him a mug of hot, sweet tea. He sipped it thoughtfully.

'Do you think they heard you?' I asked, looking down at the shuttered houses below. Still nothing stirred.

'They heard all right.'

As ten o'clock approached, the firqat began walking through the town to rout out the men. Gradually, in ones and twos, the town's men folk began to concentrate sheepishly in front of the largest house in the town until about 70 men sat along three sides of the square where Mohammed Ali Isa had marshalled them. Salim and Mohammed Said strode out of the Fort and across to the wali's house. Salim stood with his back to the large carved wooden door and began to talk. It was another long talk, but not so one-sided this time. The sitting men began to fire questions at him, which he answered at length. I watched from the roof of the fort, fascinated, as the mood of the meeting began to change from surly suspicion, to friendliness, to occasional laughter.

Children's voices sounded below me. I peered over the wall to see three firqatmen walking backwards, followed by a pack of children skipping and laughing. The firqatmen were laughing too, and encouraging the children to chant a little ditty, giving them sweets when they got it right. The charming little band disappeared up the main street, capering happily and singing. I could just make out some of the words: 'What, what are the Salahadin? They are the Army of Freedom.'

The meeting in front of the house was breaking up now and a firqatman accompanied each head of household back to his house, to drink coffee with his family and to explain further what the war was about and what the new regime had promised to do.

By the evening of that day the town was spiritually ours as well as physically. I realised that what I had witnessed was a Communist take-over in reverse. Salim had used the methods he had been taught in China. It was a perfectly executed example of indoctrination such as no SAF or British troops could possibly have achieved.

In the afternoon, one of Salim's agents came in to say that a group of twenty-four adoo were lying up not far from the town. I asked Salim to accompany me and together we climbed up to the high ground to check the pickets' state of readiness. The sangars were well-built with good thick walls made from rocks prised out of the ground. Some must have taken several men to move. They would stand up against anything the adoo were likely to use, except an RPG7, a Soviet-made anti-tank rocket launcher, probably the best of its type in the world. The RPG7 was light, sturdy and easy to operate, and its 85-mm rocket warhead would tear any but the stoutest sangar apart.

The high ground gave a good view of the town, and while we were up there we considered together the best house for the SAS Civil Action Team which would remain behind after we had withdrawn, the best place for the clinic, the helicopter pad and another house for the headquarters of the company of the Muscat Regiment which was to come in next day. Thirty-six hours had passed since anyone had had any sleep and everyone felt tired after the excitement and anticipation of the previous night, even though there had been no battle. Nonetheless, if the adoo were to regain the town, tonight would be their only chance. After the company had arrived on the morrow it would be impregnable, but tonight we must stand by our weapons.

There was no counter-attack apart from one or two men, probably scouts, who crept up to the ridge and squirted a Kalashnikov at the fort. The return fire was short but intensive and culminated in the double explosion of the BATT's Carl Gustav anti-tank launcher which blew off the top of the hill from where the adoo had fired. Their report, when they got back to Qartoob, would be worth hearing.

The following day at dawn, the infantry company arrived by boom and at noon took over responsibility for the security of the town, allowing the SAS to withdraw their pickets to help with the pioneer construction of concrete for the sangars and wire for the perimeter fence. It was hot, sweaty work, so in the evening I took my rifle and headed down through the town to the beach for a swim. As I lazed in the warm sea, I reflected on the day's progress.

It had been a day of visitors. The *naib* wali of Mirbat, Amr Bin Ali, who was to distinguish himself at the battle of Mirbat a year later, had flown in to address the townsfolk. He was an intelligent and amusing man, known as Ali Bin Foureyes by the soldiers with the intolerance of the perfect sighted, but he was also a very influential man in the Bait Umr tribe, whose tribal boundaries contained both Mirbat and Sudh. Then, there had been various officers of the Muscat Regiment, and of course Colonel Mike Harvey, the new Commander Dhofar. Until his appointment, there had been only one battalion in the Province and the Commanding Officer had held both appointments. Now there were two.

Harvey was a brave and experienced soldier and was faced with enormous problems: an inadequate headquarters, inadequate administrative back-up and insufficient troops, but he had all that could be spared. When he was replaced, it was to be with a proper brigade headquarters and greater force levels, including the war-winning Huey helicopters. But that all lay in the future.

Our first meeting in Um Al Gwarif had been friendly enough, but it had revealed differences between us over the plan of campaign. We both agreed that the war could not be won until SAF had permanent bases on the jebel. Our disagreement lay more in the time frame, than in the aim. He was rightly aware of the weakness of his force and believed that he could make best use of the limited numbers he had by throttling the adoo's re-supply route at its narrowest point near the border with PDRY. He was concerned, also, to stop the Front's construction of the 'Freedom Road', a track they were building under the escarpment. It was already wide enough to take trucks to Sarfait, and the Front planned to extend it to their great stores complex in the caves of Shershitti. Politically, too, a SAF presence near the border would enable the Government to deny that the Front had established a 'liberated area'. It was all good thinking, but the penalty would be that enough troops would not remain to establish a permanent presence on the jebel in the east. Whilst establishing a permanent base in the west, he would have to rely upon raids into the jebel to keep the adoo off balance in the east, until that is, he could get more troops as the SAF expanded.

I wanted to do it the other way round, and establish a permanent presence in the 'soft' east, from which to begin the pacification of the jebel, whilst accepting that in the west we could do little more than raid into the jebel from the *negd*. My reasoning was that the longer the problem was left, the tighter would become the adoo's control in the east and the harder it would be to establish a base at all. I believed it questionable also whether even a full battalion so close to the PDRY border would be able to do more than hamper the adoo's re-supply route, whilst its enormous administrative problems – since everything would have to come in by air – would detract from the resources needed for the pacification of the east.

A second major difference between us lay in our attitude to the firqats. We, in BATT, had to be seen by the firqats to trust them if we were ever to earn their trust – even if it meant taking risks. SAF were under no such compulsion and most of the SAF had spent too long fighting Dhofaris to accept them as trustworthy allies overnight.

The Sultan intended to visit Dhofar shortly, Harvey told me, and would visit SAF. There were to be no firqat within five hundred yards of the Sultan, he ordered; they were to act as a line of outer pickets to secure the area. It was a prudent precaution from his point of view and I suspect that, in his position, I should have done the same, but I knew it would seem a slap in the face to the firqat. Cheshire, as I had anticipated, came up hot-foot with indignation when he heard the orders. I decided that the firqat should be sent on patrol that day. We would tell them afterwards how sorry the Sultan had been to miss them.

But there had been other visitors too, furtive little Jebelis carrying notes between Salim and Qartoob. This was something else, which some SAF officers could not understand. 'Do you know,' they would confide darkly, 'we have proof that some of your firqat are in contact with the adoo?'

Of course they were. How else could they persuade them to come across to the Government's side? Often it was a case of brother conferring with brother, or almost certainly negotiation between men of the same tribe. News that a man was about to desert the adoo would sometimes reach HQ BATT days or even weeks before he actually appeared.

The negotiations on this occasion reached their climax next day. That afternoon Qartoob sent in a messenger and he was met by Salim in a small house near the entrance to the wire. Birrell told me later that the gist of the message was clear: Qartoob would not come across to the Government and said that Salim had been duped by false promises, but it was not too late and if Salim and his men would like to rejoin the adoo now, all would be forgiven and forgotten. Salim had given the messenger another note and the latter had left to return to Qartoob.

But the messenger had made a mistake. He let slip in his conversation Qartoob's present position and a Bait Umr firqatman knew the place well. Within minutes of the messenger's departure, 20 of the firqat, carrying their rifles and bren guns over their shoulders, came trotting below the sangar where I was sitting, and disappeared, still moving fast, among the broken hills and wadis stretching to the east of the town. They could move much faster than the SAS. This was a job for the firqat alone. Salim may well have decided, too, that white faces would prejudice his negotiations.

The firqat surprised Qartoob and his men completely. They had been lulled by the exchange of messages into believing that the firqat were reluctant to leave the security of Sudh and were resting in a shady wadi by a waterhole. Silently the firqat climbed on to the high ground and surrounded them. The negotiations were brutally simple: 'Agree to talk or we kill you.'

Two hours later, the Firqat Salahadin returned with the seven most important men of the adoo firqat through the main gate in the wadi bed where I stood waiting with Bill Laconde, the troop sergeant of the Firqat Salahadin's BATT. Like most of the better Arabists in the Squadron, Laconde was a Scotsman. Scots seemed to find the glottal stop and the rolling 'rrrrr' of the Arabic easier to pronounce. Salim introduced me to each of the SEPs as if they were old friends and I shook hands with them warmly.

Ahmed Mohammed Qartoob was not very tall – about the same height as Salim and, like him, looked every inch a leader. He was bareheaded but, although an older man, his neatly combed hair and bushy moustache showed no sign of greyness. A khaki shirt was buttoned to the neck over his futa. An ammunition belt around his waist and a bag slung over one shoulder held all he needed to sustain himself and fight. His feet were bare. He shook hands firmly and looked me straight in the eye. I decided there and then that I badly wanted him on our side.

We walked back to the fort where a meal had been prepared and the remainder of the firqat were waiting to greet the SEPs. I left them to it and went down to the beach where a vast amount of defence stores had arrived aboard a boom and where I was told that the 45 askars I was expecting would be aboard another boom arriving at midnight. The infantry company could not stay forever and these askars would replace them once the town's defences were properly prepared. They were Northern Omanis and far from ideal, but with the SAS Civil Action Team to lick them into shape they would serve the purpose.

The hurricane lamp in Salim's room, where he was still arguing the Government's case with the SEPs, burned late that night. These were hard-core men and they were not going to be convinced easily. I checked the guard before I retired to my own room. I had ordered maximum security. All seven of the men were still armed. I wanted these men as allies, not prisoners. Nonetheless, a certain prudence was indicated and I wedged my door and placed my loaded rifle by my side before I leant across and blew out the candle.

The next morning, a medical officer and Birrell arrived by helicopter. Each man was given a thorough medical examination and the seven seemed to be in reasonable condition though undernourished. All went well until it was Qartoob's turn. He had seemed subdued, but now as the doctor began to examine him he suddenly stiffened, his eyes rolled up and he fell to the floor, thrashing. The other prisoners and the firqatmen pressed back in alarm to form a half-circle around the twitching man and there was much muttering of '*jinns*'. It was a straight case of epilepsy, no doubt brought on by the shock of capture, and three SAS men lay on him to prevent him from harming himself while the doctor treated him. He recovered after a few minutes and could remember nothing of it.

In the afternoon Birrell interviewed each man separately, asking him about his past, his training, his knowledge of the adoo's organisation, weapons and plans. He spent about an hour with each, then gave me his impressions of them. Qartoob, he said, was the military leader, but perhaps because of his epileptic attack had not appeared as strong a character as his political commissar and second-in-command, Salim Said Dherdhir.

Dherdhir had impressed me almost as much as Qartoob. He was slightly taller than Qartoob and was dressed and equipped identically, but his moustache and hair were less well-trimmed and his eyes held the wild angry look one came to identify with newly come-over SEPs. Nonetheless, said Birrell, he was the key man. If he could be persuaded, the others would accept his advice and fall into line.

That evening Birrell sat in a small room at the top of the fort with Dherdhir and the others, together with Salim and Mohammed Said, and he argued. He argued until two o'clock next morning. He talked about the liberal ideas of the new Sultan, the plans which existed to bring civil development to the jebel, the need for the people to be able to follow their own desires and to have a say in their own government. Nobody had spoken to Dherdhir like this before except the Communists. The breakthrough came when he pointed to Birrell with a grin and exclaimed, 'You are a Communist.'

One by one the seven filed into my room and with dignity surrendered their arms to me. Over the following two days Salim and Qartoob together took out some men to return with 16 of Qartoob's old firqat whom they wanted for the Firqat Salahadin. Several more came in of their own accord and, by the time I embarked once more in the boom to return to Salalah on 28th February, there were 36. The captain surveyed the wild-looking bunch with apprehension and it was with some difficulty that I persuaded him not to mount a Browning machine-gun on the poop.

'Very well, but I shall hold you personally responsible,' he growled and retired below, making it quite clear what he thought of about 30 ex-adoo aboard his boat. I was not offered any brandy that night.

The boom anchored early off Salalah, but it was not until 0800 that the small boats could get through the surf to ferry everyone ashore. A large crowd had gathered to meet the SEPs and, after much kissing, they were led off to meet Wali Baraik. I returned to Um Al Gwarif to catch up on developments.

FIVE

ON TO THE JEBEL

Qaraitas led the Mahra, whom Raven and I had met in the wadi, out to a point called Barbezum in the negd, a place which differed from the other thousand square miles of barren wilderness only by having two or three flat-topped hills from which a sentry could see for several miles. It was food for thought that this group of ex-adoo had felt it necessary to come so far off the Jebel before they would be safe. A small BATT went in to set up a camp, and a full troop prepared to join them from Um Al Gwarif. The Mahra had decided to form themselves into a firqat. At first they chose the name Firqat Al Akhlas, but shortly after changed it to the Firqat A'asifat, the 'Storm' firqat.

Barbezum had little to recommend it, but Harvey and I were happy to leave them there. At least they could not get up to any mischief, but it did create major administrative problems. Barbezum could not yet be reached by truck from Thamrait in the north and all supplies would have to come in by air. Also, there were no more FN rifles for this firqat. Some venerable American Springfields had been found together with a large store of ammunition in Said Bin Taimur's palace after the coup and we began to issue these instead, but then it was discovered that although the weapons themselves were in mint condition, one round in six misfired. The Mahra would just have to rely on the old bolt-action .303 until we could get some more FNs.

I flew into Barbezum by Skyvan, that excellent flying truck developed by Short & Harland of Belfast. Sturdy, simple and easy to fly, the Skyvan became the work horse of the Dhofar war. A good airstrip had been laid out alongside the camp where the Troop Commander, already nicknamed 'Shams' (Sun) by the firqat because of his round sunburnt face and golden hair, stood at the side of the strip to meet me.

There was little enough to the camp: three or four tents, a few *burmails* of water and petrol for cooking, and that was all. A *burmail* was a large black, plastic 60-gallon container with two handles, which had replaced the old metal oil drum, but its Arabic name still reflected the markings on the original drum, Burmah Oil.

Shams told me his problems: in short, water and flies. Both were demonstrated within minutes. Where the flies came from and what they existed upon before the BATT arrived, I shall never know, but it seemed that all the flies in the *negd* had concentrated upon this spot. We walked up and down in the open because the flies made it unbearable inside the tents, holding our mugs of tea in one hand and waving the other over the top non-stop. Flies were everywhere; in your eyes, your ears, even up your nose. I promised him some creosote and fly smoke in the next aircraft.

'Oh, for God's sake. Now look at that,' said Shams in desperation. 'You see what I mean about water?'

An old woman had brought in three camels to be watered. Her black leather mask and black shapeless robe showed her to be from the camel-folk of the Bait Kathir or Mahra. Goatskin bladders hung from the camels' sides. One animal had already been couched by a firqatman with much clicking of the tongue and tapping of its knees with his camel stick. It sat there, looking supercilious and rumbling its stomach as the woman, helped by two firqatmen, began to fill the goat skins from a *burmail*.

Several other firqatmen had drifted over to the operation and were making noises at the camels: 'Brrr–brr–d–d–d–d–d.' There was no reason: it was just instinctive. Even when he was in the back of a moving truck, when the camels might be much too far away to hear him even if there were no engine noise, a firqatman would often mutter 'brrrr–brrrr' – more to himself than anything. Different animals received different sounds. To a cow it was 'uh–uh' and a goat received a clicking sound, 'kl–kl–k–k–k–k'.

The woman's husband was out of sight, probably no more than a mile or so away, with more camels. It was customary for him not to camp too near the water point because any raiders passing through the area would surely call at it. He would come in later when he had received the woman's report of how she had been received.

'They've no idea of water discipline,' Shams said despairingly. 'When you remonstrate with them they say it all comes from God anyway and it's their duty to give it if they have it. You tell them that it means they'll have no water for the rest of the week and they shrug and say *"Allah Karim"*. And Qaraitas, the crafty old fox, said it's essential to woo these people away from the adoo and that he gets intelligence from these people. He knew that line of argument would appeal to us. We've been supplying water to half his blasted tribe.'

He hurried off towards the water point. I could not suppress a smile at his frustration, but he was on a pointless mission. Qaraitas would continue to supply these people with water, as he would expect them to provide him if the position were reversed. If he was pushed too far, he would give that incontestable answer which brings all further discussion to an end, 'It would be shameful'.

That night we dined off goat. Several animals had been passengers with me on the Skyvan, each with its fore and hind legs bound and placed in a plastic bag with only its head and neck protruding. After a few protesting bleats as we took off, they had seemed content enough. I felt sorrier for the three donkeys that were to fly on to Mirbat. They, too, were bound and lay on their sides looking mournful, as I suppose you would with a handler sitting on your head.

After supper the firqat built a large fire and I addressed them as we sat around it. I talked on similar lines to the first talk I had given the Firqat Salahadin, but they seemed subdued. One or two nodded gravely when I made a point they agreed with but there was little reaction from most of them. It would be better tomorrow, when their BATT came in and they could begin training, I reassured myself.

The fire blazed merrily, highlighting the sharp-featured contours of the warriors' faces as they sat around it, huddled in their cloaks against the night chill. The flies had at last disappeared, and the sky was the sort of sky which you only see in the desert, awe-inspiring in its perfection. I lay back on the still-warm sand and contemplated the stars in all their crystal clarity for a long, long time, barely aware of the murmuring of the men's voices. I cannot say that any great philosophic conclusions flashed through my mind, but perhaps one began to understand why three of the earth's greatest religions had started under a sky like that.

A shape towered above my supine figure for a moment and abruptly sat down alongside me. It was Qaraitas. '*Taweel,* ureed ...' he began an impossible list of requirements.

★　★　★

I could not afford to spend too long with the Firqat A'asifat because affairs were developing elsewhere. The Bait Kathir were gradually pulling themselves together after a series of false starts and had formed a firqat, the Firqat Al Nasr. They had begun training at the old sultan's country residence at Mamurah, a large, gardened area east of Um Al Gwarif. Mamurah had been a beautiful place once, full of flowering shrubs and coconut palms, but for its water it depended on a channel which ran north across the plain to Ayn Arzat, the adoo's favourite target. Mamurah gardens had died from drought, but one or two ramshackle buildings and a circular fort manned by askars were still in a fair state of repair. I was still sceptical about the Bait Kathir ever doing anything worthwhile, so I was pleasantly surprised when the commander of the small BATT they had attached to them told me they were developing well, and that they would be ready for operations quite soon.

Developments were taking place at Sudh also. The town had been under attack two nights running by 30-plus adoo, but it had been a half-hearted effort and they had been seen off on both occasions by the BATT's 81-mm mortar and GPMG, together with the enthusiastic, if erratic, fire of the askars. I was not worried. Sudh was strong enough to resist now.

It was Salim and Qartoob who took most of my attention. I wanted Qartoob to see the Sultan to pledge his loyalty and then to get back to Mirbat with his followers in time to join the Firqat Salahadin for the next operation, Operation Eagle's Nest.

Sudh had been a valuable proving ground. Its seizure had shown that the firqat could operate alone and that they were prepared to fight for the Government, and it had shown the value of using the people against an enemy derived from the people. Without killing a man, the Firqat Salahadin had destroyed a complete adoo firqat and recruited the best of them into the Sultan's service. No SAF unit could have done that. Faced by the SAF, Qartoob and Dherdhir would have been honour-bound to fight. For the first time, Government forces had gained ground and the control of the people, instead of losing both. It was only a small step, but it represented the turn of the tide. Sudh, however, was not on the jebel, and it was there that the war would be won. We had to get on to the jebel and, most important, stay there. We could not remain there permanently, of course. That would require a major operation preceded by a long period of training and preparation, and the enthusiastic support of SAF. That support would not be forthcoming until SAF's confidence had been restored and it had been proved to them that it was possible to get up on the Jebel and remain there.

There were a number of other questions, too, which only such a reconnaissance in force could resolve. What would be the reactions of the Jebelis? Would they help us with information? What sort of force would the adoo mount against us immediately, after five days, after ten days? How would the firqat operate?

The operation had to be mounted in the Eastern Area if it was to have any chance of success, but that left the question of whether to approach from the north or south. HQ Dhofar was sceptical about the whole idea and little help would be forthcoming from that direction, so that ruled out an approach from the north; we would never be able to move the troops by air to the other side of the jebel. It would have to be from the south, but the adoo were well aware of the threat from the Firqat Salahadin by now and had strong blocking pickets along the southern scarp of the jebel. Very well, we would have to find a way up which was not a known route.

I decided on the Eagle's Nest position for several reasons; first, it was within a night's march from Mirbat; second, there was no known route up it, but, having studied the escarpment by telescope from Jebel Ali, I thought it would probably go if I put some Mountain Troop men on to the problem; third, although it afforded excellent observation of Mirbat and so might well be occupied by adoo by day, being the highest ground in the Eastern Area and lacking vegetation, it was unlikely to have water and therefore a permanent picket; and fourth, the place looked to me, when I flew over it, to be impregnable. But it meant climbing a practically sheer cliff 3000 feet high by night and surprising any adoo who might be on top, for if by dawn there were still adoo on top and our own troops were strewn over the escarpment below them, it would invite a massacre.

So, on the night of 6th March, Farran set off with a small patrol of SAS men and six firqatmen of the Bait Umr who claimed that they knew the first part of the route. It was a hard climb, with many dead ends and false routes, but by dawn they were near, though not actually at the top. That day they spent hidden in the shadow of the cliff on a ledge 150 feet below the summit. There was no cooking, nor smoking, nor sound. Any talking was done in whispers, but it was mostly a case of just lying and listening. Farran settled himself comfortably against a flat rock, took out his paperback, an essential part of any SAS man's kit, and thought wistfully about his meerschaum in Mirbat.

All day they lay there, in what little shade existed on the bare rock face, each man pressing himself into what protection he could find from the sun's rays as they slowly, so slowly, traversed their beat across the cliff face. It was a long, long day, but eventually, as the sun dropped over the horizon and dusk fell, the thirsty, cramped little group silently got to their feet, thankful to be on the move again. An hour later, they were on top and moving cautiously among the great rocks and caves of the Eagle's Nest position. It was ideal – a great semi-circular ridge with its open side on the escarpment. The plateau in the centre of the semi-circle made a secure helicopter landing point, but it was confirmed that there was no water. Farran spent no longer than was necessary to achieve his mission. Stepping carefully from rock to rock so as to leave no tell-tale footprints, he moved about the position keeping into the moon shadows until he was sure that he had it all in his mind. Then he withdrew as quietly as he had come.

Climbing downhill is always more tiring than going up. It jars the knees and ankle joints and the body misses the adrenalin it enjoyed going upward, so it was a very tired but satisfied patrol who reached Mirbat soon after dawn the following morning. Farran sent me a coded radio message straight away: yes, there was a practicable route; no, there was no adoo picket.

I left him to sleep for the rest of that day and flew down next morning. Together with Cheshire, we sat on the roof of the BATT house as he described the route and the position as he found it, pointing it all out on the ground in front and passing a telescope between us when he came to a particularly tricky part of the climb. It seemed all set to go. I did not know how long we would be up there, I told the two of them, but I was hoping for at least a fortnight. I could not spare that sort of time away from Um Al Gwarif myself, I said, particularly with the Firqat A'sifat and the Firqat Al Nasr about to begin operations and the rumour of another firqat being formed by the Bait Ma'asheni. Cheshire had already asked me if he could command this operation and I confirmed that he would be the leader with two troops, his and Farran's, under his command to support the Firqat Salahadin. They were to climb the escarpment carrying enough food and water to last two days. The helicopter was seriously short of flying hours and the first flight would bring in an 81-mm mortar and ammunition; thereafter it would bring in one re-supply of water in jerrycans, but that was all the flying time we could get for the time being. How long they spent at Eagle's Nest would depend on the enemy's reaction, but as soon as possible they were to move westwards to somewhere close to the escarpment where we could establish a donkey and camel re-supply route. And they must move near to a water hole. Food is light, but water is heavy; they could have water or ammunition flown in to them, but not both. I suggested positions above the Wadis Hinna and Ghazir.

It was a long time before all the details were decided and the time had come for me to fly back to Um Al Gwarif. For courtesy's sake, I asked to see Salim Mubarak before I went, but was surprised to be told he was sick. The BATT medic who took me over to Salim's tent explained that he was not happy about Salim's health as this was more than just one of the illnesses that the firqat were always going down with; he suspected angina pectoris. Until then I had listened with respect. Trooper Nick Dawson had been a fourth-year medical student and his father was a Harley Street surgeon. Dawson had had an expensive education and had seemed destined to follow in his father's footsteps, when he suddenly threw it all in and joined one of the Territorial Army SAS regiments. He liked it so much that he took the regular SAS selection course, passed, and joined the Army as a trooper. At his initial interview I had asked him why he had thrown in a promising medical career. He could not stand the spaniel look in sick people's eyes, he said, and could he please become an explosives expert, not a medic. I had assured him that he would not meet many spaniels in this Regiment, and we were certainly not going to waste his expertise, acquired at such effort and his father's expense. He would do an explosives course *and* become a medic.

Nonetheless, even when the finest medic in the Regiment told me that Salim Mubarak had angina pectoris, it was too much to believe.

'Come off it, Nick,' I said. 'You must be wrong. Angina is for over-fed Europeans like us. Whoever heard of a Dhofari with it? Let's go and see him.'

Salim's tent was at the end of a long line of blue Indian pup-tents. His was distinguishable only because its end-flaps were down: the others were all open at both ends to keep them cool. I knelt down and pulled the flaps aside. Salim was lying on his mat, covered by a blanket. He was asleep and breathing heavily. A deep frown creased his brow and two lines of pain were etched into his forehead between his eyes. For the first time I saw him without his shamag and was surprised at how sparse and grey his hair was; his scalp showed clearly. Suddenly he looked old.

I let the flap drop and we withdrew quietly. As we walked back to the BATT house Dawson continued to describe Salim's symptoms and his own analysis.

'He will certainly not be capable of going on the next operation. If it is angina, and I'm pretty sure it is, it may clear after a rest, but he shouldn't continue to lead the sort of life he's leading at present. I spent the whole of today with him and he knows he's ill. He kept saying he could taste blood. It's strange,' he added with a slight smile. 'Do you now what his last words were to me before he fell asleep? Salim Mubarak with all his western ways? He told me he had seen a *jinn*.'

Salim Mubarak died in the night.

★   ★   ★

I had always told the squadron not to become emotionally involved in their firqats. We were simply there to do a job and emotional involvement clouded the mind. But, although the soldiers never developed the love for the firqats which some of them felt, for example, towards the Ibans and Dyaks of Borneo during the confrontation war with Indonesia, it was impossible not to develop feelings for people who had shared your triumphs and disasters and who had risked their lives with yours, even if they were infuriating sometimes. And, here was I, prey to my own teaching, feeling grief at the death of a man who had become a friend – partly because of some natural similarity of spirit perhaps, partly because he was so dependent on BATT, partly his dignity, for he never pleaded, and partly, possibly, because he was the only firqatman I knew who never threw a tantrum when things did not go his way. He was a very political animal as well as a soldier and he fully understood when to advance and when to withdraw; he was an experienced exponent of the 'art of the possible'. But it was with a heavy heart that I returned to Um Al Gwarif.

I went to see Harvey first, to tell him of Salim's death and to give him a copy of my operation order for Eagle's Nest. It would have to be delayed a few days now, but it would still go ahead with Mohammed Said as the commander. Knowing the problem with helicopter flying hours and how critical one would be to my plan, I thought it prudent to put in writing the days on which we would need the aircraft re-supply. Harvey read it through and asked how long we intended to stay on the jebel. I shrugged. 'As long as possible.'

Next, I drove into Salalah and went to see Wali Baraik. I was shown into his office once by Abdul Aziz, a fine-looking tall young Dhofari, whose father had been killed by the adoo. He was a close friend of Baraik, spoke excellent English and had a natural charm about him. He was obviously bound for high places in the new administration. I came straight to the point with the bad news. Baraik shot a sharp glance at Abdul Aziz and then back at me.

'Are you sure it was a heart attack?' he asked.

'No,' I said. 'I'm not. My medic thinks it was and our doctor agrees with him from the symptoms he described, but we won't know without a post-mortem.'

'Could it be poison?'

'Possibly, but again we can't find out without a post mortem.'

Baraik pondered for a few seconds. 'I doubt very much they will let your doctor near him, but you can try if you like,' he said thoughtfully.

As Abdul Aziz showed me out, I was surprised to see genuine tears in his eyes. 'I have lost a good friend,' he said. 'You will have to get your doctor quickly to Mirbat. Remember that under our law Salim's body must be buried within 24 hours. That means this afternoon.'

The Medical Officer and I reached Mirbat at midday. An atmosphere of profound sorrow prevailed throughout the town. The BATT had sensibly withdrawn into their tents and the Civil Action Team into their house; this was a Muslim affair and courtesy demanded it.

The doctor went straight to the house where Salim's body was lying prepared for his funeral. He was fully dressed, lying in his coffin, protected by four firqatmen. The room was lit by candles, and frankincense burnt from vessels placed about the body. The eyes had been closed and all the orifices of the body blocked with rags. As Baraik had suspected, the firqat would not allow the doctor to touch it.

That afternoon I watched from the roof of the BATT house as the mourning little procession of the Firqat Salahadin carried their war leader in his open coffin through the silent town and out to the cemetery.

* * *

I returned to Salalah the same evening to see Harvey and Baraik again and to arrange for Mohammed Said to see the Sultan, as the new *Kaid* of the Firqat Salahadin. News awaited of both the Firqat Al Nasr and the Firqat A'asifat. The Al Nasr were behaving true to form. They had located an adoo picket in the Wadi Arzat and had asked for permission to attack it. Their BATT commander had hurried in to HQ BATT and arranged all the support necessary: artillery and aircraft, the procedure for casualties, the radio frequencies and code words – in short, all the paraphernalia needed for an operation – and had raced back to Mamurah in his Landrover to get the patrol out that evening. After he had explained all the details, the firqat commander announced that they had changed their minds and did not want to go after all.

The Firqat A'asifat at Barbezum were far more promising. Although they had nothing in the way of luxuries, (or was it because of it?) they were continually asking to go on patrol. Qaraitas had just taken seven men off for four days on his own, without BATT, and dressed as adoo. They returned tired out and high on *qat*, chewed as a stimulant and to deaden the pangs of thirst and hunger, claiming to have walked to the headwaters of the Wadi Darbat ten miles away and to have surprised a group of adoo in a cave. They said they had killed several, but they had returned with no extra weapons. Qaraitas told Shams that they had also seen another 150 adoo but had decided that discretion was the better part of valour. Whether it was true or not, time would tell, but it was reassuring that they had been confident enough to go out on their own.

Sudh was being attacked regularly now, but always by small arms or light mortar, nothing bigger. The Civil Action Team and the askars were strong enough to beat these small attacks off but not strong enough to go after the adoo. However, there were no SAF to spare, I was told and, with the Eagle's Nest operation about to come off, there was certainly no SAS or firqat. Sudh would just have to grin and bear it.

Mohammed Said saw the Sultan the next day and came into Um Al Gwarif for a final talk before he returned to Mirbat. I was struck by his self-possession. The meeting with the Sultan had paid off. He was very much the Kaid now. I noticed, too, that he carried in his belt the revolver I had given Salim.

★ ★ ★

The climb up to Eagle's Nest took place on the night of 13th March. It was a long, hard climb. The night was warm and sultry, and the two troops and 60 men of the firqat sweated freely. Inevitably, many of the firqat drank all the water they carried before they reached the top and then demanded water from the SAS, but this had been anticipated and I flew in by helicopter next morning sitting on a load of water jerrycans. Cheshire and Mohammed Said showed me around the position and as we walked among the tangle of great boulders and caves, some the size of houses, it became clear that it was even stronger than I had thought. The firqat seemed generally confident and laughed and joked as we talked, but they were keeping their heads down, I noticed, and taking no chances.

Would the adoo attack? That was the question. Or would they be content to leave us alone, reckoning that we could do no harm where we were and in one or two nights' time would conform to SAF practice and go back down onto the plain again.

'Give it three days,' I told Cheshire. 'If the adoo have not attacked you by then, we must move west to where they will, and to get a water and re-supply route established at the same time.'

The three days passed. By 17th March the adoo still had not attacked and Cheshire took the decision to move that night. The firqat told him of a position which they said was just what he wanted, a long hill in the middle of a plain and near a well with so much water that nobody could guess its depth. As usual, it was impossible to site on a map but he thought from the firqat's description that it lay somewhere north of the Wadis Ghazir and Hinna and so was in the area I had indicated.

The march took all night. It followed the normal form of SAS and firqat moves and was a direct copy of the way the adoo moved their heavy weapons. First, a small group of firqat moved to picket any defile or piece of dangerous ground, going at a trot well ahead of the main body and remaining in position until the main body had passed through. Then they closed into the rear of the column to ask for more orders. There might be four or five such pickets ahead of the main body. The SAS, with their heavy bergens and GPMGs moved behind a screen of some 20 firqat, with another 20 bringing up the rear. Cheshire moved at the front of the main column with Mohammed Said.

Gradually, the country changed as they left behind the rocky hillside of Eagle's Nest. Slowly and silently the long file of men wound its way down into thicker country until bush entirely surrounded them and Cheshire no longer knew exactly where they were. From time to time the column stopped and the SAS men eased their heavy packs off their shoulders gratefully while the firqat went to investigate a known adoo picket position. After some minutes, muffled whispers and clicks of the tongue revealed that all was well and the column moved off once more. The further west they moved, the more frequent the halts became, until the bushes became sparser and they entered the open, rolling country of the plateau. The crushed flowers and grasses left a pleasant scent as they passed, but the moon had risen now and after the closeness of the bush country it felt as if the whole world must be able to see them.

At last, with still half an hour to go until dawn, the column clambered wearily up a steep slope and found themselves on a long low hill running east to west. The feature was dominating all right, but it did not have much in the way of cover, only a few trees. There were plenty of small rocks to make sangars with, but none of the great boulders and caves of their last position.

Quickly Cheshire walked around the hill with Mohammed Said, allotting positions to the men, and then returned to the centre of the hill to begin to build a command sangar. It was becoming lighter now, and British and Dhofaris worked feverishly to complete their sangars before dawn. At last, with minutes to spare, activity ceased and all eyes were directed outwards for signs of movement as the ground in front became slowly visible.

Suddenly Mohammed Said gripped Cheshire's arm and pointed. Less than 300 yards away three men stood up and stretched themselves, then slung their guns over their shoulders and sauntered with all the confidence in the world into a shallow wadi to the right of Cheshire's position. Movement behind caught his eye and he turned to see a dozen firqat racing down the reverse slope before being lost to sight around the right-hand end of the hill. Several short bursts of automatic fire ripped out, and a few minutes later the firqat returned, exultantly carrying three Kalashnikovs.

It was a good start, but Cheshire was anxious to find out where the water lay and how many men it could support. He asked Mohammed Said to take him to it straight away, whereupon Mohammed admitted that although it was the Front's policy to mix up the tribes and post people, who lived in one part of the jebel to another, he had never come this far east. However, Qartoob would know.

Qartoob was a changed man. His eyes gleamed and he was smiling happily as he stepped over the low sangar wall and sat down alongside Cheshire. Qartoob was in his element, thought Cheshire, fighting a war in his own tribal area, in country he knew like the back of his hand.

'*Yahee*', began Cheshire. 'Oh brother' had become the common way for the SAS and firqat to address each other. '*Yahee*, where is all the water that is said to be here?'

Qartoob stroked his luxuriant black moustache and to Cheshire's surprise pointed not downhill towards the sea as he expected, but inland to a piece of broken country of bushes and shrubs 400 yards to the north. He would take Cheshire there later, he said, but it would be unwise to move yet until the adoo's reaction to the shooting was revealed.

The adoo, he explained, divided their forces into militia and fighters, soft-core and hard-core. Someone from the militia in one of the villages nearby would have heard the shooting and normally they fired warning shots to alert all the other militia in the area. These would move towards the sound of firing and try to contain the BATT and firqat column. Meanwhile, someone would be despatched to the nearest fighters, the regulars, or if these happened to be within hearing of the shooting, they would move towards it of their own accord. The fighters would try to contain the column with what they had at hand, while the heavy weapons crew went off to collect their mortar or recoilless gun and ammunition which would be cached somewhere, usually in a cave. How long it took them to bring it into action would depend on how far away it was cached, Qartoob went on philosophically. It might be hours, it might take them days to move it, for a heavy weapon could not be carried far easily. The column might be lucky, he said. They were too far from the adoo in the Wadi Darbat and those in the Wadi Ghazir and Wadi Hinna might not want to leave the routes up unguarded. By taking the route they did, the BATT and firqat had come round behind them.

The reaction, when it came 20 minutes later, was unimpressive, a few bursts of fire at long range which were answered by GPMGs, and then a long silence. Cheshire felt it safe enough to ask for the 81-mm mortar and ammunition which had been helicoptered out of Eagle's Nest shortly before they had moved out the previous night, and this was flown up to him from Mirbat, although it took a little while for the pilot to find the position. Cheshire was reluctant to use a smoke grenade and tried calling him in by sarbe and by using a flashing mirror, but to the pilot he was on just one hill among many.

At last, reluctantly, Cheshire had no choice, but to throw out smoke. The helicopter spiralled down and as the weapon and bomb cases were hastily unloaded, the pilot was able to give Cheshire a six-figure grid reference. At last he knew exactly where he was, some 5000 yards north of the escarpment and too far for a donkey route. But there were compensations. A long, flat piece of ground to the south of the hill could be made into a satisfactory Skyvan strip with not too much engineer effort and the position was certainly strong; it dominated the flat plain for a mile in each direction. The adoo would find it very difficult to advance at them across that.

The first adoo mortar bomb exploded near where the smoke grenade had gone off minutes after the helicopter had left and sent everyone scuttling into the sangars for cover. After two or three rounds the adoo gunner had the range and kept up a steady slow bombardment, which hit nobody but kept people confined to their sangars. Over the days that followed, the SAS developed a respect bordering on admiration for the adoo mortar man. He knew his work. He moved frequently, keeping his mortar out of sight so that neither he nor his weapon could be located, and caused maximum disruption of work with the minimum number of bombs. Our own mortar could not find him. He was accurate, too.

On the fourth day Farran and his radio operator watched from their sangar as the adoo bombs moved inexorably closer: explosion, delay of a minute whilst the adoo gunner worked out the necessary alteration and applied it to the sights, then another explosion, nearer this time, another delay, then another explosion still nearer. Finally, when a bomb landed just outside the sangar, both men grabbed their rifles, vaulted the wall and pelted up over the hill into dead ground. They were just in time; the following bomb hit the sangar itself, blowing the radio to bits and shredding their bergens and sleeping bags with shrapnel.

By now several tail fins had been recovered and identified. It was a 60-mm mortar, the Soviet and Chinese light mortar, that was causing the trouble. The British light mortar is little more than an overgrown hand grenade, although the British 81-mm is one of the finest ever made, but the explosion of the 60-mm was not always easy to identify, as against its larger brother. It was a weapon which quickly won the soldiers' respect and indeed the SAS used it themselves whenever they could lay their hands on one. Two weeks later the adoo mortar man walked into Taqa and gave himself up. He was a fine-looking man. As an officer in the Trucial Oman Scouts, before he had deserted to the adoo, he had been top overseas student at one of the courses held in Britain's Mons Officer Cadet School.

During one of the lulls in firing, Cheshire insisted on being taken to the water. He found himself confronted by an amazing sight: the ground had collapsed in some distant millennium to leave a huge natural hole 150 feet across and 300 feet deep. As they approached the cavern's lip a flock of doves clattered into the air; hence its name, *Tawi Atair*, the well of birds.

Cheshire stared with dismay at the distant black water deep in shadow at the bottom of the hole, and at the sheer walls of rock all around.

'But how do we get down to it?' he asked in bewilderment.

'It is not easy,' Qartoob agreed. 'The villagers send their women. There is a route which spirals down the rock but it is very dangerous. Several women have perished,' he concluded helpfully.

The following days proved just how difficult it was. Several SAS men and firqat did succeed in climbing down the precipitous route but could carry so little water back up and became so exhausted by the sheer climb that they needed to drink most of what they had carried. Efforts to fix up a rope and bucket were frustrated by an overhang. Water became a very scarce commodity indeed.

Then began the vicious spiral of dehydration. The less water, the more tired the men, the less energy to expend in fetching water, the less water, and so on. To add to the problem, the one helicopter had been grounded and despite my pleading could not be made to fly. 'There are men up there pissing treacle,' I raged, but it was no use. The helicopter had run out of flying hours and that was flat. There would be no water re-supply for Tawi Atair.

Nonetheless the operation was achieving its aim, and every day the firqat and BATT spent up there was proving a point: the adoo were not all-powerful, and even with just the one mortar we could see them off. The firqat were also very tired. The continual shooting and shelling and the patrolling and sentry duty kept sleep at a premium, but they could get out on patrol as no SAF or SAS alone could. As a spin-off, they also received confirmation of the results of Qaraitas's raid from the north. He had indeed done as he said and had killed three, including two important adoo leaders.

The reactions of the Jebeli civilians were disappointing. Although they were sympathetic, they did not dare to help.

'You say you will be here a long time,' one old man told Cheshire. 'But what is a long time, one week, two weeks? And the geysh have never stayed here during the monsoon. The Communists are here the whole time. As soon as you leave, they will come back and punish anyone who helped you.'

As the days passed, the adoo closed in and the battle became more intense. Cheshire asked to be reinforced by the thirty-five Firqat Salahadin still under training at Mirbat. These marched up in one night, killing six adoo who tried to stop them in a sharp contact at dawn, and joined up with the remainder. Cheshire's position was numerically much stronger after this infusion of fresh men, but his water problem was heightened. It was now too dangerous for the helicopter to land, so an airdrop was arranged from a Skyvan using improvised parachutes. The drop was successful but it was a short-term expedient. We might get away with it once but to try it again would be inviting the loss of an aircraft. There were two alternatives: to move somewhere else according to the original plan or to abandon the operation and withdraw. I resolved to get in to see Cheshire by one means or another and to my surprise my request for a helicopter met with immediate agreement.

It did not take long to decide which of the two courses to choose. The hill was charred black in a great swathe a thousand yards square where phosphorous bombs had set the grass alight, and the men's faces were black from rescuing their equipment. All the bombs from the mortar pit had been evacuated just in time before the fire swept over it. The soldiers were willing to go on but their lined and gaunt faces betrayed the effects of lack of water and sleep. The firqat, even Mohammed Said himself, sat about dispirited and unhelpful. Only Qartoob did not seem affected as he sat humming happily to himself and fingering his moustache.

Cheshire's appearance horrified me. His cheeks were sunken, his eyes were yellow and his talk was in the slur of a man nearing exhaustion. He looked not only extremely tired, but very ill. He clearly could not go on, no matter how willing, and later it was found that he had in fact contracted jaundice. Farran, however, looked weary, but still fit. He sat puffing his pipe and chatting to Qartoob, looking as healthy and phlegmatic as ever, his long fair hair contrasting with Qartoob's black. I played briefly with the idea of taking command myself and introducing fresh energy, but discarded it. These men had done all that could fairly be asked of them. They needed relief.

On the twelfth day the Tawi Atair position was abandoned and the Firqat Salahadin and SAS withdrew south to the high ground above the Wadi Hinna where the Muscat Regiment were mounting a one-day operation. Fire was exchanged with a group of adoo at long range, but otherwise the withdrawal was uneventful.

It had been a valuable operation, nonetheless. For the first time the SAS had been on the plateau itself. They and the firqats had taken on the adoo on their own ground and beaten them. They had killed nine confirmed and probably wounded more without loss to themselves; and had caused a sharp rise in the number of SEPs. The reactions of the Jebelis had been studied and confirmed that it was essential to establish a permanent presence before we could expect the whole-hearted support of the civilian population. The problems of inadequate maps and the firqat's inability to read them had been highlighted, together with the need to examine what they said very carefully before committing oneself to a course of action; and above all, it had been shown that any permanent base on the jebel must have an airstrip established alongside it.

The support received from SOAF had been superb, whether from the helicopters, Skyvans or Strikemasters, and set the tone for the friendship that was to develop between SOAF and BATT in the coming years, a friendship based upon mutual respect and professional admiration. It said much too, about the qualities of modern RAF pilots, once they are freed from the inevitable restrictions of peace-time rules and economy measures.

These were all lessons to be taken into account when the major drive to establish a permanent base took place. Such an operation, I was now convinced, would be feasible after the monsoon, in September or October.

SIX

METAMORPHOSIS

Matters had not come to a halt elsewhere. Whilst the Firqat Salahadin was earning its spurs at Eagle's Nest and Tawi Atair, the raising of the other firqats was creating full-time problems at Headquarters BATT in Um Al Gwarif. Weapons and equipment were critically short. The Firqat Al Nasr in particular had reached the stage where they would soon be ready for operations, yet all they could be supplied with were old .303 rifles. Brigadier Graham was well aware of the problems and flew down to Dhofar to be brought up to date. His visit instilled a new vigour and enthusiasm in Headquarters Dhofar, but even he could not provide weapons which did not exist. Besides modern rifles, the firqat badly needed some form of automatic fire-power. I asked for bren guns but there were none. Instead, we were offered heavy-barrelled automatic FNs. These were not as good as brens, but they were excellent weapons nonetheless and I accepted them gratefully.

The number of SEPs had risen dramatically and almost every day brought in three or four more. Often they carried Kalashnikovs or Simonovs, both much superior to the .303, but these tended to disappear into the maw of the Intelligence Department. We managed to prise several of these weapons out of them but, even so, the problem of providing Soviet or Chinese ammunition remained. The best way was to go out and get it and soon, carrying a Kalashnikov became the status symbol of a firqatman who had 'got his man'.

The Firqat Al Nasr had nothing else: no trucks, no uniforms, no equipment, nothing. Some cooking pots and lamps were bought in the souk for them, but otherwise they wore and carried what they had always worn and carried. Musalim Bin Tufl thought this was a deliberate policy of mine, and I must admit that I did not disabuse him.

He sat glowering in the BATT operations room and demanded to know why the Bait Kathir were being treated like paupers while the other firqats had everything they needed. He begged me to give them a full BATT troop, like the others, instead of the little three-man training team they had, although, he added hastily, he was very happy with the BATT men he had.

'You get the Firqat Al Nasr to fight, Musalim, instead of talking about it, and I will see if I cannot provide you with better weapons and more BATT men,' I said, 'but we only have so many good weapons and those must go to the men who fight, like Mohammed Said's firqat and Musalim Qaraitas's firqat. What have the Bait Kathir done so far? Nothing.'

The firqat's BATT commander sat on a chair alongside Bin Tufl looking almost as dejected and disappointed as the old man. It had become noticeable over the past weeks that living and working together had forged a bond between the BATTs and their firqats, even as trying a firqat as this one. I could see that the SAS soldier considered himself to be almost one with the Bait Kathir. A reverse for them was a reverse for him.

I could not help smiling as I looked at the huge man sitting alongside the sparrow-like Bin Tufl. Corporal 'Paddy the Ditch' was living proof that the Vikings reached Ireland. His chest was a barrel and his hands like hams, yet I knew him to be one of the gentlest men you could meet. His strength also made him one of the finest GPMG gunners in the squadron, handling the heavy machine gun as most men handled a rifle. He had one of those very fair skins which never go brown, just fiery red and when the other men stripped off to let the sun get at them, the Ditch just put more clothes on. He had grown a long moustache and beard in an effort to keep the sun off his face and his ginger hair flopped over his ears. He described his nose as 'a blister on a blister on a blister'. Now he waited till the old man shuffled off to the door.

'Don't be too hard on the old sod, sir, he's not too bad. They're a good lot, really they are. But this young Salim Gharib, now he's the man we want to lead them. It is only a good young leader they need, like Salim, and they'll be off after the adoo like a dose of salts, but can we not give them just something? You saw yourself, their families are just living in the bottom of the wadi below Adonib with not even a tent between them. Can't we get them a truck even? Then at least they could get water from Rayzut. I know it's their war but after all why should they do anything for us if we can't do anything in return?'

★ ★ ★

Next day I went to see Harvey with a paper I had prepared during the night, with frequent interruptions from the 5.5s. BATT were now running two operational firqats, the Salahadin and the A'asifat, and the Bait Kathir Firqat Al Nasr was under training. In addition, news had just come in that 39 men of the Mahra from Western Dhofar were in Muscat and about to return to the Province. These were all men who had gone to Kuwait and Bahrain during the reign of Said Bin Taimur. They had apparently been collected by a small dapper man whom I had seen at the final dinner of the Firqat Salahadin before they went to Mirbat for training. Salim Mubarak had not introduced him and I had asked no questions. Now I knew why he had come. It was looking a long way ahead, but one day a firqat who knew the Western Area intimately would be worth its weight in gold. And we were likely to be asked to raise two more firqats. Mohammed Musalim Ahmed of the Bait Ma'asheni had suggested to Wali Baraik that the tribe should raise its own firqat, based upon Taqa, to be called the Firqat Khalid Bin Waalid after the great Moslem general. Then too, during my last visit to Sudh, the *naib wali* there, after an excellent meal of goat and rice, had suggested the possibility of raising not so much a firqat as a defence force of Sudh citizens. They were becoming disillusioned with the Government askars.

The problem of administering these firqats was going to become too great for a SAS squadron. Already I had had to create a separate administrative cell to deal with firqat re-supply and I had radioed to England for reinforcements from the Quartermaster's staff; and because equipment was short, it was natural that a SAF administrative organisation would get better service from SAF resources than a British unit like ourselves. The one responsibility I did want to retain was that of paying the firqats, for in the Arab world as in any other, he who pays you demands your allegiance.

The time had come to put the firqats on a more regular 'irregular' footing, I suggested. By May, I estimated, there would be something like 400-500 men under training. How many firqats did we want? How many men should be the maximum, how many the minimum? What should their organisation be? What weapons should they be issued with and what transport? How should the unit for administering the firqats be organised? What would its relationship be with the SAF, with the *Wali*? A hundred and one matters had to be resolved.

Harvey greeted me affably. I brought him up to date on developments and gave him the paper I had written. He agreed with almost all of it and promised to back the proposals it contained when it reached CSAF. We agreed that the strength of a firqat should not be allowed to exceed a hundred, which was the most we felt one man could control, but whereas I wanted to see as many firqats raised as there were men to fill them, he felt that 700 should be the maximum number of firqatmen under arms. He said that SAF could not provide arms for more, but I could tell that he was still more concerned about the possibility of raising a Frankenstein's monster.

Part of the problem, I decided as I walked back to the BATT compound, was that he had never had a chance to talk to the firqat leaders properly. I resolved there and then to arrange such a meeting and to let him listen himself to their ideas about how to win the war and to their problems. Already his attitude showed a distinct mellowing. It would be wise to strike while the iron was, if not hot, at least warm.

★   ★   ★

The Firqat A'asifat was in a fine mood, but Qaraitas's small success seemed to have gone to his head. He had been throwing his weight around and had taken on the BATT in open confrontation over a number of minor administrative points, so when he announced that he was going to become the political leader and go to Muscat for more support, nobody shed any tears. The firqat, in any case, were mustering more and more behind the man who had led them out, Sheikh Ali Salim Saad. He was a grey-bearded man, older than I should have liked, but he was still fit and held undoubted authority over the firqat. He had an even, confident manner which contrasted with the fits of temperament and hysteria Qaraitas was beginning to throw, and he had the bearing and eyes of a soldier. The firqat had been reinforced by another group of SEPs who had recently fled the jebel closely pursued by the adoo, and now numbered 38 fighting men. They had a long way to go to reach the 93-strong Firqat Salahadin but nonetheless they were an operational unit.

They were apparently keen to get out again on another operation, but it was already becoming clear that one of the principles in the successful handling of a firqat was 'coincidence of aims'. There was absolutely no point in tasking a firqat to do something that they did not wish to do or which would bring no profit to them; these were not disciplined regulars. The BATT aim and the firqat aim must be close enough for both to be achieved. It was in the firqat's interests to fight the adoo in their own Mahra tribal area and to be seen to do so; it was in BATT's interest to examine the *gatn* for a possible location for a firm base on the northern side of the jebel. The adoo's eyes at present were directed towards Mirbat and the south. A threat from the north would make them look both ways.

However, it was a long way from Barbezum to the *gatn*. Much of a foot patrol's energy would be taken up in getting there and back, leaving less time for the productive part of the patrol on the *gatn* itself, and the long approach march would increase the risk of detection by the enemy.

Shams had opened up a route into Barbezum from Thamrait which made re-supply much easier, but the going between Barbezum and the gatn was both unsuitable and too dangerous for a three-ton truck. However, the last few days had seen the arrival of three SAS Landrovers driven down across the desert from Sharjah where a small number had been kept by the SAS for desert training. With these versatile vehicles, Shams and Sheikh Ali could approach the *gatn* by a variety of routes, drop the firqat off and rendezvous again with them later. I tasked them to explore in an area known as Jibjat for a position which offered strong defence, which had its own water and where an airstrip could be easily constructed.

Mines were the main worry; the adoo were cunning mine layers. If they came across regularly-used vehicle tracks they would lay a mine in one of the tracks and roll an old piece of tyre across the spot to make it seem that the tracks were continuous, and old SAF sangars were often mined in the hope that they would be used again. The SAF were still laughing over a soldier who went to use an old sangar to relieve himself one morning. As he squatted with his trousers around his ankles, his eyes focused on the three prongs of an anti-personnel mine protruding from the ground between his feet. Ribald speculation abounded about the effect it had on him.

★　★　★

The information service and civil action side were developing well. The first leaflets had been dropped encouraging the adoo to join the Government cause, and money had been provided to establish a permanent information office in Salalah itself and for a new, more powerful radio transmitter. The SAS Civil Action Teams at Taqa, Mirbat and Sudh were well established and had begun to get on top of the medical problem at last. The flood of people needing medical attention in the early days had reduced to a steady trickle, so the medics could set about improving the overall state of health of the people instead of having to concentrate upon the immediate alleviation of pain.

It was time, I felt, for another visit to Taqa. Mohammed Musalim Ahmed did not strike me as a military leader in any sense, but he appeared to have the ear of *Wali* Baraik and if he could produce enough Bait Ma'asheni to form a firqat, I should be very happy to raise it. But I wanted to talk to the naib wali there and to the Civil Action Team commander before deciding whether it was a practical proposition. I drove to the airport and drew up alongside the single-engined Beaver aircraft which was to fly me. Standing alongside it was a figure I recognised instantly. Sheikh Mohammed Ahmed had strolled into the operations room a few days before, an impressive portly figure with a fine beard and moustache, wearing the same clothes as now, I noticed, a smart khaki drill with the red shamag and black rope *argal* of most Arab armies. The SAF were unusual in not wearing the argal; instead they wore a green shamag wrapped around the head like a turban; not so impressive perhaps, but far more practical in jebel country. On his shoulders Sheikh Mohammed wore lieutenant-colonel's badges of rank and a pistol belt was buckled round his ample belly. He had announced grandly that he had been made 'general of the firqats' by the Sultan, to whom he was distantly related. It was the first I had heard of it and Baraik grinned impishly when I mentioned the matter to him. The message was clear – humour him but give him no responsibility.

We shook hands and exchanged greetings before he eased his bulk into the back seat and I squeezed my six foot six frame into the co-pilot's seat up front. We took off. The aircraft was heavily laden with spare parts for a 3-ton truck and the BATT Landrover at Taqa, and it seemed a long time before the pilot eased the stick back and the aircraft pulled itself into the air. It was only a short flight to Taqa and soon the town came into view ahead of us with its fort perched on high ground on the landward side. The town itself was a comely sight from the air with the blue sea lapping a long silver beach that would put most seaside resorts in the Mediterranean to shame. Beyond the town lay the long inlet of Khor Rawri; and the walls of the ruined Sumerian city of Sumhuram, bordering the far side of the *khor*, stood out clearly.

The Beaver straightened up on its final approach into the narrow landing strip marked out with white stones and parallel to the sea alongside the fort. A puff of green smoke drew my attention to a knot of SAS soldiers standing at the side of the strip.

We appeared to glide forever. The red stall light glowed brilliantly as the aircraft drifted interminably over the strip until, with a bone-jarring crunch, it seemed to drop like a stone. The pilot slapped the throttle forward and the engine roared once more as the Beaver struggled upwards again. A low ridge ahead filled the windscreen. I could see every stone. The pilot hauled back desperately on the controls and we lurched over it with inches to spare.

Having gained height we doubled back over the strip. One soldier stood in the middle of it triumphantly holding our tail wheel over his head whilst the others crouched alongside him grinning broadly.

The aircraft flew back to Salalah, made a low pass in front of the control tower to allow an expert view of the damage, and began its final approach. I took one look at the pilot's face, pulled up the anorak hood over my head and shouted above the engine's noise to Sheikh Mohammed to do the same in case of fire. The plane touched down very gently and not until we had almost come to a stop did the pilot let the tail drop on the tarmac with a teeth-setting screech and a trail of sparks.

As soon as we touched, the pilot switched off the engine and even before the Beaver came to a halt he and I had our straps undone and the doors open ready to shoot out quickly into the fresh air. Sheikh Mohammed clambered out with slow dignity and eyed the torn tail-plane for a second. '*Allah Karim*' he tossed away confidently and strode off without a care in the world. His fearlessness eventually allowed him to be perforated by an adoo machine-gun, when he insisted on standing whilst everyone else considered it prudent to lie down, but the world is a poorer place without him.

The only other way to reach Taqa, unless you wanted to wait for the weekly convoy, was along the beach. Fortunately the tide was right and we reached the town that same day without difficulty. Although the town had recently been mortared frequently, it was a quiet night and, after an early start next day, I had finished by noon. The Firqat Khalid Bin Waalid was, without doubt, feasible and a house had already been set aside by the naib wali for them. He put on a show of enthusiasm but I suspected that his subordination to Wali Baraik masked his concern for the loss of his own status if he should have a powerful firqat leader living in the same town. The Civil Action Team were delighted. It would mean more SAS.

As the tide was not right for the return journey until the evening, after lunch I set out on foot with my driver to visit Sumhuram. The possibility of meeting adoo made us move carefully, covering each other across the shallow wadi beds that had to be crossed to reach the ruins.

Little is known of the history of Dhofar before the last thousand years. It has been suggested that there is a connection between the ancient 'Ophir' and 'Dhofar' although there is better evidence to place Ophir near Aqaba. Certainly if Dhofar is Ophir, Masefield's Quinquereme of Nineveh must have had serious navigational problems; either that or a remarkable cross-country performance. But Dhofar was almost certainly part of the Queen of Sheba's kingdom, a rich and powerful state that rivalled Solomon's. The geographer Pliny the Elder, in the first century AD, described the South Arabians of his time as the richest people in the world.

Sumhuram lies on the eastern side of a great inlet, the *Khor* which is now blocked from the sea by a sand bar like the Loe Bar in Cornwall. The *Khor* is about a mile long by 200 yards across, narrowing as it runs north towards the jebel until it disappears into a deep wadi; this in turn runs up to the wall of the great Wadi Darbat, the second largest wadi on the jebel, 800 yards across at its entrance. A river, in places 30 yards wide, runs down its centre all year round. The entrance to the wadi is now a path which runs up the eastern side of a great cliff wall, a hundred yards high and five times as wide, all that remains of a vast waterfall in times past. It must have been this great mass of water that scoured out Khor Rawri. Where the Khor meets the sea, a prominent headland on either side must have provided perfect look-outs and defence posts in times of danger for the inhabitants of the city. Nothing remains of these fortifications now, but a visitor still looks straight down from the headlands into deep water and you can see the fish and dolphins cruising below clearly in the gin-clear sea. It must have been a safe, deep-water entrance.

The city itself has been excavated several times. The American archaeologist and entrepreneur, Wendell Phillips, and archaeologists from the American Foundation for the Study of Man had both carried out major archaeological work on it. Most of the rooms of the inner city had been dug out and the walls were still in good condition, rising 20 feet high in places and formed of great blocks of carefully-masoned, local stone. A deep well had been sunk in the centre of a courtyard and the rope marks still showed clearly on the sill stone. Indeed, the well looked better-made and in a better state of repair than many in current use. Most impressive of all were the two great stones set into the tall narrow entrance and covered with hieroglyphs so plain that they might have been carved this century. It was these hieroglyphs, SMHRM, that gave the clue to the city's history and its name.

Archaeologists still argue over whether Dhofar is the ancient 'Bay of Sachalites' where, according to one contemporary author, incense lay along the bay in unguarded heaps, or whether the bay was not further south in the Hadramaut of present day PDRY, but there seems to be general agreement that Sumhuram itself is the 'Moscha' of classical writers. It seems probable too, that the town was founded by the decree of King Il'ad Yalut I in about the first century BC. It was certainly there three hundred years later, because I myself found a silver coin which was identified by the British Museum as of the third century AD.

The texts of the stones and of a bronze plaque found by the Americans show that the King of the Hadramaut wanted to extend his control of the incense trade to give himself a monopoly. Since the incense shrub only grows in the mountains of Dhofar and the Hadramaut, and an inferior type in Somaliland, the entire trade would drop into his hands if he could establish a major port in Dhofar. It may have been the decline of the incense trade which caused the Sumhuramis to neglect their dredging or the unpreventable silting up of the entrance that brought about the decline of the city – who can say – but by the end of the tenth century AD it appears the city was no longer in use. By then it was called Mirbat or in the Shahari language, Sik, which Thesiger associated with the radicals of the word Moscha. It was still the largest town in Dhofar but, as it became unusable, the inhabitants established another town by the same name 20 miles further east, where it stands to this day.

A series of temporary dynasties followed which tried vainly to impose their authority on the Dhofaris, but none lasted for much more than a century. By the 16th century, the capital had moved westwards from Mirbat to nearer the modern Salalah; the ruins of that capital exist still in a number of *tels*, mostly still unexamined, but easily identifiable to the east of the modern city.

Many of the Dhofari rulers seem to have come from the Hadramaut and it was not until the beginning of this century that the people of Dhofar turned to the north for protection in the shape of the present sultan's great-grandfather, Seyyid Turki Bin Said. Even so, his authority, like that of his successors, relied less on his ability to impose Government power than on the playing off of one tribe against another. It was, and is, to the tribe that a Dhofari owes his first allegiance. There has been none of the slow forging of a national unity over the centuries as one finds in the countries of Europe, or even the exposure to those countries' social backgrounds, which at least brought some advantage to the ex-colonies of former European imperial powers. Dhofar's social background is uncomplicated: incessant tribal warfare pursued for centuries with an unrelenting zeal.

★ ★ ★

The meeting between Harvey and the firqat leaders went well. Just the three firqat leaders were present, Mohammed Said, recently down from the Tawi Atair operation, Musalim Qaraitas representing the Firqat A'asifat and Mohammed Musalim of the new Firqat Khalid Bin Waalid. I had asked Said Bin Gheer to be present, too. Harvey appeared smartly dressed in khaki drill, his three rows of medal ribbons gleaming. He was making the point that they were not talking to an amateur at the game.

A marquee had been set aside at Um Al Gwarif and a carpet spread on the floor to sit on. After sweetmeats and coffee – a lot better than the Army biscuits and mugs of sweet tea they received when they came into my operations room, I noted – the discussion began. Harvey started by explaining his plan of raiding into the jebel and ambushing the water holes. Mohammed Said waited patiently until he had finished speaking and then told him in a flat unemotional voice that the SAF were playing into the adoo's hands. Every time they went on to the jebel and withdrew, whether they had been forced to do so or not, the withdrawal was represented by the adoo to the people as another adoo victory. Tawi Atair had proved that even the firqat, their own people, would not receive the support of the civilian population until SAF established a permanent presence on the jebel. Once they had done that, the firqats could move among the people and deny their support to the adoo. Without the people's support, there would be no more adoo. He moved the palm of his right hand swiftly across his left in the Dhofari sign for 'finished'. That was all there was to it, he said.

He had spoken with such utter certainty and such total confidence that for a little while there was silence. After some seconds had passed, the other two firqat leaders felt they must say something, and Qaraitas began to talk a hundred to the dozen in his excitable manner and missing the point completely of what either Harvey or Mohammed Said had said. Then Musalim, too, had his say – and was equally irrelevant. Harvey was impressed by Mohammed Said, I could see that, but he closed the meeting firmly saying that it was out of the question to think of a permanent presence on the jebel that year, although no doubt it would come eventually. So it was a disappointed little group that repaired to the BATT operations room for a cup of sticky tea.

I was surprised, therefore, when Harvey called me across to see him later that afternoon and told me that, on reflection, he agreed to the idea of a permanent position, but that he wanted not one but two. The positions would go in after the monsoon, and after a proper training and administrative build-up. Meanwhile, he wanted proper reconnaissance made for possible sites. We discussed the Firqat A'asifat's next operation into the Jibjat area and he suggested a co-ordinated operation by all three firqats, once the Khalid Bin Waalid were ready, into the Wadi Darbat area to look for the second position. I returned to the BATT compound jubilant. The strategy was right at last.

But even though the Commander Dhofar and the Commander of the SAS Squadron were now seeing eye to eye, I was concerned that the firqats and SAF should begin to understand each other better. Even though the two had worked together in the closing phase of the Tawi Atair operation, when the Muscat Regiment moved into the Wadi Hinna, there had been mutual recriminations. A group of adoo had been trapped between the two forces and the firqat claimed that if the SAF had known their business, the adoo would never have escaped; no doubt the SAF levelled similar accusations at the firqat. So at every opportunity that presented itself, I suggested that firqatmen should accompany the SAF on operations, in no matter what role. On one occasion the Firqat A'asifat were used as donkey handlers, something which almost caused an inter-firqat battle, because whenever a member of the Salahadin met one of the A'asifat he would raise both hands to his ears, bray like a donkey, and fall about with merriment.

This particular operation was a one-day, one-night affair on to a much-used hill alongside the Midway Road, known as Jebel John. The SAF battalion moved out at night from Um Al Gwarif with a few members of the Firqat Salahadin in front as guides, led by Mohammed Said, and the Firqat A'asifat at the rear. When they reached the jebel, the leading company commander, who was meant to seize the hill, decided that it was likely the hill was occupied by the adoo and declined to advance up it with his company. In exasperation, Mohammed Said climbed the hill himself with five of his men and having found it unoccupied, invited the battalion to join him. It was not the sort of performance likely to impress hardened ex-adoo. But then the firqat did something which, had it reached the ears of SAF, would have confirmed their worst suspicions of the untrustworthy firqats.

The route to the crest lay up the northern side: in other words the companies had to go past the hill and then swing right in a U-turn to begin the climb to the top. The last company commander in the column decided he could see no point in going the long way round and started to climb straight up the southern side of the hill. It was a silly thing to do and nearly received the punishment it deserved, because as he neared the top two shots rang out. One of the firqatmen had opened fire after, he claimed, having challenged and received no answer. The company commander was clearly in the wrong in deviating from an agreed plan without warning and he apologised profusely. Everyone agreed that it was fortunate that the incident had not resulted in death and no more was said about it.

Shortly afterwards, Staff Sergeant Bill Laconde, who had taken command of his troop after Cheshire's medical evacuation to England, heard stifled laughter coming from one of the firqat sangars. He walked across to find four of the firqat, including the man who had fired, with their hands over their mouths giggling like schoolgirls. One of them explained that the man who had fired had in fact dozed off; he awoke to hear Baluch voices coming up the hill towards him and instinctively shot at them before he remembered that he had changed sides. Laconde was furious, not at the fact that he had fired, but that he had missed, and muttered darkly to me about the need for more training in night shooting. We decided that this was one tale that should not be retold outside BATT.

The Firqat Al Nasr, who were now concentrated at Adonib, finally went out with an SAF company on their first operation to try to stop a convoy of 200 children who were being forcibly moved to Hauf to attend the Lenin School there. They failed to intercept the convoy, but they did succeed in blowing up one of the main enemy re-supply routes where it ran along the side of a hill, so making the route impassable. The alternative route would add two days to the adoo's re-supply time, so it was a significant success. The commanding officer of the battalion, Lieutenant-Colonel Fergus Mackain-Bremner, took the trouble to come over to the BATT compound to say how well the Al Nasr had performed. It was a small matter and partly due to his natural courtesy, but nonetheless I went to bed that night heartened at the first words of appreciation spoken by a SAF officer towards the firqats.

Paddy the Ditch was, needless to say, delighted. 'I told you, Sir, once we got that Salim Gharib in command they would be all right.'

He was probably correct, as so much depended on getting the right man in command. A firqat's attitude could change overnight from one of surly non-co-operation to positive and cheerful enthusiasm. The election of a commander was something we were watching very carefully at that time in the Western Mahra, who were now under training at Mamurah and calling themselves the Firqat Tariq Bin Zeead, but it would be some time before they were ready for active operations.

The Firqat Salahadin could have operated into the Wadi Darbat at any time but the other two firqats in being, the A'asifat and Khalid Bin Waalid, were not yet ready, so to keep the Salahadin occupied in the meantime I decided to use them to eliminate the adoo who had been pestering Sudh. The operation turned out to be a game of musical chairs over the Sudh plain. For five days the firqat and BATT chased the adoo, always one step behind, until just as the draw-string was about to be pulled tight, the adoo group slipped out back the way they had come, towards Mirbat. Only one small contact occurred and one adoo was captured. The only real value in the operation was that it gave Lieutenant Colonel John Watts, newly arrived on a visit from Britain, his first chance to see the firqats in action and to assess their abilities, something that was to stand him in good stead later in the year.

★ ★ ★

In retrospect, it should have been apparent with the raising of the Eastern Mahra Firqat A'asifat, the Western Mahra Firqat Tariq Bin Zeead, the Bait Kathir Firqat Al Nasr, the Bait Ma'asheni Firqat Khalid Bin Waalid and even the Bait Umr Sudh Defence Force that the days of the multi-tribal Firqat Salahadin were numbered, but its collapse still took me by surprise and I think I was not alone.

I arrived at Mirbat on the afternoon of 21st April 1971, after a radio call from Laconde had said that 20 of the firqat were refusing to take orders from Mohammed Said, Laconde, or anyone else. I was not over-worried and assumed it was one of the minor tantrums which Dhofaris threw from time to time. I was reassured to discover that the leader of the mutiny was Qartoob; if anyone would listen to reason, surely it was he. I walked over to the marquee where he and four of his henchmen were waiting, and began by asking him what was his problem. It quickly became clear that this was to be no afternoon for logic and argument: the shutters of his mind were down. He could give no reason why he refused to serve under Mohammed Said, or why he was inciting those men of his own tribe, the Bait Umr and their neighbours the Bait Ma'asheni, to mutiny.

It was Said Bin Gheer, speaking in English and pretending to interpret, who explained it to me. In the first place, Qartoob had been as important an adoo leader as Mohammed Said, possibly more important: and in the second, he was a member of the Bait Umr whose tribal town was Mirbat. The Bait Umr were a powerful tribe and controlled most of south-eastern Dhofar; it was against Qartoob's pride to serve under a man of the Bait Gatun, a minor tribe of the Central Area. And, doubtless, he had been taunted by other Bait Umr in the town itself.

Nonetheless I did not despair. We talked for two hours and by the time there was no more to be said, it was dark. One by one the five men rose to leave and hand in their rifles to the BATT house. It was disappointing, but not disastrous. I also rose stiffly and walked out of the tent to the town square, where the majority of the firqat, some 60 in all, were seated around a blazing fire in a large circle. It was a night set for drama. The stars glittered with that unbelievable desert ferocity. The moon had risen and glimmered on the waves as they broke with a gentle hiss on the sandy shore. The fire exploded in miniature sun flares, some six feet high, leaping into the night sky to dissolve in showers of sparks, making shadows dance on the walls of the houses. The flames exaggerated the shadows and highlights of the men's faces and accentuated their hawk-like features. I squatted down cross-legged in a space in the circle and began to make small talk to the men on either side.

Mohammed Said was sitting a few places to my left, flanked by the lanky form of Mohammed Ali Isa, his sergeant major, and several of his principal supporters. Some men on the right were arguing angrily across the fire at him, to be answered in turn by Mohammed Ali Isa. Mohammed Said occasionally answered himself, but for the most part sat staring into the fire. Suddenly a man leapt to his feet. He stood with arm outstretched pointing across the fire, spitting abuse. Mohammed Ali Isa's face tightened and his eyes flashed, but I saw Mohammed Said seize his arm and prevent him from rising. The accuser turned his back and strode into the night. Now, several more sprang to their feet, all talking at once and all accusing Mohammed Said.

I was aghast; this had gone too far. I got to my feet and told them they were behaving like women. Mohammed Said was the Commander of the Firqat Salahadin and had the complete trust of BATT. The only people who would benefit from this sort of talk were the Front. I announced that there would be a parade at 0700 hours next morning and anyone who wished to leave the firqat could say so then. I walked away from the fire leaving Mohammed Said and his supporters sitting disconsolately in a little group on one side, the flames flickering on the many empty spaces which had been occupied by fighting men only minutes before.

The naib wali invited Laconde and me to supper but it was not a happy meal. None of us talked about the events of the evening and indeed I still did not believe the firqat would break up. They were always arguing about something or other and, after a night to cool off, I thought most of them would decide to stay in the firqat the next morning. How wrong I was.

At 0700 hours next day there were 68 men on parade. I ordered those who wished to remain in the Firqat Salahadin to stand fast, the remainder to fall out and hand in their FNs to the armoury. All but 28 fell out.

It was a disaster; three months of dedicated hard work wasted, or so it seemed. The Firqat Salahadin was back to Salim Mubarak's original number, almost exactly. My disappointment must have shown because as he passed, one of the departing firqatmen stopped and took my arm. '*Ma'fee hof Taweel*, don't worry, they will all go to join other firqats. Don't look so sad.'

SEVEN

THE GUN ON THE JEBEL ARAM

May 1971

The collapse of the Firqat Salahadin was a major setback. It would take two or three weeks before those who left fitted themselves into the firqats of their choice and before those firqats were ready for a major operation into the Wadi Darbat of the sort that Harvey and I had envisaged. For the five ringleaders it would take even longer. They had been interviewed by *Wali* Baraik and had emerged very chastened men. He decided to let them stew for a while before allowing them to join another firqat.

In any case, an immediate problem had come to hand which demanded attention. For several days past Taqa had been under fire by an adoo big gun from the jebel escarpment. A number of shells had landed in the town itself although, fortunately, they had done less damage than expected. A woman had been killed and several injured, but the mud walls of the houses seemed capable of absorbing much more of the shrapnel and blast than modern brick and glass buildings. One shell had even struck the corner of the BATT house whilst a soldier was sleeping in the room behind, showering him with dust but leaving him otherwise unhurt.

The pieces of shrapnel the BATT had recovered suggested that the adoo weapon had a calibre of 75 mm, but included among the pieces was an unexploded VT fuse. VT stands for Variable Time, which means that the fuse can be set to explode the shell before it reaches the ground so that the explosion showers shrapnel on those below. It is used normally against troops in the open or in slit trenches, but it would also be lethal used against an Arab town, where the walls provided good protection against shells that explode in the street outside, but which often surround open courtyards. Even the flat roofs of the houses could do little to stop shrapnel penetrating from above.

The pieces were collected by the BATT and sent for analysis to the artillery intelligence cell in Muscat. Most of the pieces were easily identified as coming from a Soviet or Chinese-made recoilless gun, but the VT fuse was puzzling. Artillery intelligence had no record of either the Soviet or Chinese gun having a shell with a VT fuse, so they suggested that the adoo might also have a 75-mm artillery piece on the jebel above Taqa. It was difficult to believe. The recoilless gun was a big weapon, but broken down into its component parts it could be carried on a camel train without too much difficulty. An artillery piece was quite another matter. Whereas a recoilless weapon works like a rocket launcher and disperses the recoil blast of the shell into the atmosphere behind the gun, an artillery piece has to absorb the energy itself. The barrel and breech alone of a 75-mm piece would be too much for a camel to carry. But it was just possible that the weapon had been towed across country all the way from Hauf; it was unlikely, but the possibility could not be ruled out. Fortunately the adoo seemed to be short of ammunition. The gun, or guns, seldom fired more than three or four shells at a time, and never fired when the jets were overhead. Nonetheless, the morale of the townspeople was sinking fast.

At least one SAS man was now always on duty in the fort above the town, and whenever incomers began to arrive, his job was to study the jebel through powerful glasses to see if he could spot the gun firing. So far he had been unsuccessful. A recoilless gun tends to kick up more dust when it fires than an artillery piece and the absence of any sighting at all by the man in the fort tended to confirm artillery intelligence's theory.

After every attack the Strikemasters would come streaking over and fire some rockets in the general area of the adoo gun. The BATT, too, had set up their mortar as far forward of the fort as it was safe to go. Even then the jebel was still in theory out of range, but by dropping a teaspoonful of petrol into the barrel first, the mortar was registering hits at over 6000 yards. It was highly irregular practice and would be severely frowned upon at the School of Infantry. It was dangerous, true, and there was a chance that the mortar might blow up, but the alternative – being shelled by a 75-mm gun – was not without risk itself. At least it meant we could hit back.

Plans existed to move down two 90-mm guns from Muscat as soon as they had been reconditioned and when some ammunition could be found for them. These were old French tank guns which Sultan Said Bin Taimur had procured for reasons of his own and were discovered in their original grease after the coup. They were in fact eventually positioned at Taqa and Mirbat but after the one at Taqa had blown up and killed the gunner they were replaced by 25-pounders, one of which served so well at the battle of Mirbat the following year and was the last 25-pounder to be used by British troops in action. The British Army has adopted a more modern field piece.

The adoo gun was being fired from the Jebel Aram, a feature some 7000 yards long and shaped like a French loaf. Its eastern end ran down to the Wadi Darbat and its western end and most of its northern side fell away into the Wadi Ethon. The southern side of the jebel was almost sheer, but the northern side, although it ran away steeply, was easily climbable. The jebel rose to a height of 1500 feet in the centre and it was covered with trees and scrub which became denser as the ground fell away into Wadi Ethon. A good well, Tawi Ethon, lay somewhere down in the wadi but attempts to get the firqat to indicate it exactly on a map resulted in half a dozen positions spread over a length of 2000 yards. The Jebel Aram had always been a favourite adoo area and it was easy to see why.

The task was too large for the depleted firqats and, remembering Mackain-Bremner's enthusiasm over the Firqat Al Nasr's first operation, I approached him. He was enthusiastic and together we set about planning a joint firqat/SAF operation. If it really was an artillery piece up there, we stood a good chance of capturing it. The more manoeuvrable recoilless gun was another matter, but it was just possible that if we could surprise the adoo and catch them in the act of firing then we might get that, too. Either way, an operation on to the Aram would achieve the aim of getting the firqats and SAF to work together, it would show the people of Taqa that something was being done to protect them, and it would throw the adoo off balance.

Surprise would be essential. The approach would have to be by night and up routes which the adoo would not be guarding. The single pass made by Mackain-Bremner and myself over the jebel in a Beaver showed that there were two possible routes: one led in from the west running parallel to the bed of the Wadi Ethon and halfway between the wadi and the crest, and the other involved a wide sweep around the east up to a narrow pass, the Aqbat Aram, which also led to the crest. We agreed that as few people as possible should know of the plan, but that

I should have to take Mohammed Said into our confidence.

Two firqats and two SAS troops were available, the Firqat Salahadin and its BATT and the Firqat Khalid Bin Waalid and its BATT. The Khalid Bin Waalid were still young and I would have preferred to 'blood' them on a simpler operation, but after the break-up of the Salahadin, most of the Bait Ma'asheni had joined the Khalid Bin Waalid, and the Jebel Aram was, after all, Bait Ma'asheni territory. I played with the idea of bringing in the Firqat A'asifat from the north, but discarded it because, first, they were going through a 'difficult' period, second, most of them were on leave and, third, they would not easily forget the donkey episode. In any case, there would be little in the operation to attract a Mahra firqat so far from their own country.

Although the Firqat Khalid Bin Waalid were already at Taqa, a convoy with armoured car escort moved them the twelve miles west to Mamurah, the old sultan's gardens, which I had selected as an assembly area for reasons of security and deception. The move would support the hints of another operation in the Central Area that had been allowed to circulate over the past week.

Mamurah contained a high-walled courtyard with palm-roofed shacks set about the wall inside. It was not much of a place and had not been used for anything for a long time, but it served to keep the sun off. The open trucks pulled up outside the courtyard, filled to the brim with the firqat happily singing one of those haunting Jebeli songs which go on and on repeating the same refrain, but to notes and a cadence so strange to Western ears that the mind fails to retain it within minutes of it stopping. They clambered down off the trucks carrying multi-coloured bags of food and extra clothing and sat themselves down around the walls to talk and rest. I was pleased to see that they all carried FNs.

Half an hour later, the Firqat Salahadin and their BATT arrived from Mirbat by Caribou at Arzat Camp, a short distance away. As they filed over the aircraft's lowered tail ramp and jumped lightly to the ground I noticed some young Baluch soldiers watching them with respect. The difference was marked. The firqat were no 18-year old Baluchis; they looked a harder lot altogether. A British SAF officer came up to see me.

'So those are the firqat,' he said, obviously seeing them for the first time. He studied them for a while as they climbed aboard the trucks for the short journey to Mamurah. 'Murderous-looking lot, aren't they?' he chuckled. 'All I can say is I'm glad they are on our side.'

The two firqats mixed freely at Mamurah. There seemed none of the chill I had half expected and soon they were so hopelessly mixed up that it took a little time to separate them for their different briefings. Most of the Khalid Bin Waalid were to go with the Muscat Regiment up the western route, whilst the remainder accompanied the Salahadin and the two troops of SAS up the eastern route.

The afternoon passed slowly. It was a stiflingly hot day. The briefings over and all questions finally answered, the whole force lay down to try to get some rest. The SAS tended to separate into their different troops on opposite sides of the courtyard, knots of men sitting talking quietly around two or three tommy-cookers crowned by mess tins of water about to be brewed into tea. It was important to drink as much as possible to fill the body cells with water before the climb. Here and there individual SAS men lay back reading books or studying their maps to fix the lie of the ground firmly in their minds. The firqats, too, had regrouped into little parties of men talking and laughing together, with here and there a figure curled up under his cloak with his green shamag thrown over his face trying to sleep.

The afternoon droned on until at last the shadows began to lengthen and a *mullah* among the firqat began quietly, almost in a murmur at first, to call them to evening prayer.

'*Allaaaaaaaaaaaahu akbar. Allaaaaaaaaaaaahu akbar.*'

One by one the men rose to their feet and knelt down behind him until a line stretched nearly the length of the courtyard. Their solidarity as they knelt in unison and the deep throated '*A-a-a-llah*', almost a sigh, impressed me deeply. I thought of the pathetic little cluster of worshippers at my church in Hereford and envied these men their faith. They were about to go into battle and such faith could only be fortifying.

The SAS were concerned more with affairs of this world. All round the courtyard mess tins were bubbling with curry and rice, each man adding his own little dainties to the standard Army pack: an onion here, some raisins there, taken from little bags stowed with loving care in the bottom of his bergen.

The trucks returned as dusk was falling, the troops climbed aboard, and guided once more by the armoured cars, the convoy moved off back towards Taqa. We paused as we reached the rendezvous, and were joined by the trucks filled with Muscat Regiment soldiers, and then the long column began to bump and roll its way slowly eastward with all lights extinguished and engine revolutions kept as low as possible.

At the end of an hour, a small light could be seen blinking ahead in the darkness: it was the rendezvous at a wadi junction three miles south of the entrance to the Wadi Ethon. The trucks drove up nose to tail and the soldiers clambered down, grateful to stretch their limbs after the rough ride. Weapons clinked as they were given a final check and radio operators muttered into their sets. Here and there two or three men talked in low voices, but for the most part men stood silently waiting. Although still several miles from the jebel, it seemed natural to talk softly and the clatter of breeches as each man cocked his weapon sounded painfully loud.

The SAF were the first to set off towards the dark line of the jebel to the north. A few minutes later Laconde reported that the firqat were all set and we moved off in single file north-eastwards. It was a clear night, but that did little to help the tedium, for the force had to march seven miles across the plain before it could even begin to climb. Small wadis running from north to south inundated the plain so that every few minutes the column had to scramble down one side and up another. Time passed very slowly and the outline of the Jebel Aram to the left barely altered as the long line of men plodded its way eastwards.

At last, after four hours, at first almost imperceptibly, the ground began to change and the column edged its way to the left to move more northwards. Gradually the ground steepened until, with surprising suddenness, the jebel was no longer before us but above us. The climb had begun.

The move across the plain had been accomplished with one halt: from now onwards the column halted regularly at each hour to rest. Soon it became less rocky and grass and bushes appeared, until the column was snaking its way across meadows. From time to time it halted, and men sank into the shadows of the bushes while the firqat in front checked out a known adoo picket position.

The slope began to flatten out; we were near the top. Everyone was very weary by now and I ordered a break as we were nearing the area of greatest danger and I wanted everybody to be fresh if we should have to fight. I sat down against a rock, eased the straps of the bergen off my shoulders and checked my watch: 0300 hours. Four figures appeared. It was Laconde and the three guides.

'They say they're not sure of the way from here and that there's a village ahead. They think we should wait until first light.'

'Out of the question,' I answered. 'I know they're tired, but we must push on while we still have the cover of darkness. It'll be light in two hours.'

From now on the going became slower, with more frequent stops as the leading firqat moved carefully forward. At last the ground in front evened out and began to go downwards. We had reached the top of the ridge running up to the *aqbat*. The column turned west and began to file along the high ground towards the dark mass of the Jebel Aram's peak.

I had agreed with Mackain-Bremner that the firqat and BATT would not move up to the peak until after dawn so as to avoid an accidental contact between ourselves and the SAF. By 0500 hours we had reached a small plateau from which it appeared we should have to descend slightly to get on to the pass itself. It was too dark to see much and a morning mist had begun to shroud the hill. Twenty minutes still remained before first light. This would do, I decided; we could adjust our position as it became lighter. I gave the order to halt and take up defensive positions around the hillock, the firqat to the east and south, the BATT to the north and west.

Little cover existed, apart from bushes and long grass, but I did not intend to stay there long. Laconde and Mohammed Said with two or three others set up the command group alongside a cattle fence of thorns shaped like an L with the shorter bar facing the *aqbat*, or at least where the *aqbat* should be, since it was too dark to see yet. In the middle of the plateau, a large tree stood 25 yards north of the low sangar that Laconde was busy throwing up. From it, further north, I could see a low line of bushes the same distance away, and beyond them and lower, the dark shape of the saddle between the Wadi Ethon and the Wadi Darbat.

The tree seemed to be a good observation point. I sat down against it facing towards the pass and took off my bergen. Then I took out the air photograph of the area. We were within a hundred yards of where we wanted to be, but I tried unsuccessfully to pinpoint our exact position on it. There was no need of a torch as it was light enough now to see the men quite clearly in Laconde's group, but the mist was becoming thicker and I decided to wait a few minutes longer until it had cleared. Contentedly, I settled back against the tree.

The world exploded. It was broad daylight and I realized that I must have dozed off. Bullets seemed to whip-crack from every direction punctuated by long bursts of machine-gun fire from very close at hand. A grenade exploded. A chip of wood clipped off the tree above my head.

It had seemed quite a substantial tree before; now I began to wonder. The breath was knocked out of my body as three firqatmen hurled themselves flat on top of me. One kept glancing up to the left to the high ground, muttering, 'This is not good. This is not good.'

He was right. It was not good. We were in clear view of the top of the jebel 300 yards away and if the adoo were up there and they were attracted by this shooting, we could be in difficulties. The high ground dominated us completely.

The shooting began to slacken. One by one, each of the firqatmen behind the tree waited for a lull and then sprinted for the nearest sangar, Laconde's, until I was left alone. A small voice said, 'Remember your Sandhurst training. You should set an example. Get slowly to your feet and walk calmly across to the sangar,' but another smaller voice said, 'Remember, no casualties. What do you think the effect will be in Whitehall if the Squadron Commander gets himself killed? The SAS will be out of Oman tomorrow.' The voice of pragmatism shamefully won. I eased into my bergen straps, rose to my feet and ran pell-mell for the sangar, where at last I learned how the contact had happened.

Salim Said Dherdhir, Qartoob's political commissar, had not gone with Qartoob when the Bait Umr war-leader decided to break away from the Firqat Salahadin. Dherdhir remained loyal to Mohammed Said and was taking part in this operation. He had been lying in a dip in the ground with some other Firqat Salahadin men when he felt a need to answer the morning call of nature. He put his blanket over his head, picked up his rifle and wandered off into the mist following the line of the cattle hedge. It was not a long hedge and no sooner was he lost to view by his comrades, than he came into view of a five-man adoo picket in a trench, standing-to at dawn in the best British-trained military tradition. One of them challenged him, but immediately he heard another man say that it was a woman; the blanket over Dherdhir's head must have deceived him. Dherdhir turned round and walked back with mincing steps to the hedge, where he pulled out a hand-grenade and threw it at the adoo picket. The grenade rolled to a stop on the edge of the trench. The five men ducked until it went off and then opened up automatic fire with their Kalashnikovs. Dherdhir replied with his FN and then anyone who could bring a weapon to bear joined in.

All was quiet in front now, but sporadic bursts of fire were still coming from the north-east and I recognized the disciplined bursts of GPMG fire. An SAS gun-team had the adoo pinned in the bottom of the valley where they had fled. But the fire was not all one way and every time anyone showed his head over the high ground it was greeted by a burst from below.

It was not that which claimed my main attention, however, but the high ground to the west. It was ominously quiet and our sangars were little more than scrapes in the ground. Unworthy thoughts about the SAF were just beginning to enter my mind when there came the sudden mixed crackle of fire. I felt a flood of relief. The SAF had arrived and I knew that as Mackain-Bremner wanted the top of that hill, he would take it. I walked over to see how the gun group were getting on with their adoo and, despite their pleadings, called them back up to the main position. The aim was to close up with the SAF, not to go off after adoo in the valley below. On the way back I dropped in at Dherdhir's position. The blue and red mark of a bullet graze stood out on his neck, and another had nicked his shoulder. I joked with him about it.

'You must be more careful, Salim,' I grinned.

He shrugged. 'A man can only die once,' he said.

Most of the firqat leaders possessed this sort of bravery, and it took a little getting used to. SAS soldiers performed many acts of conspicuous gallantry during the Dhofar campaign but they were usually calculated. The SAS soldier is, above all, a professional and he knows that there is a time to expose himself to enemy fire and there is a time to take cover. The bravery of the firqat leaders on the other hand seemed based upon a mixture of fatalism and faith. A Moslem killed fighting for Islam can expect certain benefits in heaven, and no doubt this helped many men to risk death, but Dherdhir was not a very religious man. Nonetheless, whatever his motivation, the idea of taking cover seemed cowardly to him.

Shooting was still going on around the SAF position, but Mackain-Bremner came on the air to say that they were firm and ready to receive us; one soldier had been killed and three wounded. The saddle showed itself to be S-shaped with little cover except near the top, so the move up was carried out prudently, with one group always firm on the ground covering the other. When we arrived, Mackain-Bremner first pointed out a position to the west and separated from the SAF position by 300 yards. I examined it and declined. The two positions were not mutually supporting and, besides, I had unpleasant visions of a battle taking place between the two by mistake, especially at night; it would be too easy to start.

The second position was better, part of the SAF position and extending towards the north-west into thick bush which began to run down into the Wadi Ethon, including the clearing where the SAF casualties had occurred. The battalion had sent a patrol forward to check the crest just as dawn was breaking. The patrol had found it unoccupied and, instead of securing it, had all returned to report their findings. When the leading troops reached the position 20 minutes later, the adoo were waiting and of the five men who crossed the clearing, four had been hit in one burst by a light machine-gun.

The firqat were now showing their tiredness and, in any case, clearing ground like this was not one of their strongest points. It would need close control in the thick country, again not the firqat's forte. I decided to use BATT alone in a T-formation, one troop to each of the two bars, with the command group where the two bars met. It was a good formation, easy to control and allowing at least half the patrol to return fire immediately in any direction without risk of hitting the other.

The leading troop, advancing in extended line, came out of the scrub on to the edge of the clearing quite suddenly. Without orders, the line naturally swung into two horns moving around its edges, but as the right GPMG team were halfway around, a long burst again crackled out from the other side of the clearing 25 yards away. Incredibly, the bullets passed between the two men and neither was hit. Both dived for cover behind a log and scarcely after the adoo's fire had stopped, their ripping GPMG bursts were tearing into the bushes on the other side of the clearing.

I flung myself flat behind a bush and shouted to the second troop to swing around to the left to see if they could not get behind the adoo. Across the clearing nothing moved. To the left came the noise of bodies thrusting themselves through the bushes and the shouts of men trying to maintain contact with each other.

Suddenly a figure appeared, moving quickly in the edge of the bushes at the left-hand side of the clearing. His green shirt and shamag with khaki webbing pouches around his waist identified him as a firqatman. Within seconds he had disappeared and I cursed my stupidity. No firqatmen were with us and, anyway, they would not have been running like that towards the enemy. Something else moved across the clearing and I glimpsed a khaki peaked hat. I called out to the GPMG team and asked if anyone was forward of them. No one. I took careful aim at the hat, dropped six inches and fired two rapid shots. Not a sound came from the bush, but when I looked up, the hat had disappeared. The shouts and the noise of firing were getting further away now as the left-hand troop pursued the adoo down the hill. Again I radioed and again had to haul on the reins until the group gradually disengaged and returned to the clearing, exhilarated from the chase.

Eventually the position was cleared and, with sentries lying silently 20 yards forward, the two troops and the firqat began to chop down the bushes in front to clear the fields of fire and build sangars. As soon as these were ready, an attempt was made to move forward into the Wadi Ethon by a company of SAF with SAS and firqat in support, but by now the Wadi Ethon group of adoo were well alerted and after an hour it became clear that there would be no chance of getting into the wadi without heavy casualties. The adoo fought fiercely and for some minutes intense machine-gun and mortar fire was directed at nobody in particular in an apparent waste of ammunition. Only later did we realise that this was probably to cover the withdrawal of the big gun.

Meanwhile, a BATT and firqat patrol had gone in the other direction towards the escarpment, where they came across the firing position of the gun and a small stockpile of shells. It was easy to see why it had been impossible to spot the firing position from Taqa. The gun had been cleverly sited on a flat area between two large rocks and roofed over with bushes for camouflage. Only the muzzle could be seen from Taqa and the back blast would be masked by the rocks and bushes. There was no sign of an artillery piece. The shells were all of Chinese manufacture for a 75-mm recoilless gun, and to cap it, one of the shells was found fitted with a VT fuse. The mystery was solved. Dherdhir, who had been trained in China, confirmed that he had never been taught how to use a VT fuse, which perhaps explained why the adoo had fortunately continued to use them as ordinary high explosive shells against Taqa.

The advance into the Ethon having failed, the SAF, firqat and BATT all returned to the main position for a rest. Everyone had been marching or fighting non-stop for 18 hours by this time and the mental tension and physical fatigue were beginning to make themselves felt. An enemy mortar in the wadi found the range of the main position and the rest of the day was spent in receiving mortar fire from, and returning counter-mortar fire into, the Wadi Ethon. The same helicopter which took out the dead and wounded SAF brought in the one SAS mortar and the two SAF mortars and these were now co-ordinated as a fire group by an SAS NCO.

The pattern was much the same next day. Both the SAF and the firqat moved towards the sort of work they were best at, a division of labour that was copied by and large over the next five years of war and an arrangement to the benefit of both. The SAF were best at seizing a piece of ground and securing it to provide a firm base from which the firqat patrols, supported by SAS when necessary, could operate, and into which they could retire in safety, or comparative safety. After Laconde and a firqat patrol coming back in had been fired at – and missed – by a SAF bren gunner 15 yards away, I insisted that all patrols were met outside the perimeter and led in by a SAF officer at the front. It should have been, and later on in the war was, unnecessary, but at this time the SAF soldiers were too unfamiliar with the firqat or BATT to risk even an obvious European like Laconde being mistaken for an adoo.

The firqats, on the other hand, did not like static warfare or straight infantry work. They were at their best on patrol, when they could take advantage of the natural lie of the land and use it to out-manoeuvre their enemy.

On the second afternoon I took Mohammed Said and Laconde to the north-eastern side of the position and sat on the edge of the bushes, looking down on to the meadow land that ran down to the village we had passed on the climb up. Forward of the village and to the left of where we sat, was the saddle between the Wadi Ethon and the low spur which ran into the Wadi Darbat. It was important to regain the initiative. Though the firqat were busily involved destroying the main adoo supply dump they had discovered – nearly two tons of rice, sugar and corn – I wanted to use them against the enemy in person.

We sat in the shadows of the bushes studying the ground in front of us as three women wearing black shawls appeared from the dead ground and began to walk about the village. Mohammed Said explained that they were checking the village for our presence and insisted on my calling down fire from the 5.5s, which had been moved to a position near Taqa to support the operation. He clicked his tongue in exasperation at the strange ways of Europeans when I said I would do no such thing. Instead, I asked him what he thought the adoo would do next. He explained that they were just containing us with these little sniping attacks at present and identifying the flanks of the position, but that night would see a major attack up the spur we were now looking down. The adoo firqat from Wadi Ethon would join up with the adoo from the Wadi Darbat, who were known to be a particularly strong unit, and they

125

would come up the spur to try to take out a couple of SAF sangars.

The spur was long, shaped like an L as we looked at it, running first eastwards for 300 yards and then north for another 400 down to the saddle between the two wadis. I decided that if what Mohammed Said said was correct, and it seemed to make sense, we should be waiting for them. Together we sited five ambush positions which should successfully intercept the adoo from whatever direction they might come. The top three positions, manned by the SAS, would be placed at the top of the spur, at the elbow, and a hundred yards down the northern arm; the lower two positions, placed at hundred-yard intervals down the northern arm, would be firqat alone. The SAS positions would each have a GPMG firing one tracer in five ball; I would have mortar and artillery on call from the top position and Laconde would move to the lowest. The elbow would form an intermediate firm base should we have to withdraw in a hurry, and since a hundred hard-core adoo were reputed to be in the Wadi Darbat alone, this was a possibility.

It was getting dark as the long line of men filed past out on to the first arm of the spur. I eased myself into the top sangar and settled down alongside the GPMG gunner, Corporal 'Mule' Gilairi, another Fijian, whose nickname reflected his immense strength, and Corporal 'Tosh' Hampton, a blond-haired Adonis from London. I followed the column of men with my eyes to the spur's elbow, but lost them in the gathering gloom as they turned north. Soon the two BATT positions radioed quietly to confirm that they were in position. A few minutes later the first firqat position reported that all was well and the remaining 15 men of the firqat, led by Mohammed Ali Isa, set off for the bottom ambush position.

Mohammed Ali Isa, a tall, gangling man with a long nose, a huge grin and an immense sense of humour, was a favourite with the BATT. He was also a very effective soldier and leader, and had been one of Salim Mubarak's original firqat. His appointment as sergeant-major had been popular among the SAS and firqat alike. He was still short of his ambush position, with his men strung out five yards apart behind him, when a voice challenged from his right.

'Halt. Who are you?'

The voice spoke in Jebeli. Mohammed stopped and stared into the darkness. Thirty paces away he could make out a figure with many more shuffling up from behind. He was pleased to see that his own men had sunk to the ground.

126

'We are friends,' he answered also in Jebeli. 'Who are you?'

'We are the army of the forces of freedom,' came the reply.

Mohammed took careful aim and fired, then dived flat. It was the Darbat adoo. They must have mistaken the firqat for the adoo group they had come to meet from the Ethon and now they paid dearly for their mistake. Whereas they were bunched up in column, the firqat were strung out in line, and in a contest between column and line, line always wins. Only the front few men of the adoo could bring their weapons to bear, whereas every man of the firqat could fire, and did.

It was at too close quarters for any of the other positions to help and Mohammed's patrol in any case did not need help, yet. After a minute of intense fire the Darbat adoo began to fall back into the dead ground from where they had come, carrying their dead and wounded. The shooting was just beginning to die down as the adoo retired, when the side of the Wadi Ethon suddenly erupted with automatic fire at Mohammed and his men. Fortunately they were still lying down and, in the darkness, most of the adoo fire went over their heads, but Mohammed was hit in the side just below the armpit. The shooting put fresh heart into the Wadi Darbat group, who pressed forward once again so that the firqat now found themselves with enemy on two sides. I heard Laconde's voice on the radio ordering them to withdraw.

Dherdhir was meant to be commanding the upper firqat ambush, but as soon as the shooting started he left his position and ran forward down the hill to help. His voice now came over the air frantically to Laconde telling what was happening. Laconde's voice was a model of calmness. Again he told Dherdhir to withdraw through him. Dherdhir's voice came in gasps; he sounded exhausted, and it was not until his blood-soaked figure staggered into Laconde's position with Mohammed's dead body over his shoulder that I understood why.

The adoo followed up closely and it was some minutes before the supporting positions were able to work out which flickering groups of fire-flies in the valley below belonged to which side. Occasionally, an adoo would rip off a burst of automatic fire and, as the firqat were armed with semi-automatic FNs only, he would immediately receive long streaks of red tracer from the GPMGs, but it was some minutes before the firqat got clear enough for the adoo to be identified positively. Then the GPMGs sent tracer hammering in amongst the adoo positions and ricocheting skywards. The mortars, too, now began to thud away into the valley, but still the adoo followed up, until Laconde was forced to roll up on to the elbow position. Here the adoo broke contact at last, and the firqat and BATT were able to make their way back up into the main position.

It had not quite gone as planned, but the adoo had been intercepted and had had the worst of it. There were no more attacks that night.

Dawn found me back in the same sangar with Gilairi and his GPMG as Laconde went out again with some of the firqat, this time towards the village. When they were within range, the BATT split into two groups to cover him, and Dherdhir walked confidently down into the group of huts with four of the Firqat Salahadin.

It was a typical Jebeli village. Perhaps a dozen houses were scattered about, each built on the traditional round-house lines, a wall of large stones built in a circle topped with a beehive roof of blackened wood and straw thatch. A U-shaped piece of timber usually formed the low entrance or sometimes a stone lintel was supported by wooden or stone uprights. Between the houses stood smaller ones for goats and large thorn enclosures and hedge-walls for cattle.

I watched Dherdhir through the binoculars as he examined the houses. Suddenly, he lifted his rifle and fired at a target the other side of the village and out of view from my position, then leant back against the wall quite casually as the fire was returned. I felt as if I were watching a television programme. The five firqat were in full view the whole time, ducking behind walls and sometimes running, sometimes walking between houses, peering around corners, occasionally firing a shot or two. It all seemed very remote.

The skirmish did not last long. There were 15 adoo in the village but they sensibly did not argue the toss. Dherdhir came up on the radio to report that he had recovered Mohammed Ali Isa's radio and rifle from just above the village and he was returning to the main position. Many bloodstains and pieces of flesh stained the ground where last night's adoo had been when the firqat opened up on them.

While I still watched Dherdhir and his men climb back up the hill, a group of five adoo came into view some 2000 yards away over the other side of the Wadi Ethon, probably from the same group that Dherdhir had chased out of the village. Now they strolled nonchalantly across our front carrying their rifles over their shoulders by the barrel.

Gilairi screwed his sights up to the 2500 figure and let go a long burst, but the figures did not even falter. Another burst drew an

Right: The author visits the Firquat Salahadin at Mirbat (Introduction).

Below: Strikemasters of the Sultan of Oman's Air Force (Introduction)

Left Mohammed Said dressed as an adoo (Chapter 2).

Below: SAS and firquat embarked for the Sudh landing (Chapter 4).

Right: Mohammed Said, Salim Mubarraq and Mohammed Ali Isa raise the flag at Sudh (Chapter 4).

Below right: SAS picquet above Sudh (Chapter 4).

Above: The surrender of Qartoob and Dherdir (Chapter 4).

Below: A machine gunner on Eagle's Nest (Chapter 5).

Above: Withdrawal from the Jebel Ara (Chapter 7).

Below: Wadi Darbat (Chapter 7).

Left: Mirbat Fort (Chapter 9).

Middle left: A patrol sets out on the central plateau (Chapter 11).

Bottom left: End of a patrol (Chapter 11).

Right: Isa and son (Chapter 11).

Below: A 'Hearts and Minds' patrol at Shuhait (Chapter 12).

Above: The three elements of victory: firquat, SAS and Civil Action (Chapter 12).

Left: A captured Katyusha rocket (Chapter 12).

answering wave from the leader before the group disappeared into dead ground. They could not get away with that. I picked up the radio.

'Hullo, Golf nine, this is Tiger nine. Fire mission 5.5s, over.'

The great shell sounded as big as a dustbin as it came rumbling overhead. A huge pall of black smoke rose lazily from behind the hill where the adoo group had gone from view, followed a few seconds later by the 'crump' of its explosion. Another shell followed. There was no point in firing again. It is usually the first shell that kills because it catches the enemy by surprise. By the time more shells arrive, they will have taken cover.

I returned to my sangar, a small low circle of stones that Tosh and I had put together under a large tree to provide some shade close to battalion headquarters. Many a soldier believes that if you want to upset a peaceful life, start to brew some tea. It is usually the sign for something to happen to stop you drinking it, the enemy start shooting or your commander decides to move suddenly. So it was that as soon as our brew was beginning to boil, a message came over the radio that Mackain-Bremner wanted an orders group. My own sangar was only ten paces away so I asked Tosh to bring my mug across as soon as tea was up and walked over. Small skirmishes were still taking place around the battalion's perimeter and now the adoo mortar opened up again, placing six bombs unpleasantly close to the battalion headquarters' sangar.

Mackain-Bremner was unruffled and began his briefing. He had decided, he said, to withdraw that evening, starting to thin out at 1700 hours and leaving the position altogether by 1730. The firqat and BATT would lead. The route was to be the direct one that we had avoided climbing, straight down the escarpment and across the plain to Taqa. I foresaw no difficulties as the firqat had already led a BATT patrol to the beginning of the route.

During a lull in the shooting I walked the hundred yards across to Laconde's sangar, which he shared with Mohammed Said, climbed the wall and squatted down alongside them . As soon as he heard the plan, Mohammed Said shook his head. The SAF always withdraw at about that time, he said. The adoo would be expecting it and would work around between us and the track to wait for us. Let us go soon after midday; the adoo attacks would lessen about then and by 1300 hours they would all be having their midday siesta before the evening's entertainment.

I looked at my watch: eleven o'clock, two hours, plenty of time. I walked back to battalion headquarters. Everything Mohammed Said had predicted on this operation so far had proved correct and Mackain-Bremner saw the sense of his new idea at once. He changed the time to 1300 hours; all the other details would remain unaltered.

A withdrawal is probably the most difficult of all military manoeuvres and must be timed to a nicety. The technique is to make things appear to the enemy as normal as possible, whilst secretly all those not needed to maintain the appearance of normality are slipping away quietly. The first danger point comes when the forward positions are being held by just a crust of men: if the enemy attacks then, he will smash through the crust and catch the battalion out of its defences like a crab without a shell. The second period of danger is during the withdrawal itself: the aim is always to manage a clean break so that when the enemy wakes up to it, it is too late for him to do anything. The last thing any commander wants is a running battle during the withdrawal.

With 15 minutes to go, helicopters came in to take out the mortars and ammunition; they had been coming in frequently with supplies over the last three days so there was nothing unusual about that. The firqat and BATT rose to their feet and buckled on their equipment, having checked that anything left behind was unusable by the adoo. The sangars were not booby-trapped. The aim was to persuade the adoo to join us. If we had to, we would kill him, but not maim him. Besides, it was quite probable that some old Jebeli would come scrabbling amongst the empty tins and litter of war to see if there was anything salvageable; empty mortar bomb tubes made good water containers.

I sent the Firqat Khalid Bin Waalid first, since this was their area followed by their BATT, then my own headquarters, both of us, then the Firqat Salahadin and lastly their BATT. After five minutes of moving through the thick bush, I sent a message forward to speed up; we were going far too slowly. Five minutes later, things still had not improved and I went forward myself to find out what was causing the hold-up. The BATT commander was a very experienced senior non-commissioned officer who had seen service all over the world, but he could just not bring himself to break with years of training in moving through jungle. He was moving cautiously forward step by step, watching every bush in model SAS manner, but this was no time for dawdling. The risk to the battalion of delay was far greater than the risk to the BATT/firqat of moving too fast. I called forward Laconde and the Firqat Salahadin. They came past at a trot and at last we began to move forward briskly.

The last of the Firqat Salahadin and BATT were disappearing down the sheer track over the escarpment as Mackain-Bremner and the leading company of SAF arrived; the timing could not have been better. We exchanged a few words and then I too scurried down the track after the BATT and firqats. The track was very steep indeed, a series of sharp U-turns almost vertically above each other. A single man could have stopped a brigade coming up it.

I caught up with the others just as they reached the bottom and began the long walk to Taqa. An hour later, I looked back to see the whole battalion moving across the plain in column of arrowheads behind us; it was an impressive sight. We had achieved a clean break and, as if to vent their disappointment, a single adoo shot sounded faintly from the jebel top.

The three miles to Taqa were a long plod in the heat of the day. The firqats until now had worked magnificently. Perhaps it was too much to expect the whole operation to go without a show of temperament. With only one mile to go, they sat down and refused to go further without some water to drink. I left them to it.

★　★　★

The effect of the operations in the first half of 1971 upon PFLOAG became apparent from a document captured later in the year. It was a copy of observations written by the First Political Commissar of the Ho Chi Minh Unit of the Central Area. He had attended the Third National Conference of the Front held at Rakyut in the Western Area in June, together with 74 other top Front members. The document made interesting reading and gave a very good idea of the disarray caused by the firqats' activities. It was remarkable for containing very little political diatribe and an honest attempt had been made to assess where they had gone wrong.

A number of ex-regular soldiers who had deserted, like the adoo mortar man at Tawi Atair, from the Trucial Oman Scouts or from Gulf Armies, had now returned from their courses in China and the Soviet Union and were making their presence felt. They had been properly trained and had little time for the hard-core 'cowboys' who had not had a proper military training. They criticised the lack of discussion or any form of de-brief after battle, so that lessons were never learnt and the same mistakes were made again and again; they were unimpressed by the way the young fighters blazed off their ammunition, particularly at aircraft flying hopelessly out of range; they thought that commanders did not insist on enough reconnaissance to enable them to arrive at an accurate estimate of the SAF strength; they criticised liaison between units, although this would improve now that each adoo unit had a radio, and the lack of technical knowledge of many of the fighters; and they demanded more materials in the shape of personal equipment instead of the hand-stitched home-made pouches they were equipped with. In short, theirs was the criticism of professional soldiers who found themselves, so they thought, amongst a bunch of amateurs.

On the political side, also, there were a number of significant criticisms. The Front realized that they had alienated the population, particularly in the Eastern Area, and decided to announce a six-month amnesty for any firqatman who wished to return to the Front. In the event, the number of people who took up this offer could be counted on one hand, for the Front had lost the trust even of its own members by its cruelty and spying. Observation posts, for example, were never less than three men strong, lest one man should persuade the other to desert with him. The People's Courts which had built up a noxious reputation for judgement and execution before trial, were to be disbanded and replaced by a new court to consist of elements of the People's Army, the militia and civilians. It would contain between seven and eleven members, and new, more liberal punishments were devised. In the past, most people who appeared before a People's Court were simply shot.

The Front was unpopular in the west, too, in PDRY itself, and so a virtue was made out of necessity by stating that all the Front's equipment in Hauf, just across the border in PDRY, should be moved into the 'Liberated Area' of Dhofar.

The Government's Civil Aid Policy and the BATT civil action teams were discussed and it was decided that the standard of medical training amongst the adoo units should be improved so that they could also give medical help to the civilians. In fact, the standard of the adoo medical orderlies was abysmally low. If a wounded adoo could manage to reach Hauf, and many of them made incredible journeys across the mountains often of several days' duration that would have killed most Europeans, he would probably live; otherwise his chances were slight. A cave at Shershitti where a Lebanese woman doctor looked after the less badly-injured contained the main adoo hospital in the Western Area, but those more seriously wounded or diseased had to go into

Hauf where her husband was practising, or were even evacuated from there by boom to Aden.

The new Government schools in Mirbat and Taqa provoked a statement of intent by the Front to improve literacy on the jebel although it was not said how this was to be achieved. Proof was provided that the Government's restrictions on the movement of food were beginning to tell when the document talked of a Husbandry Committee to be formed to promote the growing of crops by adoo soldiers in order to replace the food they could no longer obtain from the towns.

An atmosphere of distrust permeated the entire document. The militia in particular were singled out as unreliable and requiring more indoctrination. Surprisingly, it recorded that the women were more readily converted than the men, which is perhaps not surprising after all when one thinks of the life that women led; the prospect of equal rights must have seemed very agreeable. It was recorded also that the monthly payment to 'martyrs'' widows was to be increased. A fighter did not at this time receive payment, which may be one reason why service in a loyal firqat seemed more attractive to so many, but if he were killed the Front paid his widow a pension.

Finally, the paper contained two particularly revealing statements. The first mentioned the lack of information the Front was receiving from people in the Eastern Area and concluded sinisterly that the people must be *made* to tell about counter-revolutionary activities. The second agreed to freedom of religion. Islam was to be tolerated, although a man would only be allowed one wife. This was a major change of policy and reflected the success of our information services in driving a wedge between Islam and Communism.

★　★　★

The Jebel Aram operation was the last carried out by my squadron and the last operation of any size before the monsoon of 1971. Already, the advance party of the squadron that was to relieve us had arrived, and we were faced with telling the firqats that we were about to return to Britain.

Six firqats were now in being or under training: the Salahadin, the A'asifat, the Al Nasr, the Khalid Bin Waalid, the Tariq Bin Zeead and the Sudh Defence Force, soon to rename itself the Firqat Gamel Abdul Nasr. They were all aghast when they heard the news of our departure, until it was explained that those who were to replace us were from the same regiment; they were BATT just like us, (not as good as us of course, but BATT nonetheless). It was to be the first of many such changes which, in time, were to go perfectly smoothly, but this first one was traumatic for many of the firqatmen for they had come to rely upon BATT for almost everything. BATT armed them, fed them, paid them, trained them and fought alongside them and some very close personal relationships had been built up. There is little difference, however, between the men of one SAS squadron and another, no matter how much they like to think there is, and within a fortnight relations between the new BATT and the firqats were back to normal. Nonetheless, never again was there that very close relationship which existed between the first squadron and the first firqats. The first squadron had witnessed the firqats' birth pains and nursed them through their childhood: the incoming squadron was faced with firqats who were already established and beginning to flex their muscles.

It was with mixed feelings that I clambered aboard the aircraft for home, leaving behind the many friends I had made and the country I had grown to love and which I thought I should never see again. It had been a hard but satisfying tour. A lot had been achieved in the time and the groundwork had been laid for further expansion in every one of Watts' five fronts. A long way remained to go, but at least we had made a beginning.

I had no idea that three years later I should return as Commanding Officer.

EIGHT
OPERATION JAGUAR

October 1971

The operation to seize a firm base on the jebel was mounted in October of the same year. The *Khareef* had been spent in building up the firqats to operational strength and preparing them for the coming offensive, and the inevitable slowing-down in the pace of operations had allowed ample time for commanders to consult, plans to be drawn up and stores to be stockpiled. It was a heavy monsoon and not until September did it begin to break. If this operation was to succeed, as it must, the troops would be heavily dependent on air support, both for supply and for fighter-ground attack, so there could be no question of mounting it before air support could be guaranteed. The next problem, however, was religious. The month of Ramadan was due to begin on 20th October, when good Muslims should refrain from eating or drinking between sun-up and sun-down, but to postpone the offensive until the end of November would mean an unacceptable delay. The senior *Qadi*, the religious leader in Dhofar, was consulted on the problem and it was agreed that he should broadcast the absolution permitted by Islam to warriors involved in a holy war. The Sultan, who is both the religious and secular head of state, would also publish a letter authorising the firqat and all his forces to disregard the fast.

It was to be a big operation by Dhofar standards: two squadrons of SAS, over a hundred fighting men; two companies of SAF, another 250; a pioneer platoon and a platoon of Baluch askars, a further hundred, and five firqats: the A'asifat, Khalid Bin Waalid, the depleted Salahadin, the Firqat Gamel Abdul Nasr from Sudh and another firqat which had formed during the monsoon at Mirbat, calling itself just the Firqat Al Umri, a total of 300 firquatmen in all. The Firqat Tariq Bin Zeead, being

135

Western Mahra, had been despatched to the battalion in the far west, and similarly it was felt that the Bait Kathir of the Firqat Al Nasr would be best left out of the Eastern Area. The whole force would be commanded by Watts.

It was a commonly-known secret in the souk that a major operation would take place after the monsoon, although the scope and aim of it had not been anticipated. It was generally assumed that it would be another two or three-day operation, followed by the inevitable withdrawal in the normal pattern of operations over the last few years.

So, since the timing of the operation could not hope to achieve surprise, several deception measures were taken to distract adoo attention from the actual direction of attack. For two weeks before, hints were dropped in casual conversation of a major operation into the Wadi Darbat from the south. The Darbat had always been a main adoo stronghold and such an operation made sense, particularly to the firqats based within striking range at Taqa, Mirbat, and Sudh. Leaflets were dropped from aircraft into the Darbat with lurid diagrams of the wadi being struck by those great curving arrows, so beloved by military men, from the direction of Taqa and Mirbat. A 5.5-inch gun was rumbled in full view of the jebel across the plain to Taqa and set up facing northwards.

Probably the most effective deception of all was the force of Bait Umr from the two firqats at Mirbat and Sudh who climbed the jebel far to the east of Eagle's Nest and began to move westwards the day before the main operation began. The Bait Umr were accompanied by a strong BATT led by Captain Sean Branson. Branson was a tall, fair-haired impressive man, intellectually an idealist, a curious mixture of dreamer and pragmatist, who had always appeared easy-going but who was now to drive his firqats to the limits of their endurance. He moved steadily west, covering sixteen miles in the first 24 hours but, inexplicably, not until the afternoon of the second day did the adoo try to stop him. Branson attracted the adoo's eyes firmly to the south, with the result that the main operation from the north was unopposed.

It was mounted to seize an old SAF airstrip known as Lympne on the gatn four miles east of Jibjat. A squadron of SAS, the Baluch askars and the Firqats A'asifat and Salahadin marched all night to reach the strip on the morning of 2nd October. It was a terrible march. The route itself lay across the *negd*, winding its way through the boulder-strewn wadis and across the flinty little plateaux between, an area devoid of water and breeze. The night was hot and humid and before long, the combination of wrenching ankles and knee joints, the weight of their bergens and ammunition and the lack of water began to make itself felt even upon the SAS. The much less heavily equipped firqats began to throw away their rations to lighten their loads still further. The pace became slower and the final climb up the steep slope to Lympne seemed endless. At last, no more than half the force stumbled on to the airstrip at 0435 hours and set about making it secure, but they were in no state to fight without a rest. Fortunately, the adoo were conspicuously absent and remained so for the rest of the day. By the time they awoke to the fact that a force was establishing itself at Lympne, it was too late. SOAF had risen to the occasion as usual and lift after lift of Skyvans and helicopters had brought in two companies of SAF, two 75-mm guns and the hundred strong Firqat Khalid Bin Waalid.

The troops had arrived. The question was whether they would be able to stay. The airstrip was breaking up fast under the number of aircraft flying in, but the adoo's reactions had been slight. Watts decided therefore on the afternoon of the second day to move the base the 7000 yards west to Jibjat where there was a better landing strip and he ordered a strong BATT with the three firqats to set out to clear the route and secure the position for the main body.

The Firqat A'asifat flatly refused to move. They were tired, they said, and they had no food, having thrown away their rations on the march in. Besides, they had been promised support by a thousand geysh and here they were, being told to go out with a mere 20-30 BATT – 'Abadan!' It was Watts's first experience of a recalcitrant firqat. The Khalid Bin Waalid, on the other hand, were happy to go; was it not a step towards Bait Ma'asheni territory?

So a reduced force set out. It was not far, but the adoo put up a strong resistance. Nonetheless, after a sharp little battle, Jibjat was secured and the base moved from Lympne.

Branson, meanwhile, had been continuing to tramp about the Eastern Area and though the adoo tried their best to make him pay for his impudence, the Bait Umr were in their own country and they gave as good as they received. At this time the adoo were more worried at what they saw as a penetration deep into their area than by the main operation, which they still believed to be just another SAF two-day wonder up on the gatn.

By now two days had already passed and Watts, having secured his base, decided to begin his second phase, to spread out on the plateau and carry the war to the enemy. He split his SAS into two groups. West Group with the Firqat Khalid Bin Waalid and what was left of the Firqat Salahadin would move down the western side of the Wadi Darbat, and East Group with the Firqat A'asifat, who had reluctantly agreed to play again, down the eastern side of the wadi. Five days of continuous fierce fighting followed as both the Government forces and the adoo fought to retain the initiative. The Khalid Bin Waalid, led by one of the ex-mutineers from Mirbat and one of the original 27, Mustahail Said, fought like tigers as every step led them further into their own territory. The Firqat A'asifat also overcame their tantrums for a while and fought well, once they realized that they were to remain east of the Wadi Darbat, and on 4th October they linked up with Branson's Bait Umr on the plateau. The adoo fought back with everything they had against both groups, and it was touch and go as to whose morale would break first. A particularly fierce attack was mounted on the afternoon of 5th October against Branson's united force, at what became known as Pork Chop Hill, when both sides were close enough to exchange grenades and insults. Meanwhile in the west, the Khalid Bin Waalid had killed and wounded twenty in one skirmish alone, before they themselves were cleverly led into an adoo ambush.

By 9th October, however, the battle was won. The enemy had stopped coming and contacts only occurred when the BATT/firqat groups went looking for them. The enemy, hunted off the plateau, withdrew for shelter into the thick bush of the wadis. The Khalid Bin Waalid were exultant and established themselves with a SAF company in the Bait Ma'asheni heartland at a place nicknamed White City, but later re-named by the firqat, *Medinat Al Haq*, the Place of Truth.

It was at this critical time, the time when the enemy were shaken, when the successes of the past week should have been exploited by keeping the adoo on the run, driving them out of their sanctuaries in the wadis, that the Firqat A'asifat decided not only once again to show temperament, but worse, this time they infected the Bait Umr firqats also. Despite the Sultan's and the Qadi's dispensation, the three firqats announced that they wished to observe Ramadan. Wali Baraik's clerk, Abdul Aziz, flew in by helicopter to Pork Chop Hill to argue with them but it was no use; they were adamant that for them the war was over, at any rate until after Ramadan. There was nothing for it but to abandon their key position for which they had fought so hard, which dominated the area and threatened the main adoo supply caves in the Wadi Darbat, and withdraw them north back to Jibjat.

With total success so near, it was a bitter pill to swallow. Watts seethed with anger. Two days later he met the leaders at Jibjat. They opened the meeting by demanding more rations as they had burned those they had at Pork Chop Hill to avoid having to carry them on the march. It was the last straw and Watts exploded. By the time he had finished, the firqat leaders were in no doubt at all about what he thought of them and their firqats' behaviour. He ended by saying that he could see no point in British troops losing their lives to help people who were not worth it, and that he was considering withdrawing BATT altogether and leaving the firqats to their own devices. It was a powerful argument. The firqat leaders knew full well that they relied on the BATT entirely. Without BATT in the first place there would have been no firqats and without them now the firqats would lose all the air, artillery, mortar, GPMG and medical support they now enjoyed; and if left to SAF, it was questionable whether they would exist at all for very long. SAF did not have the manpower to look after them even if they had the inclination to do so. Most SAF officers had more than enough to do running their own Arab and Baluch companies to have time to spare listening to the interminable wrangles of the firqats. He would give them one more chance, and one alone, concluded Watts. The Bait Umr would be sent on leave to Mirbat and Sudh, while the Mahra Firqat A'asifat could spend Ramadan at Jibjat. Jibjat was in their tribal area and they could defend the position at the same time.

Meanwhile, the Firqat Khalid Bin Waalid and West Group were still fighting hard from White City, and news came in from some civilians of 200 adoo in the Wadi Darbat, where they were said to be resting and recovering from the actions of the last fortnight. A fierce discussion broke out over how to get at them; SOAF wanted to bomb them and the Artillery wanted to shell them. Watts vetoed both, arguing that the Darbat had far too much cover for bombs or shells to have much effect, and he was certainly not going to send troops blundering down into the wadi without a thorough reconnaissance first. The first step, he decided, was to send a strong patrol against the village of Shahait on the rim of the wadi. The force moved out from White City early on 20th October. Shahait was seized after a short skirmish and two adoo messengers were killed. Their documents provided valuable intelligence and the Bait Ma'asheni firqatmen had the chance to talk to their tribes people in this very hard adoo village.

The results were more than enough to justify the patrol, but Branson, who was commanding it, decided to exploit further into the Wadi Darbat itself. As the force struggled down through the dense thickets, clinging to the nearly sheer wadi walls, the task they had set themselves became clearer. Branson ordered a turn about. The climb back up was doubly exhausting and it was a very different patrol that re-appeared compared with the confident force that had started down several hours before. A valuable lesson had been learnt. Any operation into a wadi that size would take days rather than hours.

White City was proving an ideal operational base; moves could be made in any direction; so a week later Watts decided to move his headquarters there from Jibjat. Nobody doubted that the adoo had taken a hammering, but intelligence reports suggested that they were pausing only to regroup and await reinforcements and more heavy weapons from the west before returning to the fray. Harvey and Watts came to the conclusion that if their precarious hold in the Eastern Area was to be maintained, something must be done to halt, or if that was not possible, at least hinder, the adoo re-supply line. The battalion in the west had been doing its best, but was having little effect on the flow of men and arms from PDRY. The best place, it was agreed, was where the mountains narrowed between the western end of the plateau and the beginning of the great stark jebels and wadis of the Western Area.

On 2nd November the first of three positions was established from the north of the *gatn* above the Jebel Khaftawt. But after a week, adoo were still getting through. Although the new position was stopping the adoo's favourite route along the *gatn*, it could not influence movement near the foot of the jebel. So another position was put in lower down the hill, and finally, a third position was needed. These three positions became known as the Leopard Line. Each position was wired and mined thoroughly and each was secured by SAF to allow the Bait Kathir Firqat Al Nasr to operate out of it with BATT and sometimes SAF support.

The adoo recognized the threat immediately and since the positions were too strong for a frontal assault, launched heavy stand-off attacks with mortars and recoilless artillery. But convoys still managed to slip through the gaps between the positions for there was nothing to prevent them. Minefields and dummy minefields were placed and marked on the most likely routes, but even these could not stop men determined to get through. Nonetheless, the ferocity of the adoo's reaction indicated the importance they placed on the Leopard Line. It was still more important to the SAF, for the lessons being learnt on the Line were to lead to the strategy of linear blockade that was eventually to impose military defeat upon the adoo. The Leopard Line, although it was not realized at the time, was the prototype of greater things to come.

Information services mounted a strong campaign throughout the operation to persuade the Jebeli population that the Government forces had arrived to stay, but they met with little success. The theme of every broadcast and every leaflet was 'permanence', but as the Tawi Atair operation had shown, the civilians were not going to climb off the fence until they were sure which side would win.

The Civil Aid programme was lagging behind also. The blankets and food distributed from Jibjat and White City were very welcome, but something more substantial than blankets was needed to prove that the Government was there to stay. The two pressing needs were for water-wells to be drilled and for some form of semi-permanent building to be constructed. Only then would the population come across to the Government for good.

Nonetheless, progress was being made. By October, responsibility for the protection of the three coastal towns had passed to SAF in the form of the Dhofar Gendarmerie, and by December the three SAS civil action teams handed over to teams from the Dhofar Development Department. The standard of medical support dropped markedly as the experienced SAS medics were replaced by half-trained Omani and Indian nurses, but by this time the Salalah hospital had been properly opened and one of the Indian doctors was always on call to fly down from the coast to serious cases. At least it was a step in the right direction, forcing the Omani authorities to accept responsibility and relieving SAS resources to start new civil action teams in the primitive and dangerous conditions on the jebel.

On the jebel the firqats were persuading their own families and neighbours to bring in goats and cattle to Jibjat and White City. It was an astute move on their part, however annoying flocks of goats and herds of cattle might be to the SAF and BATT, with their more strictly military minds. If the Government was serious about helping the people, the firqat said, then they must provide water for the animals and a market for their meat. Otherwise, they ended with a favourite phrase: 'What profit is there?' How would the Jebelis be any better off than they were under the Communists? By 27th October 1400 goats were concentrated at Jibjat alone and the firqat laid down an ultimatum: no sale of goats, no operations. To emphasize the point, three days later, 45 of the 54 Firqat A'asifat at Jibjat resigned and handed in their weapons. They had called Watts's bluff, for they knew full well that the Government needed them to win the war as much as they needed the Government to regain their homeland. The A'asifat had made the point that a counter-revolutionary war was not just a case of defeating the adoo militarily. Civil development had to move into liberated areas right alongside the Army with plans already made to accommodate both the immediate problems of water and agriculture and the longer term problems of roads, buildings and education. The two sides had to move hand in glove.

While the British military leaders saw this 'mutiny' as yet another example of the unreliability of the firqats, Wali Baraik took a broader view and looked at the problem with an Arab mind. The Government had said it would look after the people, and look after the people it would. The Government was being tested. Inconvenient as it was, damaging as it might be militarily, and whether a market for the animals existed or not, they would have to be brought off the jebel and purchased by the Government. He ordered that SOAF's priority the very next day would be to fly out the goats to Salalah and he asked Harvey to begin plans to get the cattle down also. In return, he agreed to Harvey's request that the firqat leaders and seconds-in-command should be interviewed by the Sultan and given a lecture about indiscipline.

Several days passed before Operation Taurus was ready and, in the meantime, the adoo proved that the past few days had indeed been merely a pause to catch their breath. Watts had now formed another group, North Group, comprising a BATT, the Firqat Salahadin and a company of the Jebel Regiment. These had moved west of Jibjat along the *gatn* to a dominating ridge looking down into the headwaters of the next great wadi west of the Darbat, the Wadi Arzat. West Group meanwhile, had seized a waterhole west of White City, which was also vital to the adoo, and the middle two or three days of November saw the hardest fighting since the start of the operation, with concentrated adoo attacks on the water-hole position and North Group and heavy 75-mm shelling of the Leopard Line. On 27th November, West Group had to give up the water hole and withdraw to White City, fighting a running battle all the way until they came under the protection of White City's 25-pounder guns and mortars.

Next day saw what must surely be unique in military history: a Texan-style cattle drive supported by jet fighter cover and 5.5-inch artillery. Amidst scenes like shots from a Boulting Brothers comedy mixed with a John Wayne Western, fire fights between pickets and adoo on the high ground, whoops of delight from the firqat and expressions of amused disbelief by the SAF and SAS, 500 head of cattle were driven across the plateau and down the jebel to Taqa. Most of the animals were owned by firqat families, but many of them also had been owned by men serving in the adoo and were 'confiscated' by the firqat during the drive. Next day the herd, surrounded by armoured cars, arrived at Salalah to be met by the rejoicing inhabitants. As one SAS soldier described it, 'Salalah looked like Abilene'.

The Firqat Khalid Bin Waalid were jubilant, and there was no doubt that this signal demonstration of Government power did more to impress the people than all the broadcasts and leaflets put together. It proved to those on the jebel and plain alike that, whereas three months ago the adoo were supreme on the jebel, now they could not even stop the Government removing cattle when they wished. The story of the cattle drive became the main talking point in every village in Dhofar.

Having made their point, and Ramadan now over, the Firqat A'asifat and the Bait Umr got down to work again and the year ended on a high note with the Sultan visiting White City to open formally the new buildings for the Civil Action Team. It had been a momentous year. At the beginning of it, the Government could only claim to control effectively Salalah and part of the plain. By the end, the three coastal towns were totally under Government control, the plain was secure, although roads were still mined occasionally, over 700 Dhofaris were under arms fighting for the Sultan, the SAF presence in Dhofar had doubled, and the Government had two firm bases on the jebel itself. The foundations for medical services, an agricultural policy and an information department had been laid and good plans existed for the development of the Province. The one thing lacking was a Civil Aid policy to follow on the heels of military success and fill the immediate needs of the people until development plans could come to fruition.

It had been a composite effort in which many people had played their part towards the same end, but if any one man could be given more credit than others it must surely be Lieutenant Colonel Watts. The 'Five

Fronts' plan had been his, it was his SAS Regiment which had raised the firqats and secured the three towns, and it was he who had personally led the Government forces on to the jebel to seize the two firm bases at Jibjat and White City. It was an impressive record and more than enough to satisfy most men, but he was a man who set and demanded the highest standards. As far as he was concerned, the Mahra and Bait Umr firqats had let him down just as he had the chance of inflicting an even greater defeat on the enemy. They had wasted most of the advantage which the first week's heavy fighting and casualties had won. His tour of command at an end, Watts handed over to his successor and returned to Britain an angry and disenchanted man. He need not have been, for more than anyone else it was the strategy he had devised and the groundwork he had completed that was to lead to the ultimate defeat of the enemy.

NINE

MIRBAT

19th July 1972

The last few moments before a dawn attack are always ones of tension. So they were now. Two hundred and fifty men lay or knelt, silent except for the occasional chink of weapon on stone, a low cough or quiet whisper, staring into the darkness. Behind rose the great blackness of the jebel massif hidden in the monsoon drizzle. Before, 1200 yards away, lay Mirbat.

As the seconds slipped away, commanders, like commanders anywhere, would be going over the plan in their minds yet again to make certain that nothing had been missed out. Did every man know what he had to do? The weapons had all been checked and they worked. The radios were netted in all right. The artillery sights had been checked for range and elevation. The correct ammunition had been dumped by the correct guns. Everything seemed 'go', but what if ...? What if the enemy knew and, even now, were standing to their weapons, waiting. It was unlikely. Security had been good. The fighters, all young, all well indoctrinated in the cause, all heavily motivated, had moved over the jebel in parties of 40 with a security screen in front to clear out the villages they would have to pass through. In any case, they did not even know themselves where they were going until they had been briefed up on the jebel the previous night.

Ironically, the enemy had helped, too. It was a year since they had identified the party cell in town and rounded it up, and their grip was now too tight on the town to establish another. So there could be no leak from there.

With luck, few enemy should be left in the town to defend it anyway. They had fallen nicely for the decoy patrol sent down on the plain two days before and most of them were now chasing a will-o'-the-wisp, near the jebel. But that 'what if' always remains at the back of a commander's mind.

The fighters would be concerned with more immediate matters, like keeping warm in the pre-dawn monsoon chill. All along the line men would pull their shamags tighter around their heads or flap their arms against their sides, half wanting to get up and get moving, half frightened at what the next hour would bring. Riflemen would seek relief from their nerves by checking their weapons and equipment for the tenth time. Were safety catches on 'safe', bayonets properly fixed, pouches buttoned up? Gunners leant forward to check their dial sights yet again by the little lamps that glowed faintly above them, and the gun numbers felt to see that the shells were properly fused and easily to hand.

To the left, the drab sky was slowly lightening. To the right sounded a faint crackle of small arms, a burst or two of machine-gun fire and the dull thud of exploding grenades. That was the enemy picket forward of the town on Jebel Ali being taken out. It was time.

All along the line arms swept downwards and men turned away from the blast with their hands over their ears as the barrage began. Shells and mortar bombs began to rain down upon the town. At the same time 200 determined young men clambered to their feet and began to move steadily forward in line abreast. The battle of Mirbat had begun.

* * *

The commander of the eight-man BATT in the town was Captain Mike Kealy, who was to win the DSO for his exploits that day. To say that Kealy was worried about how he would behave when he heard his first shot fired in anger would be an over-statement. Nonetheless, commanding a platoon of 19-year-old fusiliers in Germany was very different from finding yourself in command of a troop of 28-year-old, hardened SAS veterans, experienced in battles fought across half the world during the British Empire's death throes. It was a neurosis at the back of the mind of most newly joined SAS troop commanders. So his feelings when he woke with a start as the first shell exploded, he told me, could not have been unlike those of the young men already advancing, unknown to him, towards the town – half apprehension, half relief.

As he fumbled for his torch, a second explosion shook BATT house and pieces of dried mud fell on top of him. Dust filled the room. Coughing, he grabbed his rifle and belt, slipped on his flip-flops and stumbled out into the fresh air. A makeshift bamboo ladder led up to the roof where most of his team were already waiting. It was just beginning to get light. He glanced at his watch - 0530.

The lean, hard figure of Corporal Bob Bradshaw paced over to him. Instinctively, although the enemy were far away, he talked in a low voice, pointing out the flashes of the enemy guns on the Jebel Ali and explaining the layout on the roof. Two machine-guns, a GPMG and a heavy Browning .5, had been mounted in sand-bagged sangars.

Kealy looked over to the two dark figures of Lance Corporal Pete Wignall and Corporal Roger Chapman and the long barrels of their machine-guns silhouetted above the sand-bagged walls against the lightening sky. It was just light enough now to see the fort also, a large square 'Beau Geste' affair, 700 yards to the north-east. A motley group of Dhofar Gendarmerie and askars manned it, tribesmen brought down from the north under the reign of the old sultan and armed with old bolt-action .303 rifles.

Nearer, to the north-west and almost within hailing distance stood the *wali*'s house. Its roof stood at the same height as BATT house and Kealy could just make out some figures moving about it. To the south two hundred yards away lay the houses of the town, now covered by a pall of mud dust from the incoming shells. He could hear screams, and some men were shouting.

A shell screeched overhead and they all ducked as it exploded behind the house. Then came a succession of explosions a few seconds apart from the base of the house. They shook Kealy for a moment until he realised it was the BATT mortar returning fire. Behind Bradshaw the bulky, reassuring figure of Trooper Savesaki was talking in Arabic on the radio. He reported that the firqat leader had just told him he had 40 men out towards the jebel somewhere. Only greybeards and children remained.

'Where's Labalaba?' Kealy asked, knowing that where one Fijian was, the other would not be far away. Bradshaw looked up from his mortar plotting board and jerked his head towards the fort. Trooper Labalaba was manning the 25-pounder with the Omani gunner, he said.

A burst of heavy machine-gun bullets crack-crack-cracked close by, followed by a long burst from the BATT .5 Browning. Empty brass cases tinkled brashly on to the roof. The air was rent by unending continuous noise now, the mind-bending explosions of incoming shells, the crashing thuds of the BATT mortar returning fire, the spitting crackle of enemy machine-gun fire and the steady booming of

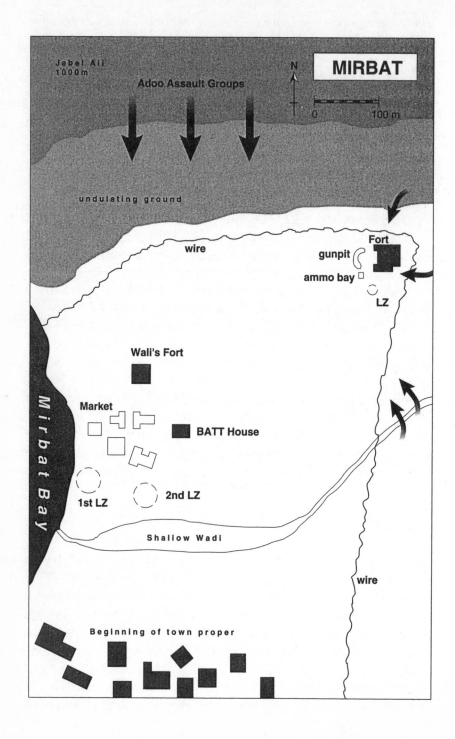

the BATT heavy machine-gun in reply. Kealy forced himself to think above the racket. He knew the firqat leader had sent a strong patrol out after the small enemy group reported at the base of the jebel, but he had not realised that so few firqat remained. There was nothing anyone could do but if the patrol fell foul of the sort of firepower now being directed at Mirbat …

Then, what was this? The adoo had never attacked with this intensity before. Was it just a stand-off attack or would they combine it with an infantry assault? He told me that he felt his first real pang of apprehension as he counted up his defences: say, 30 men in the fort – they would fight back, but they would be no use for anything except a threat to the fort itself, the few firqat left behind in the town, the eight SAS men including himself, and the Omani gunner with the 25-pounder artillery piece dug into its pit beside the fort. He ducked as an explosion sent pieces of shrapnel thudding into the sandbags by his head.

Savesaki was listening intently to the radio. He turned to Kealy, his face as impassive as ever, but his eyes betrayed him. Labalaba had been hit in the chin, he said. Kealy nodded to his suggestion that he should go and help his countryman at the big gun.

'Take some extra medical kit and keep low.'

For all his muscular bulk, Savesaki was one of the finest rugby forwards in the West Country. If anyone could make it, he would. Nonetheless all those at the BATT house stared with nerves tingling as the big Fijian raced towards the fort swerving and dodging between the explosions while bullets kicked up spurts of sand at his feet. A cloud of dust obliterated him – but as it cleared he was still seen running, until at last he disappeared from view behind the gun's sangar wall. At BATT house men breathed again.

Chapman was the first to see them and pointed out to Kealy a group of 20 men walking confidently towards the perimeter wire fence that surrounded the three sides of the town not bordered by the sea. The fort lay inside the north-eastern corner of the wire and within 40 yards of it. Kealy studied the group through his binoculars. It was now light enough to see them clearly, but still he was uncertain. They could be some of the firqat returning, or a patrol the Gendarmerie might have sent out without telling him. They appeared too cool and confident to be adoo.

Suddenly all doubts were removed. At a signal, the men started to run into an extended line, raising their weapons to their shoulders. The crackle of small arms fire sounded paltry against the ear-splitting noise of the bursting shells. Chapman did not wait for orders. Short sharp bursts of fire ripped through the haze like a succession of tiny comets into the groups of running men, the ricochets bouncing and arcing gracefully into the air until they burnt out. As if it was a signal to begin, the whole corner near the fort erupted with the sound of machine-guns and rifles mixed with the explosion of shells. All the enemy's fire seemed to be directed at the fort and the SAS men looked on with disbelief as it disappeared from sight. A cloud of brown smoke and dust, lit up in spasms by the bright flashes of shell bursts against the walls, hid the fort entirely. Above it all sounded the vicious cracking explosions of the big gun by the fort as it fired its 25-lb shells, point blank, at the wire 40 yards in front of it.

The radio crackled, but Kealy could not hear what it said above the racket. He thought it was the gun pit but could not be sure. In any case, Wignall and Chapman, their over-heated gun barrels sizzling in the wet, were shouting for more ammunition. Together with the two uncommitted men, Corporal Reynolds and Trooper Tobin, Kealy hauled up the heavy steel boxes from below until their shirts were as soaked from sweat as from the steady monsoon drizzle.

The plain was now full of groups of ten to twelve men, sometimes in full view, sometimes hidden as they crossed a dip, all moving steadily towards the town. The battle still raged around the fort, and keeping the GPMG firing in that direction, every other BATT weapon was brought to bear on the approaching infantry. But the enemy now realized where most of the return fire came from and had ranged in on BATT house with machine-guns, the bullets thudding into the mud walls and sandbags or cracking viciously about the soldiers' heads. But nobody had yet been hit and still the BATT machine-guns hammered back.

The enemy reached the wire and began to breach it. Men tore at it with their hands. Others threw a blanket over it and scrambled across; it was little more than a cattle fence and could not hold them for long. Bradshaw told me that his attention was taken by the leader, standing in full view astride the wire, shouting and waving his men on, his rifle held out full stretch above his head. In his khaki uniform, his peaked cap and his bandoliers across his chest, it struck Bradshaw that he looked like a hero from some Red Chinese poster. For a moment he watched in admiration, then reluctantly lined up his rifle sights on the man and fired. Missed! Again he fired, and missed. Damn! He paused a second to steady himself, forcing his body to obey. Breathe in … breathe out …

hold it ... a nice steady pressure ... the rifle kicked, and the man crumpled.

Several men were across the wire and running towards the fort. Others were caught. Kealy recalled that a figure lay doubled up over it like a rag doll. Bradshaw remembered that another hung head down, his arms and legs spread wide in grotesque crucifixion. Two others crossed the wire and fell immediately, one his leg jerking frantically. Another staggered about, both hands pressed to his face.

Kealy fought to think, think, think, his head a great drum of noise. Suddenly he realised that, apart from a terse contact report at the beginning, he had not told BATT headquarters 30 miles away what was going on. He scrambled hastily down the rickety ladder into the courtyard and to the long range radio, forcing his voice to sound calm as he described the situation as clearly as he could. The mist was still down to about 150 feet, he said, but nonetheless he wanted a helicopter to evacuate Labalaba and no doubt there were more casualties, and the jets were to be stood by to fly as soon as the weather allowed.

Back up on the roof a minute later, the fighting had died down. Although the cracks and thuds of battle still sounded spasmodically, it seemed very quiet, as if the whole battlefield were waiting for something. Bradshaw told him that he could still get no reply from the gun pit.

Kealy picked up the radio and called the gun pit yet again. Now very worried, he told Bradshaw to take over command at the house while he went over to the gun pit to find out what had happened to the others. A violent argument followed for a minute as all three men began to buckle on their belt equipment. Bradshaw and Wignall were needed at the house, Kealy insisted, but very well, he would take Tobin. He was a medic and would be useful.

'You won't get far in those,' grinned Bradshaw and Kealy flushed as he realized that he was still wearing the flip-flops he put on when he got out of bed. He dropped down into the courtyard and made his way quickly back to his room.

When he came out, Tobin was waiting, his medical pack slung over his shoulder, his drab green shorts and shirt grimy with burnt oil and dust. Like all of them he was bare-headed. He carried his rifle easily in one hand and his belt order, containing all an SAS soldier needs to fight and live with, was clipped about his waist. They opened the wooden gates and stepped out past the sand-bagged pit where Trooper Harris fussed over the mortar sight.

A shallow wadi, perhaps two feet deep, ran parallel to the direct route to the fort, but 75 yards to the right. The occasional bullet still came near, but it was quiet enough to set off up the wadi, trusting to its low rim if they should have to take cover. A brick laundry house stood a hundred yards up and the two men stopped briefly to shake hands with the ancient in charge.

They had not gone more than another hundred yards when a burst of machine-gun fire crackled viciously between them, the breeze of the passing bullets plainly felt by Kealy. Both men flung themselves flat for a few seconds and then, one man firing, one man running, with bullets cracking and humming about their ears they dashed in short sprints for the protection of the gun pit. Tobin reached it first, vaulted the wall and disappeared. One glance told Kealy that there was no room in the gun pit itself, but a few feet to the side and dug into the ground was a sand-bagged ammunition bay. He leapt over the body of a dead gendarme and threw himself into the bay, where he lay gasping from the final sprint. Suddenly he realized that he was not alone. He spun round. Crouching under the lip of the sandbag-covered lid was another gendarme, his lips pulled back over his teeth, his face a mask of terror.

Glancing over to the gun pit again, Kealy saw that Tobin was applying a drip to the seriously wounded Omani gunner at the side of the bay, whilst Trooper Labalaba was crawling across towards him, his face grey and bloodstained under the khaki shell dressing that covered his chin. The Fijian tried to smile with his eyes and his mumbled words were barely distinguishable, but he explained that Savesaki was badly hit in the back and had lost a lot of blood. He was still conscious, however, and was covering the left side of the fort.

A huge explosion hit the edge of the bunker. Both men were thrown against the edge of the pit and stinging sand cut their faces and hands. The crackle of incoming bullets rose to a crescendo and put an end to any more talk as the two men thrust their rifles over the crest of the pit. A series of double cracks, the hallmark of an SAS rifleman, rang out from the other side of the gun pit.

'Boss, they're through the wire.' Savesaki's voice sounded faintly above the din. The enemy had pierced the wire and were now crawling and running up to the fort itself. Labalaba dashed to the gun, traversed it as far right as he could and fired. Its deafening crash, smoke and recoil filled the pit. He slapped the breech handle back and the empty brass case dropped smoking on to the sandy floor. Turning, the big Fijian reached for another shell, slammed it home with one hand and, as the breech clanged shut, pitched forward without a sound.

Kealy lifted his head above the pit and in half of one second registered two things: first, several enemy had crept around his side of the fort, and second, a small green grenade was fizzing two feet from his head. He ducked and, a split second after the explosion, raised his head again. A man was leaning around the wall, aiming a Kalashnikov at him. He took a snap shot and the man spun and fell. Another replaced him. Kealy fired at him, too: a double tap, crack-crack. A chip of stone fell off the wall and the man ducked.

'Sav, take the left, I'll take the right,' he shouted. Another crash and more smoke as the 25-pounder fired again. He looked around to see Tobin reloading. Within seconds Tobin fell too, mortally hit. Urgently, Kealy spoke into the radio and told Bradshaw to get both machine-guns to spray either side of the fort and to fire the mortar as close in as he could get it.

Bradshaw's cool voice acted as a tonic. The jets were on their way he told him, but already Harris was hugging the mortar clear of its bipod against his chest to shorten the range while someone else dropped the bombs down the barrel. He could not get closer.

The SAS machine-gun fire crackled and spat about the fort and Kealy stopped firing for a moment to let his rifle cool down. He realized he was running short of full magazines and then he remembered the frightened man. He turned to look at him. For a second, he later told me, he thought of telling the man to fight, but their eyes met and he suddenly knew the man would kill him if he tried. Instead, he thrust his empty magazines at him. 'Fill those,' he snapped. The gendarme set to work feverishly.

Another flight of grenades came bouncing and hissing towards the gun pit. In horror he watched one roll to the lip of the pit and then drop in, to lie smoking out of reach. He pressed his body against the side of the pit and screwed up his face at the pain he knew must come ... until with a tame little 'phut' it went out. A dud. Desperately, he put his rifle over the top again and searched for a target. The air was full of the stench and noise of battle. Something passed through his hair. Another fanned his neck. Suddenly the thumping of cannon fire sounded alongside and shells hissed overhead as the first Strikemaster jet made its run.

His fingers clumsy in his haste, he dragged out a fluorescent marker panel and placed it over the body of the dead gendarme, but the cannon fire was striking well the other side of the fort. As a second jet came in to strafe, adoo began running back into the wadi behind the fort for shelter. A black bomb detached itself from the aircraft and plummeted into the wadi, where they were hiding, to explode in earth-quaking thunder and a cloud of black smoke.

★ ★ ★

The jet strike did its work and gradually a second lull crept over the battlefield as the noise of men trying to kill each other died down. Kealy scrambled over to where Savesaki was leaning wearily against the far wall of the gun pit and from where he could best see the left side of the fort. The side of his head was matted with blood and his shirt was caked a dull brown but his face was as impassive as ever. It struck Kealy how his steady brown eyes contrasted with the whites of the gendarme in the ammunition bay.

The two men looked up at the walls of the fort. The question was, who held it? They could only see one wall properly. One of the others could have been breached. Kealy recalled that a dead gendarme, dressed in a black shirt, lay slouched over an embrasure, his rifle pointing to the sky. There was no sign of life.

Savesaki was both a medic and an Arabic speaker. He eased himself up.

'Oh soldiers!' he shouted. 'How are you? Are you alive? Is all well? My captain wishes to speak to your officer.'

Silence.

He tried again, this time with more success: at least he was answered. 'Abadan! Never!'

Kealy decided it was not worth pressing the matter for the moment and clambered across to comfort the wounded men and re-dress their wounds according to Savesaki's instructions. He gave them a sip of water and made them as comfortable as he could, but there was little enough he could do. Then he pulled the dead men to the side of the pit, out of the way, and covered them with a groundsheet.

The jets made one more strike, this time on to Jebel Ali on Bradshaw's directions and disappeared into the mist back to Salalah to re-fuel and re-arm. Then Bradshaw radioed Kealy to say that he was sending Harris, another medic, over to him. And that reinforcements were on their way.

★　★　★

Von Clausewitz wrote 'War is the province of chance', and the chance that a second SAS squadron would be in Dhofar on that day stood at three per cent. The chance that the main body would have arrived from England only the previous day and were not therefore already in the hills stood at less than one per cent. Most of the officers and senior NCOs had been in the advance party and were already taking over positions on the jebel from the outgoing squadron, so only the younger soldiers were left in Salalah. And at 0800 hours that morning, the squadron commander, his sergeant major and 21 soldiers paraded all set to go to a nearby range to test-fire their weapons as part of the normal routine of taking over. They were heavily armed for such a small group – nine GPMGs and four M79 grenade launchers between them, and every other man carried a semi-automatic rifle.

By this time, the action at Mirbat had been going on for two and a half hours and that the attack was a major one could not be in doubt. The outgoing squadron commander, Major Richard Pirie, appreciated that the only way he could get any help to Mirbat in time was by air, despite the monsoon, and had already moved to the SOAF headquarters at Salalah airfield to set up a joint operations centre. There he could himself brief the pilots on the exact state of affairs they would meet on arrival, control the movements of reinforcements and re-supplies and arrange the evacuation of casualties.

So it was to the airfield that the 23 now went and, after a careful briefing, climbed aboard three SOAF helicopters bound for Mirbat. The mist was well down and the three aircraft felt their way cautiously along the coast only a few feet above the waves before landing to the south-east of the town, according to plan.

Quickly the force deployed into two ten-man 'hit' groups and a command group, and within minutes came under fire. The adoo must have estimated that in a little force like this, two-thirds the size of an infantry platoon, a maximum of three machine-guns would be carried. But this had nine, the fire power of an infantry company. They quickly disposed of the adoo facing them and, moving in bounds, group by group, and even within groups, two or three men dashing forward, covered by the fire of the remainder, the squadron moved towards the town, killing as they went.

The firqat also, at least those who were not out beyond Jebel Ali with the fighting patrol, were fighting hard. Not content to remain in the town, they lay scattered in twos and threes behind every rock and in every fold of the ground between the enemy and the town. The enemy were in effect in a trap, caught between the anvil of the firqat and the hammer of the advancing SAS.

It was this that worried Kealy. He had just returned from a one-man foray into the wadi where the bomb had landed to check that it was clear of enemy. He could hear the crackle of fire to the south-east and he knew that the relief was approaching the town from that direction. Unless he could get the gendarmes to understand, the makings existed of a disaster. He stood before the great wooden gates of the fort with his hands to his mouth and shouted till he was hoarse. Surely the bloody men must know no adoo would do that, he thought. And at last, after what seemed an age as the sounds of shooting crept ever closer to the town, the iron-studded doors creaked open and he stepped through into the courtyard.

Using signs and the occasional word of Arabic he had learned, Kealy explained the position to the Gendarme officer. He would like to borrow the Gendarmes' Landrover, he said, to take the BATT and the Gendarmerie wounded to the helicopter pad by BATT house. The officer shrugged and smiled sympathetically, but pointed without speaking to the riddled vehicle standing on shredded tyres in an ever-increasing pool of oil and water. As he looked about him, Kealy began to appreciate the weight of explosive that must have landed inside the fort. Yet, despite the pounding, the wall was not breached anywhere.

In despair at this latest disappointment, he was trying to force his exhausted brain to think of an alternative way to get the wounded to safety when a broad Geordie voice spoke behind him. He spun round with a surge of relief to see the grinning figure of one of the incoming squadron's soldiers framed in the doorway. A machine-gun rested easily on his shoulder. For a moment they stared at each other and the soldier's grin froze as he studied Kealy's face and the normally fair hair blackened with smoke and encrusted blood. Silently he turned and walked over to the gun pit. For a full half minute he stood there while his gaze took in the dead and dying men, the wrecked gun, the empty shell and bullet cases, the grenades, and the blood everywhere, on the ripped and torn sandbag walls, on the gun, in pools on the floor. At last he broke the silence.

'Jesus wept,' he said quietly.

Although to the north things were quieter, furious little bursts of fire still flared up to the south-east as the squadron mopped up. Machine-gun and rifle bullets still cracked overhead while Kealy, bone weary, stood peering with red-rimmed eyes at the helicopter flying towards him, almost touching the ground, from the direction of BATT house.

Barely realised by him, the support of the SOAF helicopters and jets had been superb. The first helicopter tried to get in to evacuate Labalaba, when Kealy and Tobin were still halfway across on their journey from BATT house to the fort. Chapman ran from the house to the usual landing pad on the beach 200 yards away to receive it and since all seemed fairly quiet, threw out a green smoke grenade to signal that it was safe to land. But, as the helicopter began its final approach, the adoo began their second attack even more ferociously than before. Bullets began to crack about Chapman and he identified at least one 12.7-mm, heavy machine-gun firing towards the incoming helicopter.

His heart pounding, he fumbled in his belt for a red grenade and hurled it as far as he could. Immediately, a machine-gun began to rake the landing site. He paused a second to watch the helicopter sheering off into the mist, then turned and raced back up the beach to where a low wall provided cover. He crawled along this for 50 yards and when it was safe stood up and walked back to BATT house where he knew his medical skills would be needed.

A quarter of an hour later a shout came from the roof that another aircraft could be heard above the mist. This time Chapman selected a landing site only a hundred yards away from the house and protected by buildings. The noise of engines grew stronger as the pilot found a hole in the cloud, and suddenly Chapman saw it, a brown blob streaking towards him at roof top level coming in from the sea, not a helicopter at all but a Strikemaster. He clicked on his sarbe radio.

'Hullo, Strikemaster, this is Tiger four one. Enemy are north and east of the fort. Over.'

'Roger, Tiger four one. I have it visual. How far from the fort?'

'One hundred meters and closing,' he replied. This was the strike which prevented Kealy and Savesaki from being overrun.

Chapman ran back up to the roof of BATT house and passed the sarbe to Bradshaw who took over control, directing the jets down the wire towards the fort and on to the enemy heavy support weapons on Jebel Ali.

Watching a brave man risk his life produces a breathless feeling almost akin to love. You feel intense admiration combined with an aching fear that his luck will run out. So the two men told me they felt as they watched the jets flying in under the mist, straight and level to give greater accuracy to their guns, while the enemy threw up a curtain of machine-gun and Kalashnikov fire until the sky seemed an impenetrable mad network of criss-crossing tracer. Then came the ripping sound of the aircrafts' 20-mm cannons before they pulled up and disappeared into the mist. Some jets were indeed hit, but none fortunately badly enough to prevent their limping back to Salalah.

Bradshaw radioed back to base that it was out of the question for helicopters to attempt to reach the town at this time, so the next lift brought in the relieving squadron's soldiers to the beach. It was not until a second lift had been dropped at the same place that the first helicopter, flown by Squadron Leader Baker and already holed, was able to reach BATT house. Here he landed three prisoners from the beach and loaded up the most seriously wounded for evacuation to the Field Surgical Team at Salalah. Although quieter, bullets were still cracking about and Baker knew he had to fly his helicopter over open ground to reach the fort. Nonetheless he decided to risk it, and it was this aircraft's approach that Kealy was now watching.

Harris, having done all he could for the wounded, ran out to guide it as close as he could to the gun pit. Its doors were already open and two men leapt out as it touched the ground to help lift in the wounded men. The two worst hit, Trooper Tobin and the Omani gunner, were lifted aboard first. Savesaki declined to move until they were aboard and even then insisted on walking to the aircraft with wounds that would have killed any ordinary man.

The enemy were now in full retreat back to the mountains and having seen the helicopter take off safely, Harris and Kealy walked back to BATT house. As the centre of resistance, it had attracted all manner of people throughout the battle: firqatmen, wounded or asking for ammunition or help in one form or another, townsfolk wounded by shrapnel or just frightened, and the inevitable hangers-on, mainly old men, bearded, frail and toothless who appear to offer advice and the comfort of their presence at any incident of note in Arabia. Kealy raised his eyes in surprise as he saw a figure dressed all in white, bent over a wounded man.

'Doctor' Ahmed was a civilian who had received some medical

training and who had been posted to Mirbat by the wali of Dhofar, qualified doctors being unobtainable. Anxious to assert his authority, Doctor Ahmed had, at first, been thoroughly unco-operative to the SAS men and sparks had flown on more than one occasion, but although a thorn in the side of BATT, Ahmed was symbolically important for he represented the first faltering step in the development of an Omani medical system which was eventually to cover the whole of Dhofar. Now, in emergency, he revealed his true worth.

English voices sounded outside and a group of soldiers strode into the room led by the relieving squadron's commander, Major Alistair Bowie. Bowie was a Guards officer and he had that calm, smiling authority that immediately makes things seem not quite as bad as they appeared to be. Kealy explained the situation as shortly as he could and spoke of his worry about the firqat still the other side of Jebel Ali. They would be right in the path of the retreating adoo. Even as he said it, the first crackle of small arms fire sounded to the north. Kealy felt sick with helplessness. Perhaps he could take a sarbe out and see if he could direct in jets to help the trapped firqat, he suggested.

Bowie read the despair and fatigue in the man's eyes. Very well, he agreed, but Kealy was not to go beyond Jebel Ali. The small jebel was now picketed by a platoon of the Northern Frontier Regiment that had flown in with the third helicopter at 1220.

Kealy hurried off and, after several minutes scrambling and slipping on the wet shale, reached the top. Mist hid everything but the first 2-300 yards. As he had secretly known, he could see and do nothing. He settled down to wait against a sangar wall, weary beyond words, until at last the dispirited huddle of firqat appeared out of the drizzle, carrying their dead and wounded and passed beneath him.

Once more he trudged back to BATT house, where he found that Bowie had wasted no time in reorganizing the town's defences and establishing order again. Two Landrovers had just returned with the dead and wounded and 38 enemy bodies lay in a row, their weapons and ammunition belts, all new Chinese and Russian equipment, piled in heaps nearby. A gaggle of firqat clustered about them trying to persuade some stony-faced SAS men that they needed the weapons to claim reward money to feed their families.

Within the house a medical officer and the SAS medics busily applied dressings to the minor wounded, both friendly and enemy, while in a separate room the prisoners were being interviewed by Chapman. The three sat quietly smoking cigarettes and drinking tea and Kealy was struck both by their youth and by the dignity with which they accepted their lot. These were brave men.

★   ★   ★

The battle of Mirbat was a milestone in the Dhofar War. The Front had to do something spectacular to counter the Government's successes during and since Operation Jaguar the previous year. The attack was well planned and well executed. By using the cover of the monsoon, the Front had calculated that SOAF would not be able to fly. Similarly, having decoyed the firqat out on to patrol, they had anticipated that 250 hard-core fighters supported by all the Eastern Area's recoilless artillery and mortars should be more than enough to take out the defences that remained. From the enemy prisoners we learned that the aim was to capture the town, to hold it for a few hours only, possibly for a day, to denounce and execute the *wali* and his advisors, to subject the townsfolk to a propaganda harangue, and to retire once more to the jebel. And, had they achieved it, the effect on Government plans would have been disastrous. It had been hard enough to find a *wali* in the first place. After such a catastrophe nobody would have taken the job. Townspeople throughout the province would have been terrified into total non-co-operation with the Government, and the Front could have used the towns and villages as they pleased. Eighteen months of painstaking effort to build up the confidence of the Dhofari people would have been demolished in one day.

As it was, the enemy blundered by underestimating the skill and courage of the SOAF pilots, but it was just bad luck, a coincidence no commander could have expected to foresee, that a second SAS squadron should arrive in Dhofar the day before the attack. These two factors saved Mirbat.

Back on the jebel, the adoo looked about for scapegoats. The faith of the younger men in their leaders had been shattered. These resorted to terror in an effort to re-assert their authority and a number of kangaroo courts were set up on the jebel to judge and execute those considered responsible for the failure of the plan. The death of so many of their friends (the total number of deaths, including those who died from wounds in the primitive jebel hospitals, was just under a hundred) also had its effect. It was no surprise when August and September proved to be particularly good months for enemy surrendering to the Government.

Perhaps the best man to sum up the battle of Mirbat is the Commanding Officer of the Northern Frontier Regiment. Having visited the scene immediately after the battle, he concluded his despatch:

'It may appear that an unusually large number of names have been recorded. This is because there were, on 19th July, an unusually large number of gallant actions at Mirbat.'

TEN
A SETTLING OF SCORES

June 1974

I could not repress a feeling of excitement as I pressed my face against the Andover's window and peered at the jebel below. How small it all looked, as we passed over Eagle's Nest, Tawi Atair, Jebel Aram and all those other places I knew so well from three years ago. They looked so close together and insignificant. It must be very hard for an airman to understand the sweat and labour, and often blood, it took to move about that peaceful-looking countryside below.

There would be many changes since 1971, I knew, and the first became apparent as we banked over Salalah to turn out to sea before the final circuit. The town had quadrupled in size, and the fields were green again with growing crops. The plane banked once more, the engine changed its tone, and I watched the flaps easing out of their sockets in the wings. We were losing height fast and one of the Hedgehog positions, a fort made of sand-filled oil drums, came into view under the wing. It was one of several that lay in a half circle around the airfield, halfway between it and the jebel.

The air quartermaster signalled to me to sit down and fasten my seat strap. A gentle touch-down, a lurch forward as the engines roared into reverse thrust, and the plane rolled to a halt. Scarcely before it stopped, the doors were flung open to let in what breeze there was and a minute later I looked down to see the familiar face of Shams, now the Squadron Commander, waiting at the foot of the steps, his face as red and his hair even fairer than before.

As we walked over to the Landrover he pointed out the line of helicopters, well spaced out, each with its miniature Hedgehog position around it.

162

'Hueys, ex-Vietnam. Wonderful aircraft, we use them for everything now. No more lugging mortars around on donkeys and camels,' he grinned.' In fact we have our own ATLO Team to arrange all our air moves. We've seven positions to keep re-supplied, you know.'

As we drove the familiar route to Um Al Gwarif he kept up a running commentary, explaining the various buildings going up on either side. Most still consisted of little more than foundations or even simply piles of bricks, but the shape of things to come stood out plainly. We passed a small estate of huts and bungalows and crushing and brick-making machines.

'Taylor Woodrow. Been very helpful to us. They're even building us a bar at UAG. A lot of them come along for a jar at our place in the evening. Seem to prefer it.' He caught my eye. 'I know. The jebel is still dry, but I let the boys let their hair down a bit when they come down to base.'

The Landrover turned into the main gate, past the old fort, and shuddered to a halt in the BATT compound. Headquarters BATT had not changed much except that small prefabricated huts had replaced some of the tents. I dropped my bag off in one of them and followed Shams into the operations room.

'Very smooth!' I exclaimed. 'Where did all this come from? Air conditioning too!'

'Most from SAF, with a little help from TW. The Brigadier, Jack Fletcher, is a great guy. He's really brought the wind of change into Dhofar. He's going shortly though. Do you know the new man, Brigadier John Akehurst?'

I knew Akehurst well from Staff College days. 'No problem. We seem to be putting the right people in the right place at last.'

I sat down in a comfortable soft chair facing a wall-size map of the province. To my right the operations sergeant sat at a desk answering telephones. A flap in the wall opened, allowing the high-pitched rhythmic tattoo of morse to be faintly heard. A hand appeared clasping a message. 'Signal from four three,' a voice sang out. The hatch closed again.

Shams stood by the map and began his briefing. 'Where shall I start? Safait, I think. The position in the far west went in in April '72. The aim was to establish a Government position near the border and to stop the adoo's re-supply.'

'And has it?'

'It must have hampered them to some degree. but the question is how much? It certainly didn't stop them firing Katyushas at RAF Salalah. The adoo don't like Sarfait and they fire off a lot of ammo at it. Some people say this would all be carried over to the Centre and Eastern Areas if Sarfait wasn't there to act as a sort of sponge, but, as I say, it hasn't stopped or even hindered the adoo very much. The Hornbeam Line, on the other hand, has had much more effect. The Leopard Line, you remember the line from Windy Ridge down the Jebel Khaftawt to Mugsayl, was withdrawn in the summer of '72 because we couldn't keep it supplied during the *khareef*. This left the route wide open to the adoo and as a result RAF Salalah was hit by RCL fire and later by Katyusha rockets. The Katyusha has a 122-mm warhead as you know, and it doesn't half make your eyes water when it goes off. It sounds like a jet plane when it comes over.'

'Anyway, we put out a line of positions on the high ground overlooking the wadi mouths, where these things were fired from, called the Diana positions, and they were remarkably effective. There's been scarcely a shell fired at the airfield since. But I was talking about the Hornbeam Line. You will get a chance to see it tomorrow, but this was probably the most important operation since Jaguar. When the *khareef* finished in '72, before the Dianas were put in, SAF established the Hornbeam Line here from Mugsayl on the coast for 40 miles inland to Oven here, where we have a BATT. It was a tremendous undertaking, rather like the "barrages" created by the French in the Algerian war. There's a position every couple of thousand yards and these are linked with wire by sappers, then it will be mined. The adoo can still get through of course if they are determined to do so, but only on foot, and they have to recce very carefully first or they get caught by a SAF patrol. There's not been a Katyusha fired east of the line since last November. The Firqat Al Nasr occupy the position with the SAF. Apparently they're very good now.'

'Brew, boss?' I took the steaming cup gratefully from the operations sergeant and briefly admired his retreating back covered with two intricately tattooed dragons, relics from the Borneo campaign. I turned again to face the map. Shams took a long swig before continuing.

'In early '73 the first of the Iranians arrived, a Special Forces battalion, and they were sent in to help man the Hornbeam Line. Then, in December last year another 1200 arrived and they were used to open up the Midway Road. A good deception plan had drawn most of the adoo towards the Hornbeam Line and so there was very little resistance. They had a bit of a dust-up after a few days, but it is all very quiet now. Those boys use ammunition like confetti; no adoo goes anywhere near them. It is like the Normandy Landings up there at night. We've a BATT here,' he pointed at the map, 'right on the road at a place called Qairoon Hairitti, between two Iranian positions. To begin with the idea was that they would patrol out of the firm base held by the Iranians, but the Iranians shot at them when they started to come back in. So then we insisted that an Iranian officer should accompany each patrol with the radio set. The idea was that he would come up on the radio as the patrol neared base and tell the Iranians the route they were following to come in; but the Iranians still shot at them. The firqats eventually refused to patrol at all, understandably, so now by night up there no one leaves the base. The trouble is, it is not always safe to leave by day either. They have shot at women, camels, trucks, just about anything that moves. And of course, hardly any of them speak Arabic, so from the hearts and minds point of view, they are non-starters.'

I had taken my squadron to train in Iran before we went to Dhofar in 1970, the first body of British troops to do so since the Second World War. We had trained closely with the Iranians, who were anxious to learn all they could. Their knowledge of counter-insurgency operations was rudimentary and their first attempt to emulate us practising fire and manoeuvre using live ammunition, the nearest that training can get to war (except that no-one shoots back), was a disaster. An Iranian soldier was killed within the first few minutes.

The Iranians under the Shah had been trained for normal, that is 'limited' warfare only, and had been trained along American lines; by British standards, they used ammunition extravagantly. Their discipline, I knew, was severe but unthinking, and the gulf between their officers and soldiers was vast. Nonetheless, given a job to do, I knew they would do it to the best of their ability. The Shah was taking personal interest in their performance and that would concentrate the minds of their commanders wonderfully. For all their limitations, I knew that with their numbers of infantry, their artillery and their helicopters, provided they were properly briefed and employed, they could be a major asset to the campaign. And so they were to prove.

Shams took another mouthful of tea: 'Now for the five fronts.' He counted off on his fingers. 'Medical. The FST has moved to the RAF camp, and Salalah Hospital is for civilians only now. A newer, much bigger hospital is going to be built, incidentally, just out of town. I've seen the plans and it will be huge. God knows where they will get the staff to man it. There's a "flying doctor" service about to start and a doctor visits all along the coast, but we still run clinics at our positions on the jebel. The medical system is beginning to work, but it's still fairly rudimentary. You'll meet a couple of RAMC sergeants we have attached to us who are training up firqs as medics.'

'Veterinary. We don't have a vet any more; it has been handed over entirely to the Omanis. I'll take you for a run tonight past the experimental farm. There've been various tests done to see how to improve the jebel economy, new fodder' s being grown, new strains introduced, that sort of thing, but it's still hit and miss. For example, there's a huge Friesian bull up at Qairoon Hairitti. He nearly killed the first little jebeli heifer he mounted so now the firqat won't let him near their cattle. Poor old thing gets randier every day. But there's definite progress. Just behind the camp here they're growing all sorts of different types of fodder. You probably saw it when you flew over. Then there are a couple of schemes to buy the young bulls off the jebel and fatten them up on the plain before turning them into corned beef, because, of course, the jebeli habit of killing off all his bull calves is a desperate waste of meat.'

'What about fishing?' I asked, thinking of the swarms of fish I had seen from the air.

'There've been a couple of teams out from the UK to look at the possibility of canning all those dried sardines they use for camel fodder. At the moment, when they lay them out to dry on the beach, all the oil from the fish runs into the sea. I don't know if anything will come of it.'

He counted off his third finger. 'Intelligence is not our baby any more. There's an intelligence team still, but it's attached to HQ Dhofar, not here. Similarly with information services. We still retain a team for tactical use, but the Government has opened a large Information Department in Salalah. Lastly the firqats. There are sixteen firqats now, about a thousand men in all. You remember it was already becoming difficult to administer them in 1971, so SAF created Headquarters Firqat Forces. It's still a two-men-and-a-boy concern at the moment. They're meant to have Firqat Liaison Officers to look after the firqats after we've raised and trained them, but it's hard to get the right men. Most of the ones they do have are ex-Regiment.'

'I think we can identify three phases in a firqat's development,' he went on. 'The first phase is raising and training them, sorting out their tribal problems and establishing a leader. The second phase is the main operational phase, getting a company or battalion of SAF, and as many BATT as we can, and establishing them in their tribal area and helping them to clear it. The third phase is getting the civil action going, a well drilled, a clinic, school and shop built, and so on. That's when we withdraw and hand over to Firqat Forces, freeing our men to start again with another firqat.'

He turned back to the map. 'We still control firqats, from left to right, here at Oven, at Hagaif to the west of the Midway Road on the *gatn*, at Qairoon Hairitti, at Zeak east of Qairoon Hairitti, at Jibjat, at Medinat Al Haq and finally at Tawi Atair. I've fixed for you to spend at least a night at each.'

'What are the relationships like between the firqs and SAF?'

'You'll see a great difference in the two, but not so much difference in their relationships, I'm sorry to say. SAF are already much better than they were, and of course they've doubled in size. They've carried out some first rate operations over the last few months and they're not afraid to get out of base. They spent eight days up here, not long back,' he pointed at the map, 'and here in the Wadi Dut they recovered eight and a half tons of food, ammunition and weapons just recently. But they still dislike moving about in less than company strength.'

'The firqs too have changed,' he went on. 'They're more mature, they understand more about the realities of life, what is feasible and what isn't, and their leaders tend to be older men than before. The firqat leaders are becoming little warlords, in fact. They control everything that goes on in their own areas, the grazing, watering, the sale of government food, everything. As soon as they're established in their areas you can see them change from being soldiers to politicians. Most of them spend far less time on the jebel than they should because they are all down here in Salalah, where the political decisions are made. You'll find they're a new breed. Qaraitas and Sheikh Ali are still around, but Qartoob and Dherdhir were both killed.'

'Mohammed Said?'

'The Firqat Salahadin are just a remnant of what they were. We now have a Central Area firqat at last, up here at Qairoon Hairitti, led by an old original, but the Bait Gatun are still solid adoo. Mohammed Said became disenchanted over not having enough men to form a viable firqat and he's joined the SAF. He's a captain now and doing very well, by all accounts. The firqs and SAF work together much better now and there've been a number of very good joint operations over the last few months,' he pointed at the areas concerned, 'but it would be wrong to say the two forces are fond of each other. I suppose,' he conceded, 'you could say they've grown to realise they depend upon each other.'

'What about civil aid, well-drilling and so on?'

'You'll remember that civil development just wasn't geared to keep pace with military operations: and still doesn't for that matter. So a new department was created. It's gone through various names, but Civil Aid Department is the present one. It's commanded by an ex-SAF officer, Martin Robb, and it's meant to fill in the gap with short-term projects until proper civil development can get under way. Martin works to the *wali*, but inevitably they're short of everything, cash to buy what is needed, people to organise it and trucks to deliver it. Nonetheless Martin and his boys have performed miracles. They produce prefabricated CAD buildings which are flown into a position on the jebel and reconstructed to provide a school, a clinic and a shop. CAD produce the teacher and medic, and the firqat run the shop with food and cloth provided by CAD. The Dhofar Development Committee is now a going concern as well. They meet weekly and amongst other things, they decide where the water-drilling rig should go next. Similarly, they've a good plan for a road network all across the jebel. In short,' he concluded, 'the adoo are still strong and they must be driven out of the wadis before the civilians will come across in numbers, but nonetheless the Government's policy is correct and we're winning, without a doubt. Last monsoon was the first time that SAF had remained on the jebel throughout, and this monsoon they'll do so again at all the positions they hold. Once the locals see that, it'll be the writing on the wall for the adoo, I reckon.'

★ ★ ★

I visited each of the BATT positions over the next few days and each was different from the others, with its own type of terrain, its own atmosphere, its own problems. The first, Oven, lay at the northernmost end of the Hornbeam Line, and the name was apt. As we flew along the Line itself, my admiration grew for the engineers, both British and Jordanian, who had created this obstacle over appallingly difficult country, quite different from the grassy rolling downs of the Central and Eastern Areas. This was harsh country, barren apart from camel thorn, and with steep-sided wadis between razor-backed jebel ridges, but the wire fence appeared to pay no respect at all to the lie of the land. It snaked down into wadis, across their rocky bouldered bottoms and up the almost sheer sides again, for mile after mile. Scattered along the wire, wherever there was room to do so, a SAF position had been established on high ground, its sangars dominating the wadi bed below. Small figures strolled casually between the sangars, occasionally waving at the helicopter.

The sun beat viciously off the great white boulders on the floor of the wadi as we dropped down into it. The wadi itself was not more than fifty yards across, but it was four times that to the top of the wadi walls, so that one side of the wadi was in almost perpetual shadow. I was led past drums of fuel and rolls of wire to where a tarpaulin had been erected across some poles, leaving the walls of the tent open to whatever little breeze might appear to relieve the searing heat. I stared at a large thorn bush alongside, covered in what appeared to be small rectangular brown fruits, but as my eyes adjusted to the glare, they proved to be old tea bags thrown up to catch on the thorns. I sat down on a bench and a pint of tea was placed before me. How do other armies survive without the British Army's brew, I wondered as I sipped the hot liquid. Even in temperatures of 120° F it replaces the body's fluids and sugar content without causing it to lose the benefit by sweating, as a cold drink will do.

After tea I set off down the wadi with two of the BATT, including the medic, to visit the families who lived there. At first sight, it was difficult to believe that anyone could or would want to live in a wadi that was almost bare apart from a few thorn trees and a scrap of frizzled grass here and there. The nearest water lay two miles away and even that was just a small water hole that dried up most years.

The first sign of life came after half an hour's walk, a small piece of dirty linen tied to a thorn bush. Opposite the bush in a curve in the wadi side, too small to call a cave, lay the charred remains of a small fire, a couple of saucepans, and a pile of clothes wrapped into a red shamag the size of a medicine ball – the worldly goods of a family. We came across them a quarter of a mile further on by an oil drum which the BATT kept filled with water; the CAD had not yet reached this far. The master of the household, naked above the waist, sat in the shade of a bush. He smiled and called out, but boorishly did not rise to greet us. His two wives sat opposite him and pulled their black shawls over their faces at our approach. A hundred yards away a small herd of underfed goats, guarded by a little girl, picked at the meagre pasturage. We sat down and offered the man some tins of corned beef. He accepted greedily, cackling with delight before ordering his wives to make tea.

It was a wadi similar to this one that Shams had visited a month before. He had been told of a water-hole in a fertile wadi only an hour's drive away from Oven and determined to visit it. Wherever you find water in Arabia, you find people, so he took some tins of corned beef and some tinned fruit as a gift. It was a longer drive than he expected, since the route took him in a wide arc out into the negd, but eventually he found the wadi he wanted and his two Landrovers growled their way slowly up the wadi bed. At last, as he had almost given up hope, he saw what seemed after the desolation of the negd a little paradise ahead of him. A large flock of goats fed on the scrub that had sprung up all around a large pool in the wadi bed. The pool was surrounded by cropped green grass and a tall tree provided shade from the sun's rays. Set into the wall of the wadi were one or two caves, each bricked up with rocks to provide accommodation for people and herds. The whole scene was the more impressive for being so unsuspected, an inaccessible little shangri-la in the middle of nowhere.

The head of the family sat under the tree and rose to greet Shams. He was an elderly man, already grey, dressed in a futa and shirt with an indigo cloak slung across one shoulder. They shook hands.

'*Salaam aleikum*' began Shams, '*Khayf haalak?*'

'Good afternoon,' came the reply in perfect English. 'Where have you come from? I do hope you did not come too far out of your way?' He smiled knowingly at Sham's speechless astonishment. 'You are surprised to find someone like this,' he gestured about him, 'who speaks English. Well, let us sit down and have a cup of tea. An Englishman always drinks tea when he is at a loss for words, does he not?' He called out to his wives in Jebeli.

The old man explained that he had, like so many others, gone into exile under Said Bin Taimur's rule and had learnt English in the Gulf. He had travelled widely and prospered, but always he dreamt of the valley where he had been born, and he resolved to return one day. Now he had more than enough money to buy all the goats, camels and wives he needed, and he was as happy as the day was long. He saw few people, he said, but for several hours he and Shams discussed the affairs of Oman, the Gulf and the world, and Shams was amazed at the depth of knowledge the old man possessed of affairs outside his own little wadi.

It was a fascinating afternoon and Shams was reluctant to leave, but at last he rose to go and uncertainly handed over the tins of food. The old man took them, examined them for a moment and then looked up at Shams with a twinkle in his eye.

'What, no beads?' he said.

★ ★ ★

The BATT position at Oven was like a Mediterranean holiday chalet. It had a smooth cement floor, and whitewashed plywood boards hid the revetted corrugated iron and sandbagged walls. Even the sandbagged roof was supported by white plaster board held up by thick iroko beams painted black to give an olde-worlde impression, and a talented graphic artist had painted pictures in the style of Toulouse Lautrec to compete with the inevitable girlie posters. The rooms were high and spacious to let cool air circulate.

Hagaif on the other hand, was quite different. The position itself lay at the southern end of a large horseshoe-shaped ridge. The open end of the horseshoe faced north and provided a perfect administrative area for vehicles and stores and a natural helicopter landing site protected on three of its four sides. A track ran out of the position on to the gatn and along to Qairoon Hairitti. The BATT were on the most dominating part of the southern loop of the position and their sandbagged sangars had been cut into the hill, so that only the top three feet protruded above ground. All windows were blacked out at night, and a communication trench, supported by revetted corrugated iron walls and iron pickets, led forward to the sandbagged Browning sangar. The heavy machine-gun's barrel projected from a slit a yard long by a foot high so that it had a good traverse and covered the barbed wire and trip flares laid all along the front. You approached the position from the north, up a long staircase built of old ammunition boxes set into the earth. The whole place gave the impression of being very much in the front line, as indeed it was.

Qairoon Hairitti was different again. Being located on the Midway Road, and dominating, as it did, all the tracks running east and west along the *gatn,* it was already becoming a popular calling-place for travellers between Thamrait and Salalah. The place could not avoid becoming a prosperous community.

The Iranians maintained a tight grip on the area and no adoo came anywhere near. The firqats were glad about this, of course, but annoyed at the sometimes arrogant attitude shown by the Iranians towards the civilians, so an uneasy state of affairs existed. Although not as frontline as Hagaif, the BATT sangars were solidly built huts of sandbags and corrugated iron set into the shelter of a small ridge. The medical centre had been built entirely by the BATT, as had all the other buildings, but this was a craftsman's work of plywood and wooden beams set on a cement base, and the firqat cast envious eyes towards it, thinking of the protection it would provide against the monsoon rains.

I found the atmosphere at Qairoon Hairitti very different from the other two. There, you were aware, the whole time, of the possibility of an adoo attack. Here, probably because they depended entirely upon the Iranians for protection, there was much less tension. Most of the firqatmen went home in the evening to sleep in their villages, and returned for duty next morning. The place seemed to be already beginning to adapt itself to its post-war role as an administrative centre.

★ ★ ★

I decided to drive to Jibjat instead of flying. We left Qairoon Hairitti soon after dawn, myself and a two-man BATT escort in an SAS Landrover and a three tonner filled with firqat. The morning was fresh and cool, and soon the firqat began to sing their contentment at being young, healthy and alive on such a day. The two vehicles wound their way through the camel-thorn bushes of the *gatn*, purposefully keeping off the tracks made by previous vehicles. There was always a debate about whether it was better to be in a three-tonner or a Landrover when you were mined. Three-tonners were much higher off the ground and the cab carried armour-plate. On the other hand, Landrovers had often driven over mines which the heavier ground pressure of a three-tonner later set off and, though you were further away from the blast in a three-tonner, if you were thrown out, you had much further to fall; and if the truck rolled onto you, you did not stand a chance. A Landrover would be literally blown to pieces if it took the full blast of a Soviet anti-tank mine, but there were several instances of Landrovers just setting off mines with the side of the wheel and when most of the blast was expended in thin air. Almost invariably the Landrovers were thrown on to their sides or backs, but the thick anti-roll bars shaped in a hoop over the top of the vehicle helped prevent the men inside from being crushed.

From time to time we passed a small herd of camels grazing on the thorns and parched grass of the *gatn*. Invariably there would be an old man past fighting age sitting under a tree nearby, who would wave his stick and exchange shouts with the firqat. At last, three hours later, the two vehicles drove through the perimeter wire fence of the Jibjat position and the firqat leapt down off the truck to be led off by members of the Firqat A'asifat to their tents for tea and talk. I found myself on a bleak flinty plateau with more in common with the *negd* than the grassy slopes of the jebel, and yet the jebel proper began just over the skyline to the south, only a mile away. A long, rectangular corrugated iron hut, from which the hiss of a petrol burner announced that a brew was on the boil, housed the BATT. Alongside the hut, 25 yards away, a smaller hut contained a diesel engine, used to operate the water pump. The well-head lay inside a small, wired-off enclosure nearby, and thin metal water pipes led off to the picket positions.

The unprotected BATT hut contrasted with the low bunker in which I slept that night, a relic from Jibjat's fighting days. The position was ready to be handed over to Firqat Forces. The Firqat A'asifat were the most powerful firqat on the jebel at this time and had long since driven the adoo out of their area altogether. An adoo paymaster and his escort had stupidly tried to cross the firqat's territory only a few days before. The firqat caught them and killed the lot but, for some strange reason, had said nothing about their success for three days. They said later they were examining the paymaster's papers. When at last they handed the papers and weapons into BATT, they denied all knowledge of the several thousand Omani *riyals,* many thousands of pounds, that the paymaster's papers revealed he was carrying. Perhaps he had been dishonest enough to remove the money for his own purposes, they said with straight faces.

Not that the firqat were short of money. The formation of the firqats had caused inflation to run riot on the jebel, where for the first time the jebelis were able to match the prosperity boom of the plain. A firqatman was paid 50 *riyals* a month, plus his food, weapon and ammunition. He bought his own clothes, costing perhaps a riyal a month, but the rest was spending money as he had no overheads at all. Yet the jebel could only support so many cattle, goats and camels, and the herds could not be increased. The result was too much money chasing too few goods, the classic formula for inflation. In 1971 a goat cost five riyals, in 1974 it cost 60; in 1971 a cow cost 80 *riyals,* now it was 300 (and three years later was to rise to 1000 *riyals* an animal). It caused the SAS soldiers ironic amusement that, whereas they were struggling to make ends meet at home on their British Army pay, the underfed, unhealthy Jebeli whose sores they were treating might well have £50,000 worth of cattle on the hoof.

Firqat Forces did not have enough liaison officers to be able to take over responsibility for Jibjat, that I knew, but the place was tying down a BATT which could be more profitably used further west. I played with the idea of abandoning the position to SAF, who had a platoon here, but discarded it. Had SAF had a company with a company commander I might well have handed the place over there and then, but it was too big and the firqat too large to be handed over to a mere platoon commander. The firqat still needed a white face there, who could intercede for them when Headquarters Firqat Forces or SAF were being unhelpful. I decided to tell Commander Dhofar that we wished to hand it over by the end of the year. That would give Firqat Forces time to find a suitable firqat liaison officer. We would not hand over the position just yet. It was to prove a lucky decision.

★ ★ ★

The only thing that made 11th October 1974 any different from any other day at Jibjat, as far as the four members of the BATT were concerned, was that it marked the day of Eid Al Fitr, the end of the Ramadan fast. The firqat were in high spirits and even now, at ten o'clock at night, a burst of fire ripped into the sky from time to time as some exuberant firqatman let off steam.

Lance Corporal Dave Hocking was the last man to go to bed. He turned off the Tilley lamp with a faint 'pop', felt his way over the familiar few feet to his bed and snuggled into his sleeping bag. He had scarcely shut his eyes before the radio slung from a nail above his head crackled into life. Wearily he reached up and clicked on the transmitter. He recognized the voice as the sergeant of Picket Four.

'What it is, O Brother?'

The reply was garbled and Hocking had difficulty in making it out, but it appeared that there had been some kind of accident and the firqat sergeant major was dead.

'Understood, O Brother, understood. The captain and I will come immediately, and we will bring the doctor.'

Hocking put on his desert boots, picked up his belt order and rifle and walked over to the other sangars to arouse the rest of the BATT.

The commander, Corporal 'Scotty' Fergus was not unduly worried. The Firqat A'asifat was a fine firqat, keen as mustard, and held in great respect by the adoo, as was clear from captured documents. He supposed that someone had let his Eid high spirits get out of hand. The other two BATT men appeared now buckling on their belts as they crawled out of their sangars: Lance Corporal Taff Thomas, the medic, and Trooper 'Ginge' Carter, the radio operator. The four men collected outside the BATT hut. Hocking turned the radio's volume fully up so that they could all listen to the continuous flow of rapid Mahri. Fergus shrugged.

'Not a chance of breaking in there. Taff, Dave, you come with me. Ginge, get on to base and tell them what's happened. We'll give them details as soon as we know something firm.'

The three men climbed aboard the three-tonner and set off. They did not have far to go. The Firqat A'asifat was nearly two hundred strong and had split itself into four sub-tribal groups, each of whom manned a picket position of three or four sangars and a similar number of tents. Picket One lay to the east of the BATT position whilst the other three lay in a triangle 3-400 yards apart to the west. South of BATT, only 6- or 700 yards as the crow flies, a platoon of SAF had dug in, but since a huge wadi lay between them, the only way to reach the platoon was from the west in a mile-long loop through the three firqat picket positions around the head of the wadi.

Fergus stopped the truck outside Picket Four, and he and Hocking walked towards a Landrover standing in the middle of the position lit up by the glare of its own lights. A figure sat slumped over the wheel and a quick inspection revealed it to be the almost headless body of *Wakeel* Saad, the firqat sergeant major. The position was eerily quiet and, now fully alert, the two men carried out a quick search of the empty tents. They could think of only two possibilities: either the picket had gone out in pursuit of whoever killed the *Wakeel* or the whole picket had deserted to the adoo. The latter was scarcely credible, they decided. Picket Four had proved themselves time and again. Nonetheless, just in case, the BATT at Medinat Al Haq was contacted by radio and advised that it was just possible there was a renegade bunch of firqat about.

Still mystified, the three men returned to BATT HQ where Hocking raised all the picket leaders on the radio and at last began to establish some form of order over the chaos. Gradually, his cool patient voice calmed down the firqat leaders and the story became clearer. The Picket Four men were not outside at all, but hiding from the wrath of Picket Three, the dead man's picket, in the Picket One positions. *Wakeel* Saad Bakhait had been a popular and respected sergeant major and he and his driver had returned from leave that afternoon. The *Wakeel* had been driving around the pickets to bring himself up-to-date on what had been happening during his absence. On duty in Picket Four had been Muwaith Mahad Masood, whose family had a blood feud with the *Wakeel*'s dating back fifteen years, and Muwaith had decided to settle it there and then. He had shot *Wakeel* Saad through the head and then shot the driver for good measure. The driver had crawled away wounded, only to be followed by Muwaith and dispatched some yards from the Landrover, which was why the BATT men had not found him. Muwaith fled into the night and the rest had wasted no time in seeking shelter amongst the non-involved sub-tribes.

It seemed a cut-and-dried case. Fergus's main concern was the hole in his defences, but the firqat seemed to be behaving reasonably and, together, men from the other three pickets made up a guard for the night. Fergus thought it prudent that BATT should stand-to all night also.

Dawn saw the arrival of a helicopter carrying the SAS Squadron Commander, Major Alan Trant, and the ubiquitous Said Bin Gheer, my old adviser from Mirbat days, together with certain officials of the *Wali*. All still seemed under control and the bodies of the two men were flown back with the visitors to Salalah, except for Trant who remained. He, Fergus and Hocking walked across to the Picket Four position to find it milling with 30-40 of the dead man's friends and relatives, and they were working themselves into a fury. One after another they assailed the three BATT men, demanding that action be taken there and then against Picket Four who were all Communists to a man, not to be trusted, and who should all be thrown into prison and the leaders executed, or by God, they, Picket Three, would do the job themselves. One look at their faces persuaded the BATT men that they meant what they said. If something was not done soon, an intra-tribal war would destroy the most powerful firqat on the jebel. To add the final ingredients for disaster, a message arrived that thirty-five men of the Firqat Khalid Bin Waalid at Medinat Al Haq had armed and were coming to protect their friends.

The BATT commander at Medinat Al Haq was another Fijian, Sergeant Jim Takajasi. Takajasi realized that the firqat both at his own position and at Jibjat were feeling the effects of Ramadan; he had watched them becoming more irritable and unreasonable as the month progressed and the one day of Eid celebrations had not done much to restore their flagging energies. By midday most of them had been tired out. He decided to play for time.

It was too far to walk to Jibjat, the firqat said, they would need a truck. Takajasi listened imperturbably, asking a question now and then, doing anything to keep them talking. Well … he mused, it might be possible, but the petrol tank would need to be refilled and one of the tyres was not really up to the journey … why not walk? Another ten minutes was wasted explaining again why it was not possible to walk. And so on. After two hours' prevarication, the firqat decided it was too hot outside to go anywhere and retired to their tents. As the last man left the BATT hut, Takajasi reached inside his parachute smock and put a small object on the table. He looked about the room at the other SAS men with a little smile.

'Lesson one: always have a fall-back position.' It was the three-tonner's rotor arm.

The dilemma at Jibjat was complicated. The men of Picket Four would never surrender to Picket Three; Picket Three could not in honour allow Picket Four to live; Pickets One and Two would be bound to exercise the rights of hospitality and retaliate if Picket Three attacked the men of Picket Four under their protection. Stalemate. The greybeard Sheikh Ali Salim Saad cut through to the heart of the problem and proposed a solution: let BATT disarm Picket Four and escort them to the other side of the wadi to the geysh position. Once they were out of sight, Picket Three would cool down.

It was a good idea and BATT would not be alone, for another platoon of SAF were now arriving by helicopter as Trant had asked. He had also asked for the *Wali* to come in, but he had wisely declined. Hocking knew the leader of Picket Four well, Lieutenant Said Salim Baraikan, one of the original few, so Hocking, Trant and Fergus now approached the first of the two positions where the murderer's relatives were hiding. They took a truck full of SAF with them, but they need not have worried; the men in the tent were overjoyed to see them. Nonetheless, it took an hour of Hocking's quiet persuasion before they agreed to give up their weapons and accompany the geysh to the other side of the wadi. The second position took even longer. After an hour and a half, when both sides seemed to have reached stalemate, Sheikh Ali rose and asked the three BATT to wait outside for a minute. Twenty minutes later, he emerged to invite them to come in and receive the men's weapons. What he had said no one will ever know, but the old warrior had not lost his prestige. Some men from Picket Four were still out on patrol, but these were rounded up by BATT in a Landrover during the afternoon, together with the help of the Picket Four sergeant, who was re-armed for the occasion.

The situation seemed to have been restored. The *Wali* now sent in a message by helicopter with Said Bin Gheer to say that the entire Picket Four were to be sent out to Salalah immediately since it was plain they could never again stay at Jibjat. Relieved that at last some sort of decision had been taken, Fergus called Lieutenant Said Salim and his sergeant across to BATT HQ to plan the move. It was a mistake. Within minutes of the helicopter's arrival, the BATT hut was under a state of siege from Picket Three and no amount of cajoling could mollify them. They had the two men they believed most responsible for their brother's death almost in their grasp, and they were going to kill them. If the BATT did not like it, so be it, and it would be too bad if they got in the way. The firqat moved into firing positions and cocked their weapons.

Things were looking bad. The only way out, Trant decided, was to call the firqat's bluff, and to call it soon. He announced that helicopters were shortly arriving to take the Picket Four men on the other side of the wadi back to Salalah and the first helicopter would fly across to land at the BATT hut to take the two men away with them.

'If it does,' replied the Picket Three leader, 'we will shoot it down with or without the two men we seek.'

The atmosphere over the next half hour was electric. Both sides took up battle positions with weapons loaded and ready. It needed only one shot to start a catastrophe. Perhaps, as they lay there, the firqat realized it too, but they had got themselves into a position where they needed to save face before they could withdraw. Now Trant provided just that in the form of a pair of Strikemasters which came streaking out of the sun, passing over the heads of the firqat in an ear-shattering show of force. Even so, it was not until the helicopter was safely out of range carrying the two men back across the wadi to join their companions on the SAF position that the SAS men could afford to relax.

All's well that ends well, but the murder at Jibjat could have been disastrous. Had the Firqat A'asifat started to fight amongst themselves, it would almost certainly have drawn in the neighbouring firqats and the entire situation in the Eastern Area, built up so painstakingly over the previous three years, would have been in peril.

★ ★ ★

The fifth position, Medinat Al Haq, was in that ugly transitional stage before becoming a Government Centre. Great scars had been made in the pasture land, where roads and buildings were being constructed and piles of pipes and bricks and wire littered the landscape. The firqat had taken advantage of the amount of engineer and building stores to be had for the taking, to build themselves untidy shanties around the place, totally lacking the charm of the jebeli roundhouses. One of the CAD's Civil Action Teams had been set up in a prefabricated centre and was working well, although the BATT had to be ruthless in turning away people who preferred the BATT medic to the semi-trained CAD man.

The drill had struck good water and two huge Southern Cross water tanks, each containing thousands of gallons, had been built above the well, from which gravity feed pipes led down to cement cattle troughs. But despite this show of prosperity, fewer cattle came to drink and fewer children came to school than had been anticipated. The adoo were still powerful and many civilians were still too intimidated to come in. In a way this was convenient, for it gave the Government time to prepare for the flood of people and cattle who certainly would come in once the area had been cleared of adoo, as they were already doing at Tawi Atair.

★　★　★

Tawi Atair, the well of birds, was only approachable by air. A small air strip had been constructed below the southern face of the long hill, which Cheshire and Mohammed Said had first climbed after that long night march from Eagle's Nest over three years ago, and which still formed the main defensive position. For the first two-thirds of its length it ran gently uphill and so looked even shorter than it was. It was not an easy landing strip, as the two wrecked aircraft pulled off to the side of it testified. As we drew near, the Skyvan lost height in tight circles around the hill, so as to keep out of range of adoo machine-guns until it straightened out for its final approach. The stall-hooter blared and red lights flashed on the instrument panel as we crossed the white boundary markers. Trees and bushes flew past the windows and the crest of the slope rushed towards us. Still the aircraft would not touch down; the heat reflected from the strip was keeping it airborne. The pilot's face was tense and I noticed the veins standing out on the back of his hands as they gripped the control column. Still we glided, until with 50 yards to go, the wheels touched. The pilot slammed the controls into reverse and the nose dipped as he pressed on the brakes, but it seemed seconds before there was any change in speed. With a lurch we finally came to a stop well past the end of the runway markers and within feet of boulders that would surely have wrecked us.

The two men waiting to greet me were a well-matched pair, each of average height, but each built like an ox. Their rolled-up shirtsleeves and shorts accentuated their thigh and arm muscles, much to the admiration of the wiry Jebeli men who used to poke them with their fingers and mutter '*Kathir lahm*', much meat, while the girls put their hands over their mouths and giggled with delight as they let their imaginations run riot.

'Thought you were a goner there, boss.'

I picked up my bergen and followed the two men as they loped off up through the long grass, threading their way amongst the rocks, across a low barbed-wire entanglement being prepared for the monsoon, and into the BATT position. A couple of aircraft seats had been recovered from a wrecked Caribou and set up under a fig tree to look out over the firqat living area in the low ground and the Tawi itself beyond. The BATT lived in four well-built sangars sited to be mutually supporting in case of attack and impregnable to all but a direct hit from a recoilless gun. The sangars of the SAF company and artillery troop who held the position, dotted the rest of the hill and much of the plain below.

After lunch I picked up my rifle and walked down through the firqat positions to the Tawi. From a CAD hut came the sound of children chanting verses from the Koran. Opposite stood another with locked doors, but the mound of old onion skins, tubes of evaporated milk and tins of perfectly good but unused meat showed it to be the firqat's food store. The third hut, which joined the other two to form a U, was a clinic painted white with a red crescent on the door. The BATT medic inside was attending to a woman and her child, but otherwise the place was empty of people. A bed and chair were the only furniture except for a row of shelves on one wall, which held the medical stores. I exchanged a few words with the medic and the woman, and then walked on down to the Tawi until I stood on the lip of the great hole. A Royal Engineers squadron had produced what was, to me at any rate, a masterpiece of engineering. A pumping engine had been installed at the bottom of the hole with a pipe running up the sheer rock and splitting into branches at the top. These in turn were connected to cattle troughs and to pipes running into the SAF, firqat and BATT positions. Already 5000 cattle a day came to drink at the troughs and I watched a party of Sappers, stripped on the waist, busily manhandling a second pump towards the Tawi.

All along the skyline cattle stood waiting. A herd had just finished drinking and waddled away contentedly. A second herd, some 60 strong, was walking forward to replace them, moving quite slowly and pushing in alongside each other without fuss. It was a hot day and I expected them to take great draughts of water, but no, they lapped it gently, taking enough to slake their thirst, but no more. Then, without orders, they backed out and returned the 20 paces or so to the waiting herd. The herdsmen's problem seemed more to get cows to drink enough than to stop them. From time to time a few camels strolled up and after much urging from their owner and with supercilious looks at the cows, eventually condescended to drink, rumbling their distaste for the whole undignified business as they stalked away.

The troughs had become a communal meeting place, where the herdsmen congregated and sat chatting over the day's events, while the herds waited patiently for the sign to move forward. The whole scene reflected contentment and peace. Even so, many more would like to use the facilities at Tawi, but were still inhibited by the adoo from doing so. Most of these herds I was watching came from the north and east where the Jibjat and Tawi Atair firqats ruled, but strong adoo groups still operated to the south in the Wadis Hinna and Ghazir and to the west in the Wadi Darbat.

Tawi confirmed my concern over one matter which had been present to a lesser extent at the other positions I had visited. Over the previous two years, BATT had made a deliberate effort to get the firqats to become less dependent on them and to stand on their own feet. The responsibility for all their affairs had been handed over to the firqat leader, his *mindoob*, a sort of administrative officer, to SAF and to Firqat Forces. It had been a fairly traumatic experience for the firqats at first, but it had had its effect and they were much more self-sufficient now than in 1971–2. But HQ Firqat Forces, as has already been explained, were not geared to looking after so many people, and SAF, by and large, were not interested. The result was that the firqats had become second-class citizens to SAF and, without their SAS BATT commanders to go and beat the desks in Um Al Gwarif or Salalah, they simply did not get the support or materials they needed. Of course, the firqats themselves did not help matters. If one firqat could make away with the rolls of plastic sheeting reserved for another, so much the better. If they could then hand that over to their families for waterproofing their roundhouses and persuade the quartermaster that they had never received any at all, better still.

Another result of this policy of forcing the firqats to become self-reliant was that the BATT and firqats had drawn apart. At Tawi, for instance, their living areas were 400 yards from each other, a far cry from the old days when they lived cheek by jowl. In the near future, however, I knew that we would become involved in operations further west. BATT would never again be able to mount the two squadron operations of the past: first, because it was no longer necessary, as SAF had grown in numbers and experience, and second, because even gathering together enough men to mount one squadron operation would mean stripping the seven firqats we then supported of their BATTs. In the future, BATT were going to have to work with the firqats in parties of six or eight men only, and so would be more reliant on the firqats than ever before for their safety. I decided that BATT must become much more involved with the firqats again, but without returning to the old days when they were reliant upon us.

It could be achieved in two ways: by moving to live within the firqats' perimeter, and by making a conscious effort to involve ourselves more with them, visiting them in the evenings, discussing their problems, entertaining them in the BATT hut and generally aiming to return to the climate of trust that had existed in the past. It was a total reversal of the current policy and had to be explained carefully to the Regiment because many SAS were only too happy to be free at last from the firqats' bickering, but most saw the sense of the directive straight away. Even the less enlightened ones saw the point when they realized that in the coming months their lives could depend on it. The firqats in their turn were overjoyed to see BATT living amongst them once again. Although it was made clear that BATT would not run their administration for them, they knew that in the last resort, if all else failed, their BATT would intercede for them.

An opportunity to make the point presented itself within days at Zeak when I went on patrol with the firqat. The monsoon was beginning to break and it was raining heavily. Whereas SAF were wearing their excellent waterproof camouflaged uniforms, the firqat wore their usual futa and cloak and were soaked to the skin. The SAS refrained from wearing their waterproofs because they were embarrassed to do so in front of the soaked firqatmen. To be objective, I was angrier than the firqat, who did not appear at all concerned. Nonetheless, it would set a good example, I knew, if BATT could obtain the envied waterproofs for them.

At HQ Firqat Forces I was told that they had not received the waterproofs from SAF. Enquiries at HQ Dhofar also drew a blank; they had indeed equipped their own men, but did not have enough for the firqats. My spies, however, produced quite different information; the stuff was there, but it was being kept for SAF. On my next visit to Muscat I called in to see Sayyid Fahr, the Deputy Minister of Defence. The waterproofs were released next day.

The firqats seemed glad but not unduly so, since they were more concerned over waterproofing their houses than themselves. Most preferred to wear their futas than encumber themselves with the heavy and noisy waterproof trousers, but the jackets were very popular, mainly, I suspected because they liked the military appearance of the camouflage pattern, rather than its waterproof qualities. Some of the younger men wore their waterproof jackets even in the sweltering heat of summer.

Rain had a psychological effect on Dhofaris. At the first sign of rain a general feeling of pleasurable anticipation permeated the camp; the men laughed easily and were obviously in high spirits. Even heavy rain did nothing to dampen enthusiasm. Rain meant pasture land for the cattle and they talked of a 'good *khareef*' meaning a particularly rainy one. I once came across a family sitting on the hillside in the pouring rain, eating some food from a cloth in front of them.

'What are you doing?' I shouted from my Landrover.

'Enjoying the rain,' came the answer. They were out for a picnic.

ELEVEN
ZEAK PATROL

Zeak interested me most of all the positions, partly because it was new – the BATT were still blasting out the mortar pit when I arrived – and partly because of its potential. As Government control expanded eastwards from the Midway Road and westwards from Medinat Al Haq, the adoo tended to retire into the area between, some twelve miles square and out of normal patrol range from the Government bases. Zeak lay a fifth of the way between Qairoon Hairitti and Jibjat on the *gatn* itself. If it were considered the north-west of four positions, about six miles apart in the rough shape of a square, the adoo's present safe area would be completely dominated. Zeak could become the springboard, from which the three other positions would be inserted.

The position itself was fairly typical: two platoons of SAF provided the security in four sangars placed around the wire perimeter, the firqat were centred on a marquee surrounded by a rock wall with subsidiary sangars close to it, and the BATT were alongside, a six-man team who lived in pairs in three solidly constructed sangars, each capable of resisting a direct hit. They fed together in one corrugated iron hut, which served as dining hall, briefing room and recreation hut for the evening games of Scrabble and chess.

It was mid-afternoon by the time I arrived. I took a quick walk around the position and then strolled out through the wire downhill to a large solitary fig tree a hundred yards away where the SAS medic held his clinic. There had not yet been time to put up a tent, let alone a hut, which would be next in priority after the defences had been completed. A small group of people sat waiting to be treated, mostly women and children and one or two greybeards. The medic was giving a woman an iron injection in the arm whilst the others looked on and I was struck by the calm acceptance of it all. In the early days a male European Christian would not even have been allowed to touch a woman. Jebeli women were much more emancipated than women in the coastal towns or in the *negd*, but even so, it was a sign of progress.

Jebeli women were also much better looking, or perhaps they just revealed more, for they seldom wore a mask. They enjoyed colourful clothes, as against the habitual black of women in purdah, and I studied the girl being treated now. She was pretty, very nearly beautiful, with fine features, good even teeth and large brown eyes, but her skin was grey and she looked washed out. She was probably not more than 15 or 16, but already she had had her second child. A many-coloured cotton robe reached down to her ankles but her arms were bare and a shawl of similar colours to the dress, in a pattern of yellow, green and vermilion was draped over her head. In one nostril she had clipped an elaborately worked gold clasp; otherwise, her ornaments were of silver, a couple of light plain bracelets, and a pendant of silver and coral beads on a chain round her neck.

She contrasted brightly with the two old men squatting alongside her, their horny feet sticking out below their grimy kilts, now black, but which had probably held colour originally. Around his waist each carried a short knife of the type found in the souk, with a plastic handle and Solingen steel blade; jebelis are concerned more with a knife's efficiency than its decoration. Their chests were bare, but one had a little leather bag slung around his neck by a cord, containing a talisman of some sort. Their only other ornament was a greasy black rope wrapped around the head to signify their sheikhly status. The two old men argued loudly in the complaining guttural sound of the Jebeli dialect and prodded the ground now and then with their sticks to emphasize a point.

Several small children also needed treatment. They lay quietly with solemn faces in the protecting folds of their mother's robes, the little boys in long white shirts, the little girls with colourful dresses like their mothers. The little girls' heads were shaven and one or two already wore silver trinkets. Another group of children clustered nearby who were evidently perfectly healthy and who had just come to watch the fun. They were jostling each other and skylarking behind the sitting patients. Four or five girls, already knowing their places, stood smiling shyly and talking quietly to each other, whilst their lords and masters pushed forward brazenly, grinning broadly and saluting with whichever hand pleased them, and sometimes with both together.

But the person who took my attention most was sitting by himself on a fallen branch 20yards to one side watching the little clinic intently. He was a young man of fighting age, probably in his early twenties. He was wearing civilian clothes, a dark green futa and a red shirt with the sleeves rolled up. His feet and head were bare and his black hair uncombed. He carried no weapon of any sort except a light camel cane, curved at the top like an English walking stick.

I had seen that set, wild look many times on the faces of SEPs. It took several days before they lost it. I raised my eyebrows and nodded towards the man. The medic followed my glance and looked back at his work.

'Adoo. The firqat leader, Ali Tamaan, told us about him. Apparently he can't make up his mind whether to SEP or not – this is the third day he's sat here, watching. Ali wants him to see for himself that what the firqs say is true. He reckons he'll come in over the next couple of days. Just ignore him.'

He finished his clinic, and we walked back together to the BATT hut where we found the rest of the team sitting on their folding chairs around the long table. A delicious aroma of steak and fresh vegetables and newly baked bread and cheese filled the hut. Today was 'fresh' day and the helicopter that had brought me in had also brought in the weekly box of fresh food. An SAS soldier has to spend so much time eating tasteless dehydrated patrol rations that he enjoys good food to the full and the standard of cooking was high. Each man took his turn to cook and the rest of the team soon made their views plain if the food was not up to standard.

'What d'you think of the bread, boss?'

Never was a gourmet's opinion awaited with such silent anticipation as now. Most of the BATTs I had already visited had claimed to be the best bakers on the jebel and each had built an oven from old ammunition boxes: it would not do to be partisan. I passed what I hoped was an encouraging but prevaricating judgement and the conversation turned to more important matters.

Sergeant Jimmy Jordan, the BATT leader, was a short wiry ex-Royal Engineer and one of the few SAS men to wear glasses. Now he took out a map from his trouser side pocket and carefully unfolded it. A battery of pint mugs of tea appeared on the table as he began his briefing. I listened carefully because I should be taking part in the patrol, but also because this sort of occasion gave me the chance as Commanding Officer to assess the operational standards in the Regiment. Jordan leant back in his chair and plucked a blade of grass from the ground behind him to use as a pointer – a good start – no thick fingers trying to indicate detailed positions. He began with a general description of the operation and then started on the first of the list of headings: ground, situation, the enemy, own forces, troops in support, mission ... every detail was covered, every man listening knew what matters would be talked on next; the familiar liturgy of an army orders group.

'Any questions?' he finished. There was a general shaking of heads. 'Right, well I'll go and brief the firkins. Want to come, Colonel?'

We walked across the flat, grass-covered hilltop the 50 paces to the firqat marquee and went in. A dozen men were reclining on rush mats on the floor. Some large cardboard boxes were piled untidily at the other end of the marquee, but otherwise it was empty. A guffaw of laughter had sounded before we entered and they were still smiling as they stood up. Ali Tamaan came across to receive us. He was a square, stocky man with a strong face below his tightly wound green shamag. A sturdy pair of brown legs protruded from a pair of khaki shorts below an ex-British Army parachute smock. His feet were bare.

'*Ahlan, ahlan.*' He waved us to the centre pole where he had been seated and Jordan introduced me.

The other men had started talking to each other again and I caught the word 'Salahadin'. I looked around at a youngish man who was smiling at me knowingly. I remembered him as one of the later men to join the Firqat Salahadin at Mirbat and, although I could not remember his name, he was obviously waiting to be recognized.

'Ah, I remember you, you were with me in the old days at Mirbat,' I said. There was a chorus of approval at the kaid's incredible feat of memory.

'You've not changed a bit,' I said, putting the gilt on.

'You have, *Taweel*,' he replied grinning. 'You're going grey and your teeth are falling out.'

Dhofari directness! I had had a tooth pulled a few weeks before.

Jordan drew a rough map in the sand and explained with its help the route he wanted to take. Several minutes were spent while the men asked questions about the map; this mark was such-and-such a wadi, that little pile of earth such-and-such a jebel. Then followed lengthy explanations by five of them simultaneously to the inevitable numbskull who could not understand. '*Shoof Mohammed. Hada al wadi kabeer …*'

★   ★   ★

At last all was clear and Jordan continued. Ali Tamaan interrupted. He did not like the route and suggested an alteration, and a geysh picket would be needed here and here, he added.

'How many men can you produce?' Jordan asked.

'How many geysh are coming?'

'A platoon and a half.'

Ali Tamaan thought for a minute. 'You'll not need more than 20.'

Jordan bargained. 'That's not enough. Our information is that the adoo themselves number 20. I want 25.'

A period of haggling began. Many of his men were visiting villages, Ali explained, but very well, he conceded, he could produce 28.

Dusk was falling as the force formed up on the space between the BATT hut and the firqat marquee. Thirty-four firqat were on parade, but it could well have been any number between 15 and 40. Most wore shirts or camouflaged smocks of some sort. Some had acquired SAF desert boots, often several sizes too big, but most were bare-footed. All carried FNs except Ali who had a Kalashnikov. Each man's equipment was a miscellany of British, American and Chinese belts and ammunition pouches, and flung over or under his shoulder, every man carried his food and sleeping cloak in a small bundle.

There were six SAS including myself; the seventh man had gone off to the SAF mortar pit to act as fire controller. Between us we carried a GPMG, an M79 grenade launcher – an ugly weapon like a stubby shotgun but capable of putting a grenade in a man's pocket at 150 yards – and four Armalite rifles. The spread of weapons was the most flexible for the size and task of this particular patrol. We could put down more automatic fire up to 300 yards than a platoon of infantry: the GPMG could reach out to 600 yards, the Armalites could also give accurate single-shot sniper fire, and the M79 gave us a mini mortar. The SAS soldier uses his weapons as a workman uses his tools. An SAS soldier is cross-trained in them all, and in many foreign weapons as well. He expects to select the right weapon for the job in hand, or in the case of a commander, the right mix of weapons.

After radios had been checked and each man had cocked his weapon, the firqat led off, followed by BATT, with more firqat to bring up the rear. The night was chilly, but the moon had not yet risen, so progress was slow. Several times the firqat halted to listen and once six of them broke away and headed downhill into a wadi, silent as wraiths, to return ten minutes later, satisfied at whatever they had heard.

Two hours later we left the high ground and dropped into a shallow re-entrant that marked the beginning of a wadi. As we descended, the slope became steeper, the walls of the wadi rose sharply on either side, and the twisting rock path disappeared more than a yard or two ahead. The long line of men shuffled their way slowly downwards, the only sounds the scraping of feet, the rustle of clothes against the bushes and the creaking of canvas belts and packs. At last the slope eased and the path led out on to a cleared flat piece of ground. This was the place for the intermediate picket, who were to protect those going further down, and who, in turn, would be protected by SAF pickets up on the high ground. A whispered conference between Jordan and Ali Tamaan, and five minutes later, ten firqat and the BATT moved through the clearing and down once more. The moon had risen and it was light enough to see easily now. A further ten minutes brought us out on to a high rock covered with low scrub, looking down on to the sandy wadi bed sixty feet below. To the right, just out of sight, lay the waterhole we were to ambush that night. Fifty yards away, the opposite wadi wall rose steeply and then ran more gently up to a crest 300 yards from our position. Both walls of the wadi were heavily wooded.

I settled down on my stomach, into a gap from where I could look down on to the wadi bed, trying to make myself as comfortable as possible amongst the sharp thorn bushes. A hand appeared through a bush and passed me a roll of cord; I tied a loop around my wrist and pushed the remainder of the cord through to the man on the other side. Then I pulled my shamag up over my head, rested my chin on my rifle butt, tucked my hands under me for warmth and dozed.

You only catnap on patrol, so when a hand shook my shoulder I was instantly awake.

'Your stag, boss.'

I grunted acknowledgement and eased myself up to sit cross-legged. It was cold and my eyes felt gritty. The sky was already beginning to lighten and the wadi bed shone silver below. Nothing moved. I sat and waited.

Forty minutes later dawn had almost broken. A cock crew from the village beyond the far crest. All around, chirrups and snatches of bird songs began and the bushes of the wadi stirred with life. I could make out individual trees now in the wadi wall opposite. I pulled sharply on the cord, first right, then left. The answering tugs came immediately and a quiet rustling either side of me indicated the invisible men crawling into fire positions. Ten minutes passed and it was almost broad daylight. From over the hill came shouts from herdsmen; then high-pitched voices suddenly sounded nearer and, peering across the wadi, I saw a young woman and a boy hurrying down the slope, zig-zagging like skiers, towards the path which led down the wadi wall to the water hole.

If the adoo were in the village, they would either come down themselves for water or send the women, Ali Tamaan had said. I had asked him how we would know if they sent women and he had mimicked frightened women looking nervously this way and that. There was nothing nervous in the appearance of these two and, after a further half-hour's waiting, Ali Tamaan stood up and called it off. All around, men stood or sat up, grateful for the chance to stretch, and soon wisps of smoke among the bushes showed where little fires were boiling the breakfast cups of tea. Ali Tamaan and Jordan were busy on the radio talking to the SAF commander above us on the high ground which the SAF had occupied shortly before dawn. There was some re-positioning to do but after half an hour, all was set for the next phase and the entire firqat and their BATT descended into the wadi itself for the wadi search.

It was a long, hot day. The firqat split into two groups, one 20 feet up the far wadi side, the other moving down the wadi itself. Jordan stayed with Ali Tamaan with the lower group whilst the rest of BATT formed a separate fire group staying as high as possible on the near wadi side. Whenever a cave or a finger wadi appeared, the search group of firqat investigated, covered by the two fire groups. They swarmed like ants over the hillside, climbing into places the SAS men could never have reached. The larger caves received only a cursory glance; the ones with small entrances but which opened out into larger caves inside were most likely to hold arms.

By midday it had become breathlessly hot. The sun's rays beat straight down into the wadi, the walls reflecting and magnifying the heat until every piece of scrub-thorn or rock over-hang that could provide a minuscule piece of shade for a minute or two became precious. Suddenly the ground shook with an explosion. Instantly the figures below us scattered and disappeared.

The sound appeared to have come from above and the BATT began to move fast up through the bushes in extended line. There was a moment's confusion of sharp, shouted questions and orders.

'What was it, RPG?'

'Dunno.'

'Why no more shooting?'

'Can you see anything?'

'Get that jimpy up on the left, Charlie.'

The radio spoke. A booby-trap mine on the far side of the wadi had exploded as a firqatman was crawling into a cave on his elbows. The firqats were checking it out and Jordan was moving up with a body-bag. The dead man's torso was in a mess.

The find was not large, a machine-gun, a couple of rifles and some ammunition, but by the time it had all been carried down into the wadi and a helicopter had been brought in to take it out, together with the dead man's body, more than an hour had passed. The firqat were visibly shaken. The dead man had been an older, experienced and popular firqat member and the damage done to him had not been pretty. The pace in the afternoon was slower and more careful.

The cave was the only find. By five o'clock the firqat had lost interest and walked along with their rifles held by the barrel over their shoulders. Anything that had been hidden in this wadi had long been moved, they said, but their spirits bucked up as the wadi ran into a much larger one. A water hole lay under a large rock and someone had constructed a low concrete wall around it to form a shallow cistern fifteen feet long by ten feet across. A man and his two daughters were watering their cattle. Ali Tamaan and the man exchanged greetings as the firqat approached.

'*Het, het.*'

'*Bikair het, het.*'

The firqat formed into a line and passed by the old man, each shaking hands as he passed or touching noses, when both placed one hand behind the other's neck and pulled each other forward until their foreheads and noses met. The younger firqatmen were more interested though, in the elder of the girls. She stood a few paces from her father and stretched out her right arm at full length to touch hands whilst, with her left, she pulled her shawl demurely across the lower part of her face. The men kept well away and stretched their arms full length also, so that just the tips of their fingers touched. It was a chaste salute, but the brushing of the fingertips and the upward look she gave the men from under her long eye-lashes must have made the young men's blood run faster. One or two of the SAS quietly growled their appreciation, but stood discreetly back from the greetings.

Every red-blooded male appreciates a good-looking girl, yet at no time throughout the seven years' campaign was there any problem between an SAS soldier and a Dhofari woman, although many of them were beautiful. Every soldier knew that the quickest way to fall out with an ally is to interfere with his women, and even one case could have damaged the years of work done winning the hearts and minds of the people.

The meeting proved opportune, for the old man had good information about the adoo. They had indeed left a week ago and had crossed over into one of the wadis further west, taking everything of value with them.

The firqat celebrated by building a large fire and killing a cow. By now it was dark and the blazing fire threw dancing shadows against the wadi sides. Five men pulling at a rope around its head and pushing at its haunches brought the beast towards the fire; it was stiff-legged with fear, its head lowered and its eyes staring wildly. Other men sprang to help, laughing and whooping and in an instant the beast was on its back. A flurry of legs, a knife flashing in the firelight, and the firqat had meat.

Dressing the carcass took over an hour, but at the end the meat lay in its bloody pieces on the skin having never once touched the ground. The meat was next placed on skewers cut from the bushes around about and roasted at the fire that still blazed merrily. A firqatman came up as I was lying on my sleeping blanket and handed me a piece. It looked black in the flame's reflection and smelt strong. The outer part was cooked all right, charred in fact, but the centre of the lump of meat was still raw. I chewed it as best I could until it had turned to gristle and threw the rest surreptitiously away. By now the firqat were ' high' on the meat and the wadi echoed with their laughter. Meat seemed to affect them rather as alcohol affects others; they became light-headed and lost their inhibitions and next morning they would feel just as bad, but with a hangover of the stomach instead of the head.

Now four or five started to dance whilst the others chanted and clapped their hands in rhythmic unison. The dancers took mincing little steps, turning slowly around with one hand on their hip and the other extended above their head holding a knife. From time to time each man threw his knife, point first, in the ground and then recovered it without losing the rhythm of the dance. For no apparent reason, one of the dancers would suddenly lose interest and leave the circle to sit down and be replaced by another who would begin to dance to the laughter and encouragement of his friends. I saw this excitement at the slaughter of a cow quite often. Sometimes clothes belonging to old people were soaked in the blood of the animal or, if it was a calf, the carcass itself would be draped over the shoulders of an old man or woman who then cavorted about the village, scarlet with gore, in the belief that some of the animal's energy would enter him or her.

Gradually, having gorged themselves, the party broke up to sleep and the fire sank until it was nothing but glowing embers.

★ ★ ★

Next morning the march back to camp began. The long line of men wound its way slowly up the hill under the protection of the SAF pickets, whose Arab and Baluchi soldiers must have wondered at and envied the junketings going on down in the wadi the night before. At last the top was reached and the long plod across the flat pasture land began, but it was an easy walk and after two hours, the sangars and tents of Zeak came into sight. One of the firqat, named Isa, asked me if we would like to go to his village for breakfast. The village lay nearby and it would give the medic an opportunity to look at the villagers, so three of us accepted gladly whilst the remainder went on back to camp with the main column.

We reached the village in a quarter of an hour. It was of average size, eight roundhouses and a similar number for the cattle. A number of women and children stood around on the hard-baked earth awaiting our coming. Isa beckoned me over to one of the houses and I ducked and went in. It was dark inside, and my eyes took a moment to adjust before I realized that there were people already in it, an old man, who proved to be Isa's father, and Isa's first wife. The house was comfortable and dry and surprisingly roomy. The floor would have been of hardened and polished cow dung in days gone by, but now it was made of cement to reflect Isa's prosperity and laid in a terrace, a low level for the fire and kitchen area, a rise of six inches to the living area and a long bench eighteen inches high for sleeping. A fire had already been lit and we huddled around to warm our hands on it. A huge ten-foot high blackened tree trunk in the centre of the house supported the roof and from its top large branches extended to rest on the five foot high wall of rocks. In fact, there were two walls, eighteen inches apart and filled with

193

earth to make the house cool in the summer and warm in winter. These branches in turn were meshed with smaller horizontal branches and again with even smaller vertical ones. Finally a thin layer of straw covered the whole to form a very effective thatch.

Furniture was sparse: a wooden chest, some cooking utensils, some bundles of cloth containing spare clothes, and a goatskin of water suspended from a beam. The house would last twelve years, Isa explained with pride, although the thatching would need to be replaced every two or three years, he added.

An aluminium tray appeared bearing small glasses of milkless sweet tea, followed by a large bowl of milk, still warm from the cow. A few minutes later, refreshed, Isa suggested we might take a look around the village. The medic was already busy treating the old man, so I left him and joined Isa outside. Nearby was a tiny roundhouse just big enough for two, where he slept with his new wife, and beyond stood a tent the size of a small camping tent. This was obviously his pride and joy and he ushered me inside like an agent with a prospective buyer, pointing out the advantages of it and telling me how much it had cost him. We had hardly settled down on the rush matting when his Number Two wife entered, carrying his chubby young son. Isa took the child and settled him on his knee making the gooey sounds used to babies the world over. The wife was little more than a girl and retired to the entrance of the tent giggling and pulling her shawl over her face. Number One wife, whom I had seen at the roundhouse, entered with more tea, set it down on the floor and then sat herself down in the more senior position within the tent. Next, Isa's mother appeared holding a small boy of perhaps six or seven, Isa's eldest son; all proceeded to join in the cooing and chucking directed at the baby, who remained sucking his thumb and observing with unsmiling solemnity the strange-coloured, and probably smelling, green-clad figure opposite. Number One wife and the elder son showed not the slightest hint of jealousy at being supplanted in the father's affections by the baby. I took my camera from my belt and asked Isa if I might photograph him and his son. His mother became quite agitated at the sight of the camera, afraid that I might steal the child's soul, but Isa told her to be quiet and he posed stiffly, with the baby on his knee. I managed to include Number One wife in the viewfinder and looked at her carefully for a few seconds. She had been a lovely woman once, but now her skin was lined and her eyes were tired, a middle-aged woman of 25.

It was time to leave, all too soon, and I quitted the tent whilst Isa said his fond good-byes to his family. He joined me outside with rifle and equipment, once again the stern soldier, and we left his village without looking back, discussing military matters as though the visit had never taken place.

It had been a typical wadi search. Few arms had been found and no contact made with the adoo. One man had been killed, but on the credit side, the firqat's influence had been extended a little further. The last months of 1974 and the early months of 1975 were taken up in many such searches, often very much larger, sometimes in battalion strength, but the principles and methods were similar. By November 1974 the adoo had withdrawn all their heavy weapons west of the Hornbeam Line and most wadi searches recovered little in the way of important arms, but their real significance was that they showed the people that the adoo were no longer safe anywhere, not even in the wadis. In fact, it was not until February 1975 in the Wadi Ashoq at the beginning of the Western Area, that the first important finds were made, when the SAF's Frontier Force and the Firqat Al Nasr destroyed the adoo 9th of June Regiment, capturing all their heavy weapons in the process.

To begin with, many of these wadi searches were fiercely resisted by the adoo who saw them for what they were, intrusion by the Government's forces into the last adoo strongholds, and both sides took many casualties. But there were always more SAF, more BATT, and more firqat, whilst the adoo, their losses exacerbated by the continually rising SEP rates, could not be replaced. The adoo bands became weaker and weaker through battle losses, defections and lack of re-supply, until they were no longer capable of resisting in strength. By the middle of 1975 the adoo in the Central and Eastern Areas had split into small bands on the run, still with a sting, still able to punish SAF or firqat carelessness, but no longer able to call the tune.

TWELVE

WAR AND PEACE

January 1975

Major General Tim Creasey had taken over from Brigadier Graham as the Commander of the Sultan's Armed Forces. He was a big bluff man with a very strong personality, a soldier's general and just the sort of man the Iranians admired, but for some months past he had been concerned at the lack of activity along either side of the Midway Road, where patrolling had almost stopped. The trouble was that the Iranians did not patrol at all, as SAF understood it. When they did leave their bases, they moved in force. Any adoo about saw them coming from miles away and, sensibly, lay low until they had passed by. Consequently the only people who could get at the adoo were the firqat, and these refused to go on patrol because they thought the Iranians might mistake them for adoo on their return. Military progress along the Midway Road was coming to a halt.

Elsewhere, in both the Central and Eastern Areas, things were still going well. SAF, BATT and the firqats were patrolling extensively, the adoo were avoiding contact, and civil development was well under way. And the Hornbeam Line had been reinforced by a long-stop, the Hammer Line, which was established on the Jebel Khaftawt and occupied similar positions to the old Leopard Line of two years previously. In short, the east and centre were under control. Creasey decided it was now time to carry the war to the adoo in the west.

He was also taking into account the imminent arrival of a battalion of the Jordanian Special Forces. These, he believed, being Arabs, would get on better terms with the firqats and the civilians, and responsibility for the Midway Road would give their Commanding Officer a clear-cut objective. The Iranians, on the other hand, with their firepower, would

196

be ideal for aggressive operations in the Western Area. Consequently, Creasey had instructed the Iranians to develop a remote airstrip in the *negd,* known as Manston, into an administrative base.

I had flown over Manston in 1971 and knew it to be a typical barely marked *negd* airstrip with a poor track connecting it by land to Thamrait. When next I saw it, in 1974, I could scarcely believe the transformation; the place was huge. Row upon row of air-conditioned cabins surrounded a great concrete runway more than capable of accepting the heavy Hercules transport aircraft that flew in daily from Iran. Mountains of defence stores, barbed wire, wooden beams, corrugated iron, metal pickets, sandbags, petrol and water jerrycans stood guarded by steel-helmeted sentries. A row of Huey helicopters rested, parked near underslung loads ready to be hooked on. And the track to Thamrait had been turned into an excellent, graded road.

Security, as in all matters Iranian, was strict, even so far out in the negd. My credentials were meticulously checked before I was allowed to enter the airfield. The runway itself was guarded on either side by a row of soldiers placed 200 yards apart. Each man stood in a little palm-roofed sentry post, and I wondered why they all faced inwards towards the concrete runway instead of outwards where the threat lay.

It was from this base that Creasey ordered the Iranian battle group to advance upon and seize the coastal town of Rakyut and the adoo stores caves at Shershitti. Rakyut lay 17 miles almost due south of Manston alongside a narrow lagoon at the mouth of the Wadi Khais Bin Uthman. Its inhabitants had long since fled, but in more peaceful times had made their living from trade and fishing. Its stout houses, most now roofless, still remained as a reminder of its wealthy past, when the town was the centre of the slave trade in Western Dhofar. Slaves from Africa were disembarked at the smaller town of Dhalqut, twelve miles further west, where they were fattened up, and where row upon row of graves still mark the fate of many of them, before being shipped or walked to Rakyut for sale. Rakyut's importance in 1974, however, lay mainly in its being claimed on Radio Aden to be capital of the 'liberated area'. The capture of Rakyut would be an undoubted blow to the Front's prestige, but the effect of the capture of Shershitti would be greater still, for the caves were the main adoo stores complex in all Dhofar and were known to contain hundreds of tons of food, clothing, equipment, weapons and ammunition.

The advance began in mid-December, and failed. The battle group did not get beyond the *gatn*. The adoo watched the move across the negd and were waiting in carefully concealed positions, ready to hit the advancing troops as soon as they were within range of their heavy weapons. Whereas the Iranians were pinned down in the open, the adoo were able to move along the edge of the treeline. The Iranian casualties mounted, and the advance had to be called off. The worst incident was when three Iranian sangars were engaged by the adoo. As no fire was being returned, the adoo closed right up to the sangars, threw in grenades and then leant over the sangar walls to shoot dead the survivors. They then climbed over the walls, stripped the bodies of weapons and equipment, and returned to the cover of the trees without a round having been fired at them in return.

It was a major setback, but Creasey was not the man to give up. He decided to try again, this time allowing the Iranians to concentrate solely upon Rakyut whilst the SAF seized Shershitti. However, all the battalions in Dhofar were fully occupied and none could be released for this operation; unknowingly, the first ingredient of the catastrophe that was to follow was introduced: a battalion from Northern Oman, the Jebel Regiment, was given a short period of retraining in mountain operations and sent down to Dhofar post-haste.

The SAS had had their eyes on Shershitti for a long time. As long ago as early 1973, a study had been made of the caves complex to see if there was not some way of reaching them, and the air photographs and studies done then were still held at HQ BATT in Um Al Gwarif. The caves lay in a very strong position at the head of a long wadi running up from south to north and four miles inland. Several sheer escarpments protected them like giant steps. The only route to the caves lay either from the lateral track that ran along the foot of the final escarpment, or by a track that ran down to them from above. The caves themselves lay in a horseshoe and each stocked its own commodity so that camels could stop and be loaded as they went by.

Having mounted the final escarpment, the Shershitti Wadi ran off more gently to the north-west though thick thorn bush. Immediately above the caves, however, it passed through a tooth-shaped clearing 1000 yards long by 200 across, the top of the tooth resting on Shershitti itself. The wadi finally split into smaller finger-wadis that ran out south on to a long ridge running west to east. Another ridge similarly aligned dominated the northern side of the wadi.

Major Alan Trant was a dark, handsome man, with a fertile brain

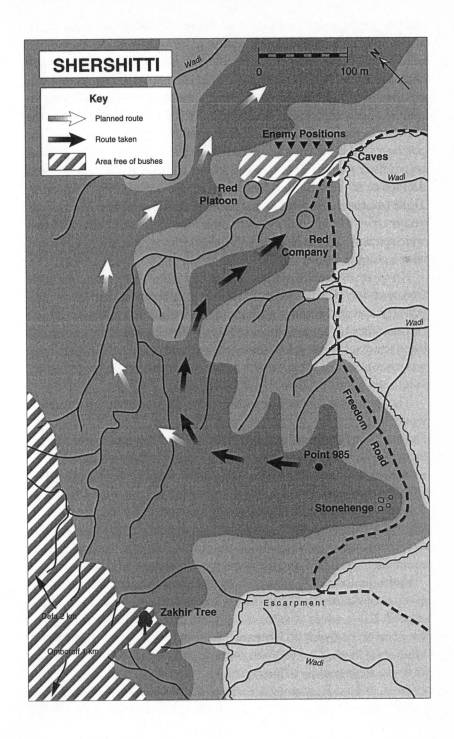

and one of the best squadron commanders 22 SAS had produced. He also held a fervent belief in maintaining the unofficial SAS motto, 'Do unto others before they do unto you' and had recently had a narrow escape as a result of it. Trant had noticed that the adoo always followed up after SAF had withdrawn, to check for dropped ammunition, re-usable radio batteries, etc. Trant decided to take advantage of this habit of theirs by staying behind in a small, well-hidden sangar off the main position so that he could direct artillery fire on to the enemy as they began their search. As luck would have it, however, an adoo patrol decided to cover their searching men from precisely the same position Trant occupied. He and his patrol were discovered and had to fight desperately to hold off the greatly superior numbers of adoo until they were rescued in the nick of time by the returning battalion, but it had been a close-run thing.

Now Trant put a plan to Brigadier John Akehurst, the new Commander Dhofar. Akehurst was a charming and very able infantryman and among his many qualities he had two essential in a commander; he always appeared smilingly confident and he would listen to advice. Now as he listened, he realized that much of what Trant was saying coincided nicely with a plan already beginning to formulate in his own mind.

The final plan for the Shershitti operation was straightforward; it would be a battalion operation, supported by BATT and 40 men of the Firqats Tariq Bin Zeead and Southern Mahra. The attack would be in three phases: first, the seizure of an airstrip on the gatn called Defa; second, an advance from there along the western ridge to Zakhir Tree and then south-east to a clearing at Point 985; and third, the advance on the caves themselves. The BATT would split into small four-man BATTs with each SAF company to manage the firqat guides, and a fighting unit, two troops strong, with the main firqat force, all under Trant's command. The BATT and the firqat would lead the advance.

By 4th January 1975 all was ready. Defa was seized easily, but the fly-in of troops and stores was poorly organised and for a while chaos reigned. It was not an auspicious start, but at last all was sorted out and the advance on Point 985 began. The route lay along the gatn to the south-west for the first 3000 yards and at Zakhir Tree turned south-east on to the ridge leading to Shershitti.

Trees, at least large trees, are important landmarks in Dhofar. They are meeting places, recognition features and observation posts, all rolled into one. Zakhir Tree was such a recognition point, and now it was here, as the column left the plain of the gatn and entered the tree-line, that serious resistance, and the casualties that go with it, began. It was close quarters work. Most of the trouble came from an adoo GPMG, identified later as having come from the former British Army days in Aden. The firqat behaved badly and showed little stomach for the fighting, but the SAS men's blood was up and they pressed on, firqat or no firqat. Finally, at 1530 hours, the first troops broke out of the bush into the clearing of Point 985 and an hour later, the helicopters brought in the first of many shuttles of defence stores. Fortunately, the main adoo band had been destroyed at Zakhir Tree and it was not until darkness began to fall that the adoo attacked. Then they managed to creep up close and opened fire with machine-guns and RPGs, causing several casualties but losing several men killed themselves.

Visibility throughout the advance had seldom been more than 20-30 yards, and often less, and the best way to see was to lie down and look under the branches at ground level. The SAS had adopted a U-formation for moving, the open area to the rear. At each of the four corners was a GPMG gunner, and every man carried a fully automatic weapon, either an FN rifle borrowed from the SAF (since the British version fired only semi-automatic), or an Armalite. Experience had shown that the only answer to the adoo's firepower was firepower. It is all very well for theorists to say that most of the adoo's automatic fire went overhead; it was true, but a man needed very cool nerves to shoot back single shots under the deluge of fire from, in effect, ten machine-guns or more, firing at him from less than the length of a tennis court. He needed a fully automatic weapon just to make himself heard.

The advance on Shershitti began next day. The plan was essentially Trant's and it was a good one. One company would remain to guard the base. Two companies would move off north, then east across the Shershitti wadi, then south-east on to positions on the ridge north of the caves. From there they would dominate the southern side of the horseshoe escarpment. A third company would not cross the wadi at all, but instead would move south-east along the ridge to a hill from where it could look down across the wadi and the tooth-shaped piece of open ground into the caves on the northern side of the Shershitti horseshoe. When the three companies were in position, the BATT and firqat would move down the track into the wadi and down the escarpment into the caves. There would no doubt be fierce resistance, but with fire on to them from three sides, and plenty of artillery, mortar and air support, the adoo would be out-gunned.

The leading companies moved out soon after dawn, but it was not until 1100 hours that the BATT and firqats left Point 985 with the battalion's tactical headquarters. By this time the leading troops, Red Company, should have been crossing the Shershitti wadi, but the company commander had already realized that he was too far south. Nonetheless, he radioed that he knew where he was and would shortly start to cross the wadi. Trant travelled with battalion headquarters with radio communications forward to the small four-man BATT teams with the companies, to the main BATT/firqat forces behind him. and back to the mortars under the control of an SAS mortar man at Point 985. Control of the operation, however, soon became very difficult in the thick bush and each man followed the one in front, with only a vague idea of where he was. Navigation had to be by direction, time and pacing and at best could only be approximate. After an hour had passed, Trant began to become anxious. The leading company, Red Company, seemed to have turned eastwards too soon. He mentioned his misgivings to the acting Commanding Officer who questioned Red Company Commander over the radio; again he assured them that he was going east and would shortly be crossing the wadi, but progress through the thick bush had become painfully slow. Trant now became very worried. They must find out where they were, he insisted, or they would arrive too late at the caves to do anything before nightfall. This would be serious because it would give the adoo time to move much of the equipment during the night and to bring up reinforcements before dawn.

Fortunately, Red Company suddenly resolved the quandary by breaking out of the bush into a cleared area and for the first time the Company Commander could see exactly where he was – his company had not crossed the wadi at all but, as Trant had suspected, had turned east too soon, an easy mistake to make in the thick bush. They were still south of Shershitti on the hill overlooking the tooth-shaped clearing which should have been occupied by the last company in the column. It was a good position and the Company Commander radioed that he felt he should stay there and provide covering fire for the next two companies who should move through him across the wadi and up on the high ground beyond.

The rest of the battalion column had come to a halt, still in thick bush with battalion headquarters 500 yards behind. Trant and the acting Commanding Officer debated. Should he accept Red Company' s advice or should he press Red Company to go on? The fact was that Red Company Commander was the only person who could see anything. He was an experienced major and the acting Commanding Officer decided to back his judgement. Red Company would stay where they were and Two Company would move through them over to the other side of the wadi. Two Company's commander was on leave and the company was temporarily commanded by the second-in-command, who now moved forward with his BATT, to the hill to look at the ground in front.

His BATT commander was Corporal Willie Watson. Watson was a highly experienced SAS soldier in his mid-thirties and in any other unit he would have been a company sergeant major, but he had turned down rank time and again. Now he took one look at the scene in front of him and gave his unsolicited advice that it would be madness to move across that open ground unless the high ground on the other side of the wadi was secured. Otherwise, if the adoo held the high ground, the clearing would become a death trap. Twice Watson, quietly and respectfully, but with all the authority of his battle experience, recommended strongly that nobody should cross the clearing. They should retrace their steps and cut up to the high ground whilst still under cover of the bush.

It is not hard to imagine the dilemma in the mind of the young acting Company Commander. Meanwhile, whilst he studied the ground before him and looked anxiously at the lowering ridge that rose opposite, Red Company sent a platoon around to the left to a hillock which rose between the roots of the tooth and from where they looked down almost the whole length of the clearing. Then when all was set, Two Company started down the slope.

The leading platoon broke cover and strode confidently in arrowhead formation across the clearing; the company headquarters broke cover too and followed them; then came the second platoon, and the third. When the leading platoon were half way across the clearing a few shots rang out. There was a pause of a second or two and then the whole of the far hillside exploded into life: heavy, medium and light machine -guns, recoilless guns, mortars, rocket launchers and small arms. The leading platoon went down as if scythed. The Company Commander and his artillery FOO dashed gallantly forward with the four or five men of his headquarters group to a low ridge 50 yards ahead. As they gained it, 20 adoo rose from the ground and, without even bothering to raise their weapons to the shoulder, cut the little group down. The weight of fire and the noise was like nothing any of the SAS had heard before. Soldiers took shelter in whatever cover there was from the racket of bullets and explosions all around them.

Lance Corporal Taff Thomas from Jibjat was BATT commander with Red Company. He now ran forward to where the leading GPMG gunners were lying and shook them to start firing, but the men just lay there paralysed. After some seconds, he and the other three BATT men grabbed a machine-gun apiece and began to return the fire. Then, leaving the others to keep the machine-guns firing, Thomas ran back to company headquarters, led the 60-mm mortar team forward to where they had a good view of the enemy and gave them fire directions. After the first shock, many SAF soldiers had started to shoot back as well now, while the continuous crackling of fire to the north-west showed that the Red Company platoon on the hillock were giving as good as they got.

Even now, after several minutes, the only information to reach battalion headquarters in a coherent form was coming from Watson's signaller, since Thomas's BATT were too busy fighting their battle to talk. The signaller's voice sounded controlled and steady. He was difficult at times to hear above the din, but he could just be made out to ask for immediate mortar fire which he would adjust and direct on to the hillside. Watson, meanwhile, decided to move back to under cover of Red Company's hill, but first he noticed a line of adoo, in single file, creeping their way around the back of the Red Company platoon on the hillock. He shouted out an order and the four men fired together in a vicious volley. Three adoo dropped dead and the remainder dived for cover, their outflanking manoeuvre finished. Watson then withdrew his BATT back across the open ground, using fire and manoeuvre in pairs, until he was in the safer cover of the hill. It was a textbook action.

Trant found himself in the position that faces every commander when he is separated from his troops in action: to go forward or not? It is a stomach-knotting question. You always fear the worst and the temptation to go forward is very strong, and indeed it is sometimes right to do so. At battalion headquarters, however, Trant could still influence decisions; forward he could not. He decided to remain where he was and sent Sergeant Jim Takajasi, his second-in-command for this operation, forward to co-ordinate all BATT action.

The battle was still raging when Takajasi arrived at Red Company headquarters. Cautiously, he edged forward on his stomach to a position from where he could see. Bullets snapped and cracked overhead, but they worried him less than the sight that met him. Lance Corporal Thomas was standing on a rock in full view of the enemy, taking slow cool pot-shots from the shoulder.

'For God's sake get down, Taff,' Takajasi shouted, and he had to continue to shout until at last he saw Thomas drop down behind a rock. His example, however, had done its work and a steady crackle of returning fire was now being directed at the enemy. Takajasi took stock. Something was missing. Then he realized that although the SAF mortars were raising clouds of black smoke on the far hill, he could not see any shell bursts. He spotted the FOO in his trench and shouted down fire control orders to him to relay to the guns. Next he asked Trant by radio for immediate jet cover. Ironically it was nearly his undoing. The first air strike came in only minutes later, but it was one of those mistakes of war which happen in the best regulated campaigns. The pilot misunderstood his directions and strafed company headquarters instead. Fortunately only one soldier was hit but Takajasi was almost the second; his smock was pierced by two bullets.

At last, with artillery, mortar, machine-guns and air support pounding the enemy, SAF's fire superiority began to tell. The adoo's fire slackened and gradually died away until only sporadic bursts were coming back. Takajasi moved down on to the clearing and with the other BATT men and SAF volunteers, began to recover the wounded. It was still dangerous and sudden flurries of shooting often forced the rescuers to take cover. Many acts of gallantry were performed during the next 20 minutes. Captain David Mason of Red Company ran, ducking and weaving among the bullets to the far side of the clearing to recover his friend, the seriously wounded FOO of Two Company. Having brought him back into cover, Mason set off again alone to try to bring in the Company Commander's body, but even he could make no progress against the scattered but still accurate adoo fire into the clearing. A sniper cracked close by as Takajasi and three SAF soldiers were carrying his third wounded man back on a groundsheet: the three promptly dropped their unfortunate comrade and took to their heels, leaving the huge Fijian to stagger the last hundred yards carrying the man across his shoulders.

Finally, only the dead were left behind, all wounded and weapons had been recovered, and the dismal column began the return journey to Point 985, passing through a firm base formed by the rear company and firqat. As the last man passed through, from the direction of the clearing came what Trant described as 'The saddest sound I have ever heard'; the sharp reports of Kalashnikovs as the adoo walked about the battlefield shooting into the bodies. Incensed, Trant called for ten rounds rapid mortar fire from all tubes, mixed high explosives and phosphorous. Every man in the column glanced backwards in a moment of satisfaction as the clearing erupted in black and white smoke, flame and shrapnel. There was no more shooting, but it was a shaken battalion who returned to Point 985 that night.

The following day passed in building sangars and flying in defence stores and reserve ammunition. Trip-wire and claymore mines had to be laid out in front and fields of fire had to be cut, stacking the bushes right in front of the sangar, so that anyone approaching had to cross the open ground and still could not see the sangar behind its wall of thorns.

As soon as the news of the SAS casualties during the seizure of Point 985 reached me, I had flown out from England and I arrived on the position at dawn next morning by helicopter with Akehurst. While he went off to talk to the SAF, I did the same with the SAS. The events of the day were still very confused. Trant gathered all the SAS men together around a little model of the ground built of earth and stones and bits of stick, and I listened carefully to each man's account. In battle each individual tends to remember vividly the events around him at the expense of the overall picture, but gradually, after two hours of listening and cross-questioning, the facts emerged.

It had been a bloody repulse and Akehurst was concerned lest the Arab troops' morale broke altogether. There could be no question of withdrawal. That would give Radio Aden far too much satisfaction, but what to do next without incurring further losses? An SAS trooper suggested the next step: the adoo were too strong for a frontal attack, so why not shoot them out of it?

The ridge extended southwards to a hillock of huge broken boulders, nicknamed Stonehenge. From there SAF could dominate the so-called 'Freedom Road' running up to Shershitti and they should be able to see the caves themselves. The range would be about 3500 yards, well within the capability of heavy weapons and I suggested to Akehurst that a 25-pounder would serve admirably.

First, however, Stonehenge had to be taken and this was done without loss, whilst two BATT heavy machine-guns were being flown in. They would be at maximum range at Stonehenge, so that night one of the guns and ammunition, together with a large night-viewing device, were loaded on to donkeys and a patrol set out east from Point 985 down towards Shershitti. Carefully, a spot was selected which looked on to the caves, the telescope was set up and the gun unslung. Only then was it discovered that the gun's back-plate was missing; it must have dropped off on the journey through the bush. This meant that the patrol was well within range of the adoo' s heavy machine-guns, but had nothing to reach the adoo itself. It was too late to return before dawn next morning and it was a very quiet patrol who settled down for the night.

The following day was more successful, with the arrival of two 106-mm recoilless guns borrowed from the Iranians; the 25-pounder had proved too heavy. These guns were placed on Stonehenge and spent the next five days firing directly into the caves by day and night, whilst the firqat swarmed down into the lower ground to the south-west to talk to civilians and to recover a large adoo ammunition dump. During this time a bulldozer was trundled down off the *gatn* and a track driven through the bush to allow a Saladin armoured car to reach Stonehenge, from where its big gun could fire shells right into the caves' entrances. But no further attempt was made to capture the caves by assault. Finally, having mined the Freedom Road, the SAF, together with the BATT and firqat, withdrew from the Shershitti area on 19th January.

Further east, the Iranians were being far more successful than on their first attempt. Using fresh troops, and with many of the adoo drawn to the protection of Shershitti, they had worked their way down the escarpment towards Rakyut. The almost continual rumble of their fire support from warships, artillery and armed helicopters could be clearly heard by the SAF at Shershitti ten miles away. Rakyut was seized and soon a series of positions were established from there up to the *gatn*. A new line had begun – the Demavend Line.

By no means could the operation be called a success, and yet it was not a total failure either. True, the attack on the caves had been disastrous and it could quite easily have become a rout. The battalion had suffered heavy casualties, but the adoo had lost many men also, and once the guns were established at Stonehenge the adoo just had to sit in their caves and take it; there was nothing they could do to retaliate and there are few things worse for morale than that. But the main effect of the Shershitti operation, as we shall see, was not apparent until almost a year later.

★   ★   ★

The next six months were a period of remarkable progress on both the military and civil fronts. The wiring and mining of the Demavend Line was completed by May and after the Frontier Force's success against the 9th of June Regiment in February, the Hornbeam Line received no further incomers. The last crossing of the Line in strength had taken place in October 1974. This had involved the adoo in quite a large operation to get men through and even then the crossing was identified so quickly and the crossing party harassed so effectively that 20 per cent of them came over to the Government soon after their arrival in the Central Area

Within days of its capture, Rakyut was visited by Wali Baraik and the town began to attract civilians to it once more, albeit in small numbers because they still had to run the gauntlet of the Iranians. It was not until a SAF unit took control of the southernmost picket and an SAS Civil Action Team was put into the town that the numbers began to increase significantly. Within days, Robb's Civil Aid Department brought in a landing craft load of relief stores for the refugees and building materials to begin the restoration of the houses.

He had also acquired two ex-SAF three-ton trucks, which he had painted bright yellow and which were intended to be used to shift the heavy stores about the town. The first one drove off the landing craft's ramp and promptly bogged down in the sand. The second managed to reach the land, but in its efforts to retrieve the first, also bogged down, and there they stayed until the tide rose over their cabs. That evening the SAS Civil Action Team's report read 'What is yellow, has four wheels and lives underwater? A CAD three-tonner!'

It was a good-natured jibe because the speed with which CAD had brought relief to Rakyut was impressive and had a major effect upon people accustomed to procrastination from any form of authority. Civil Aid was rapidly becoming one of the success stories of the Dhofar War. By June, 35 water wells had been drilled, 155 miles of motorable track linked the various jebel positions, and a new, graded modern highway had been built to replace the old tortuous Midway Road. The 21 firqats now contained 1600 men dispersed over 26 different locations, in each of which CAD had set up Civil Aid Teams. Medical and teaching facilities had improved greatly, with Egyptian, Lebanese and Jordanian teachers and nurses being brought in from abroad. I visited many of these people and was always amazed at their dedication. Many of them had come from reasonably affluent backgrounds and now found themselves in isolated and primitive living conditions, yet they set about their work with the enthusiasm of vocation.

As the war moved westwards, so did the BATT, handing over their positions in the east to the SAF, Firqat Forces and the Civil Aid Department, and setting up new firqats and new medical centres as they went, but in June an unusual request for BATT help arose off the jebel altogether, in the five islands of the Kuria Muria group which lie some 25 miles off the coast opposite Hasik, the next town east from Sudh. The islands have a strange history. In 1853 a British sea captain discovered guano there; it was a time when guano fetched high prices as a fertiliser. Britain asked the then ruler, Sultan Said Bin Sultan to cede or sell the island to Britain, but instead Sultan Said insisted on presenting them to Queen Victoria as a gift. The guano was removed the following year and with it the one source of wealth the island had ever had. They lapsed into obscurity once more until they were included as part of the Aden Colony in 1937. Then, in 1967, shortly before Britain withdrew from Aden, they were handed back to the Sultanate of Oman.

Only the one island, Al Hallaniyah, was populated and in May 83 people lived there; by June 16 of them had died, including all the babies except one and most of the old people. Robb asked if BATT could send a team to look at the problem for him.

It was a strong little team who met in the BATT operations room at Um Al Gwarif. All four spoke Arabic and were medically trained, and like the leader, Corporal Wally Warwick, two of the others had lived amongst Arabs on their own in primitive conditions before. They were tasked first and foremost to bring immediate medical help to the islanders. Having done that, they were to carry out a census, examine and report on the food and water problems on the island, improve the airstrip to enable Skyvans to land on it, and to report generally on the materials needed to improve the islanders' standard of living.

Two days later, on 23rd June, the team landed by helicopter at Al Hallaniyah. To their surprise, they were not immediately surrounded as they had expected. The reason, they discovered later, was that the last doctor to visit had refused to allow the islanders near him in case he contracted their diseases and had flown away again after an hour. But as soon as the islanders saw the team unloading their tents and realized that the BATT men were there to stay, and also discovered that they would not be treated as pariahs, they bustled forward cheerfully to help erect the two tents, one for the team to sleep in and the other to serve as a clinic.

Medical inspections began immediately, at the clinic for those who could walk or at home for the bedridden under the watchful eye of the headman, Abdul Aziz. Abdul Aziz was a young man and, in comparison with the other villagers, he was in good health. He was tall and slim with clean features and clear eyes and his sparkling white clothes contrasted all the more with the grubby rags of the remainder. But the islanders' privations and the deaths of the last month had made him prematurely grave beyond his years. His smile was the bleak smile of despair.

As they walked around the village he explained the problems to Warwick. He was an intelligent man, although he had had only a limited education, but he could partly read and write and he knew about the war. He knew too, of the civil development going on in Dhofar and was understandably jealous, but he was under no illusions about the scale of development the islanders were likely to receive. Nonetheless, he had problems not shared by any other inhabitants of Dhofar, he pointed out, the problems caused by the two monsoons, the *khareef* from the southwest and the *shimaal* from the north-east. During rough weather it was impossible to leave the islands; food became scarce and since they could not get out in their boats to fish, they had to rely on fish traps in the shallow water. They could not radio to the mainland – there was no radio – so if an epidemic broke out or if the one fresh water well on the island became polluted, the entire population could perish without the mainland even knowing.

The team became ever more impressed by the stoicism and good-natured generosity of the islanders. The SAS men had brought in extra food with them for distribution amongst the people; now in return they were offered the pathetic savings of the islanders. Killing a chicken was a feast; there were, after all, only six on the island. The islanders owned thirty-five domestic goats and about a hundred wild ones roamed the low hills, but they had only two rifles to shoot them with, and one of these had a bullet stuck in the breech. The only animals which seemed to thrive, the team noted, were cats which fed on the scraps of fish.

Perhaps the creature to arouse the team' s sympathy most was the island's donkey. This lonely, overworked animal was the sole means of transport. Robb had offered to supply another one, or two if they were needed, but Abdul Aziz had sadly declined, pointing out that the island's fodder was barely enough to support the one beast they had. Every morning at dawn all the men and youths set off for the island's well, accompanied by the donkey. The men carried tins and the donkey two jerrycans. The well lay a brisk three-quarters of an hour's walk away to the south-west and to Warwick's mind was not really a well at all, more a seepage in a hole in the sand; it was no more than two feet wide by eighteen inches deep. He helped the islanders to fill the tins and jerrycans from the one small tin reserved for the purpose and then returned with them to the village. The whole trip had taken two and a half hours. The donkey was unloaded and then set off again. So it continued until enough water had been collected for the 67 people of the village to last the day. Warwick suggested moving the village to the water supply but Abdul Aziz pointed out that the south-west was too exposed for boat operations; they might then have water, but they would have no food.

Fish, turtles and occasionally the luxury of turtle's eggs, formed the staple diet. The islanders often caught more than they needed but when Warwick asked about trading fish in exchange for rice and flour, Abdul Aziz reminded him that the only towns within reach on the mainland, Mirbat, Sudh and Hasik, were themselves fishing towns. The islanders' only source of food, other than what they caught, was that provided by CAD. There appeared to be no easy solution.

The BATT quickly settled into a routine. Two men worked on the airstrip whilst two ran the clinic. From time to time villagers came out to the airstrip to help, but a lifetime of malnutrition prevented their working for more than two hours a day, even the strongest. The medics made quick progress. Most of the islanders had never received proper medical treatment in their lives and the drugs, antibiotics and vitamins their bodies now enjoyed began to produce results within a week.

Women were the hardest to treat for several reasons: whereas at least fishing and fetching of water gave the menfolk exercise and fresh air, the women tended to stay in their houses, where hygiene was appalling; what good food there was tended to go to the males of the household; and finally, the women would not allow themselves to be touched by a male medic. Nonetheless, a general across-the-board treatment of iron, vitamins, antibiotics and anti-tubercular drugs in tablet and syrup form performed wonders, and one or two even accepted injections of streptomycin.

The islanders' living conditions were grim. Trees did not exist, so houses were built of rock and driftwood with roofs of seaweed. The single living room usually contained a bed for the man and his wife, but the children lay on mattresses of seaweed on the floor. The women cooked in a separate little room or in the open, throwing the offal and fish heads over the walls for the cats and flies. And flies were everywhere. Fortunately Abdul Aziz was intelligent enough to see the point of Warwick's advice about airing the bedding and regular washing and disposal of rubbish, but without new buildings whatever was achieved would be a temporary respite. That much was obvious.

The islanders' response was embarrassing in its generosity. Every morning fresh eggs, probably the only ones laid that day, were brought to the BATT tent. The SAS men remonstrated with Abdul Aziz about taking the islanders' food, but he was adamant that they would be dishonoured if the team did not accept what little they had to give.

Finally, their tasks accomplished, the time came for the team to return to the mainland. They left behind a people in very much better health and better prepared to stay healthy. More important, they returned with a full reconnaissance report and recommendations. Only two alternatives made sense, Warwick said; either the Kuria Murias must be set up properly with maximum help from the Government, or the population should be rehoused and rehabilitated on the mainland.

A year later there were 20 new houses, a clinic, a village hall, a school, a mosque and a radio room on Al Hallaniya. A new site for water was found nearer the village, a proper well was constructed, and more chickens were introduced. By then too, the Flying Doctor service had been established and the Kuria Murias, like 37 other Government Centres, received a weekly visit.

And to the great satisfaction of Corporal Wally Warwick and his three SAS soldiers, a Landrover was flown in to replace the lonely donkey at last. It would make a happy ending to say that it retired and lived happily ever after, but that was not to be. The donkey was eaten. Life was hard in the Kuria Murias.

THIRTEEN

THE BEGINNING OF THE END

By the time the Kuria Muria operation took place, no doubt existed in anyone's mind about the outcome of the war. It was not a question of whether the war would be won, but of when and how it would be won. In the Central Area, the second firqat position into the remaining adoo-controlled area, pivoting upon Zeak, had been put in and the third was planned. It would need only one more to complete the square.

The future of the firqats was a nettle that had never been properly grasped, but now that the end of the war was in sight, it could not be ignored any longer. The spectre of 2000 well-armed, battle experienced and politically-aware firqat uniting against the Government was a worrying one. While they had been busy fighting the adoo, the firqats were content, but already many firqats had cleared their areas. What would happen then? It was, in miniature, the problem which had faced governments and kings throughout history – how to turn swords into ploughshares, only this time it was exacerbated by having soldiers with no interest in ploughing. Manual labour they considered demeaning. Certainly something had to be done; some plans had to be laid.

It seemed to me that there were two reasons why the firqats might become restless: first, from boredom, and second, from disenchantment with the speed and scope of civil development on the jebel. I did not see a major uprising taking place, which was worrying some people both in Dhofar and Muscat, as my experience with the Firqat Salahadin had suggested that it would take a very strong force indeed to unite the firqats against the Government. More likely was a gradual dissatisfaction amongst the firqats themselves, leading to the settling of old blood feuds, to private accommodations with the remaining adoo to live and let live, or possibly a fight between one firqat and another, or even between groups of firqats.

The slowness of civil development was largely due to lack of money, and the situation was not helped by a report produced by two eminent administrators brought in from overseas to study the problems of development on the jebel. They concluded that there was no point in building houses for the firqat because they were nomads, which was of course quite wrong. The Jebelis had been forced to follow a nomadic life in the past, moving between plateau and wadi, because of the problem of water. It was not from choice. Given a permanent source of water, the people would remain in one small area. The report was, nonetheless, eagerly seized upon in financial circles and it took some time before the damage could be repaired.

Akehurst saw the matter clearest. The firqat needed houses, but let them build their own, he said. What money there was should be spent on roads. Hard-top the roads to allow the materials to reach the jebel and the firqats would soon build their own houses. They had more than enough money to do so. And if each man built his own house to his own specifications he would stop bickering.

The firqat leaders were showing a remarkable maturity. The one thing they had wanted most was year-round water, and this they now had; every firqat position had its own well and pump. For the rest, they were prepared to wait and, knowing the value they put on their water, I could not see them being prepared to sacrifice it by turning against the Government.

Boredom would be the problem. To counter it, I recommended that the firqats should be split into two, along the lines of the adoo hard-core People's Army and the soft-core militia. It was a split the ex-adoo firqatmen would understand. The hard-core would comprise the top ten or so men of each firqat. They would be properly disciplined, trained, uniformed and armed, rather like the old Trucial Oman Scouts, to form a multi-tribal armed police force to patrol the jebel. Only in such a disciplined unit could the ties of tribalism be cut, just as they had been in the Dhofari squadron of the Scouts. The remainder of the firqats would remain as they were, an armed militia responsible for the security of their tribal grounds. The whole, I recommended, should cease to be second-class citizens of SAF and come under the direct control of Wali Dhofar, Sheikh Baraik. Once a month or so, the firqats would be raised, I suggested, at a rifle meeting, with ammunition to be supplied by the

Government. All firqatmen love to shoot and it would be sure to attract them. After the meeting, they would be paid their retainers, a cow would be killed and the ensuing meal together would give them a good chance to air their grievances and to receive the Government message from the *Wali*'s representative.

It might have worked, but the idea was never implemented and, after the war was won, the chance of making it work receded. By then, the firqat leaders had power, money and prestige. They controlled everything that went on in their tribal areas. Why should they abandon all that for the discomfort of a disciplined unit? Nor would they provide younger men for such a force, as they needed the young fighting men for their own power-base.

In the end, the firqats did what everyone hoped they would do: they destroyed their power themselves. As the war receded, so did the unifying force that had brought them together. The firqats began to break into their sub-tribal groups, then into sub-sub-tribal groups and eventually into family groups of ten or twelve men only. However, that still lay in the future.

The second problem that concerned me was the next step to take in the west, and I thought a trip to the Simba position had given me the answer. It was my first visit to Sarfait because, until this stage of the war, the SAS had been forbidden to approach so close to the border with PDRY. The first thing to strike me was its size. It was a huge position, in the shape of a U, with each bar of the U three thousand yards long. Behind it, to the north, lay the beginning of the huge Wadi Sayq which ran off eastwards down to the sea 14 miles away, its great stark walls rising perpendicularly in places for 1500 feet from the wadi bed. The open arms of the U faced north-east and from between them the much smaller Wadi Sarfait hooked its way around to the south.

I stood on the edge of the escarpment at the front of the position and looked down. The cliff in front fell away for a sheer drop of a thousand feet to the first of the escarpment steps leading down to the sea. This first step ran for 2000 yards before it dropped away out of sight, but before that rose a prominent rocky hill nicknamed Capstan. It reminded me of the Stonehenge position at Shershitti. Like Stonehenge also, it dominated the Freedom Road, which lay between Capstan and where I stood, a dusty single track long since unused. In the past, the adoo had driven vehicles along it, before offloading on to camels at the Sarfait waterhole for the long journey eastwards through Shershitti to the next main stores area in the Wadi Nahiz.

It was easy to see now why the Simba position had been unable to stop adoo re-supply trains; everything beyond Capstan was in dead ground. The adoo could move a division past Simba without anyone being the wiser, and unfortunately Capstan was too isolated to be occupied as part of the Simba position.

The battalion was well spread out along the crest of the U in sangars. These were sturdily built and capable of standing up against anything other than a direct hit from the 122-mm Katyusha rockets or the 85-mm artillery shells that were fired regularly at the position from across the border in PDRY. The chances of a direct hit were fortunately remote since the adoo could not see what they were shooting at, but with a hundred shells a day landing on Simba, it was inevitable that from time to time somebody got hurt. It was an unenviable position to be in. True, it was impregnable from assault, but the same lack of routes up made it easy for the adoo to deny SAF routes down. Only two existed, one directly from the front of the cliff, where a steep wadi could be made to provide a route with some engineer help, or out of the back of the position along the Wadi Sarfait. Both routes, needless to say, were heavily mined by the adoo, and so there the battalion stayed, bottled up, waiting to be shelled. The amazing thing was that morale seemed as high as it did.

The position held a good firqat, the Southern Mahra, and the SAF Commanding Officer spoke highly of them, but they felt caged in. From time to time, they overcame their frustration by patrolling out to the north, but they were unable to get down to the civilians since they all lived in the fertile areas to the south and east. And yet this was a war for people. Somehow, the firqat had to be given the opportunity to get amongst people and spread the Government message.

The Western Area was nowhere near as densely populated as the plateau of the Central and Eastern Areas, but nonetheless it held a fair-sized population and these were in a sorry plight. They could not come across to the Government or provide information about the adoo, even if they wanted to. If they tried to come into Simba, they stood to be blown up on an adoo mine, and if they managed to run the long gauntlet of the adoo-controlled area to the Demavend Line and tried to reach Rakyut, they stood a fair chance of being shot, either by the adoo as deserters or by the Iranians in mistake. If they stayed where they were, particularly if they had camels, they were likely to be shot up by SOAF.

Akehurst, I knew, was anxious to maintain the initiative and momentum of SAF operations during the monsoon, which was almost upon us. I therefore proposed that SAF should establish a position during the monsoon on the *gatn,* where it would not be permanently enshrouded in mist, near Defa, in the same area used to mount the Shershitti operation. The aim would be to provide a firm base from which the firqats could patrol south into the populated areas. I left the idea with the squadron commander whilst I went out on patrol and told him to sound out the Brigadier. To my surprise a signal reached me the following evening to say that Akehurst had accepted the idea with alacrity. It was not until four months later, when he told me his plan for the final operation, that the reason became clear. The new position, besides allowing scope for the firqat, would provide just the diversion he wanted.

★   ★   ★

15th September 1975
Sergeant Rover Walker and Corporal Danny Bell did not think much of Defa. They were an inseparable pair, both in their thirties. Walker was one of the top free-fall parachutists in the Regiment. He had been a tearaway in his youth, but maturity, responsibility and marriage had sobered him down into a formidable senior NCO. He was a tall, brown-haired man with a slight stoop and like many SAS he had grown a long Victorian moustache, which made his lopsided grin even more menacing than normal.

Bell was slightly shorter, but still a big man. He held the rank of corporal in the SAS, having turned down an appointment as sergeant-major in the Royal Signals. He also sported a moustache, but his was more of the Old Bill model and ginger red, like his hair. Like many Scotsmen in the SAS, his Arabic was fluent.

Like Saul and Jonathan, Danny and Rover were not divided; you never saw one without the other. Not that an outside observer would always recognize their association as friendship, for much of their time was spent arguing. They were both total professional soldiers and both had minds of their own: one man would suggest something, the other would oppose it on principle. Consequently you knew that every idea they produced had been examined from several angles and, by the time it came to maturity, it was always sound and often highly unconventional.

Defa was a strong position, they both agreed, and the support was

217

good – a company of SAF, a troop of Saladin armoured cars and a pair of 25-lb guns. It was a pity most of the firqat had refused to fight during Ramadan, but there were one or two about, and besides, they had a whole SAS troop there. But something, they decided, had to be done about the Katyushas. Now that they had been in position for three weeks, they were used to being pounded, but it did not make it any more pleasant. Much of the time they were protected by the monsoon mist, but whenever it lifted, particularly whenever they could see Zakhir Tree – BLAM – in came another Katyusha. The launcher's observer, and perhaps the launcher itself, must be somewhere near that tree. Why not go out and see? They decided to talk to the troop commander.

Captain Charles Delius liked the idea. He was a taciturn, freckled man with similar red hair to Bell. A free-faller himself, he had developed a great respect for Walker, who taught him much of what he knew, and for Bell. Now he squatted in his sangar and listened intently as the two men explained their plan. Two firqatmen had said they knew the route to Zakhir Tree, so, despite the mist and the inaccuracy of the maps, they should be able to reach it. Delius would have to clear the operation with Squadron HQ, who he knew were usually adamantly against BATT going out on patrol without at least the same number of firqat, but on this occasion he thought he could swing it. In any case, he agreed something had to be done about that Katyusha. It was not in the SAS way to just sit there like dummies.

The squadron commander sympathised. Nonetheless, it was too far to go without some form of support, he directed. He would give permission, provided a support base went out with them, to consist of a platoon with a FOO to control artillery fire and the troop of three armoured cars. That way, if things went wrong, the SAS would not have so far to withdraw or, alternatively, the armoured cars could come forward to get them out of trouble.

At 0400 hours on 19th September, 13 SAS and two firqat guides slipped out, past the silent prone men of the covering platoon of Northern Frontier Regiment and the solid reassuring shapes of the armoured cars, into the night. It was a dark night and the thick mist cut visibility down even further, so each man had to concentrate hard to see even the back of the man in front of him only three yards away.

For an hour the patrol moved carefully south-westward, stopping frequently to check their bearings, but when the hour was up, Walker had become very uneasy about the route. It seemed to have meandered all over the place. He halted the patrol and quietly asked each of the guides to point out where he thought Zakhir Tree was. The two men stood back to back, like Tweedledum and Tweedledee, and pointed in exactly opposite directions. Walker raised his eyebrows to heaven. Very well, could they find the village of Omboroff, he asked. This time the two men pointed in much the same direction, so again the patrol moved off and in ten minutes, to Walker's relief, reached the rubble of the ruined village. Here he took a bearing from the map to take them to the tree, and the patrol set off towards the south-east.

Zakhir Tree, he knew, stood on the edge of a spur and the ground did not begin to fall away until you had passed the tree, but now, after a further ten minutes walk, the ground already began to fall away in front of them. Something was wrong. The patrol lay down in a circle, with everyone facing outwards, while Walker and Delius studied their maps by the light of their carefully shaded torches. There was only one thing for it – they were on the wrong ridge. In fact, unbeknown to them, the map location of Omboroff was nearly a thousand yards out. The patrol had come down the ridge slightly west of Zakhir. They were nonetheless in the right area, Delius and Walker deduced, for in front of them lay the beginning of a wadi running north to south; this must be the one immediately west of Zakhir. So, whilst Delius remained with his protection party of six men on the spur, Walker, Bell, the remaining five SAS and the two firqatmen dropped off the ridge for a further 200 yards to lower ground, from where they could look down into the wadi.

Walker checked his watch: 0545 hours, just beginning to get light. The mist lay still thick but swirling, clamping down to nothing one minute and suddenly clearing for up to 200 yards the next. During one of these clear periods, Walker realized that their position was tactically untenable and moved his patrol a further 200 yards to the north-east, right on to the edge of the main wadi. At the same time, Bell offered to take one of the firqat to look for Zakhir Tree so that they could fix their position exactly.

The two men moved carefully across the low wadi and up the gentle climb to the ridge on the other side. Bell sniffed.

'Do you smell meat, O Brother?'

The firqatman shook his head. Bell shrugged and the two men walked forward a few more paces. Both of them saw the footmarks in the soft soil simultaneously; the edges were sharply etched and the sides of the imprints still damp. Four or five men had passed from south to north minutes before. The smell of drying meat became stronger and now the firqatman could smell it too. He touched Bell's elbow and with wide eyes beckoned to him to retrace their steps, but Bell was curious. Cautiously, his rifle at the ready, he crept forward into the mist and in the next ten minutes found several more paths, all well trodden. The firqatman was now very nervous, clutching at Bell's shirt-tail and appealing mutely to him to go back. Suddenly the mist cleared for a few seconds and there only 50 yards away stood the Zakhir Tree, before the mist closed as quickly as it had lifted. Satisfied, Bell took another bearing with his compass and led the firqatman back westwards down into the wadi and up the slight rise, back to where the patrol were lying.

Walker was annoyed. Neither he nor Delius could get any response over the radio from the SAF covering platoon a thousand yards to the north. They were a good platoon with a first-rate platoon commander, so he was sure it was not their fault. The sets had been all right when they checked them before leaving, so the patrol was probably in too low ground: they would have to move up a little.

Whilst Walker was fuming over the set, Bell's eye was caught by a movement above them. A man was walking through the mist, parallel to the wadi northwards, towards the protection party. He carried his rifle slung over his shoulder, but the mist and the fact that he was seventy yards away prevented a firm identification. The man disappeared. Walker clicked on the radio.

'Boss, have you anyone forward of you?' he whispered.

'Nobody,' came the low reply

'Then I think you've got visitors,' Walker whispered.

Delius had scarcely time to pass this news to the other men in his patrol when they heard voices. Three figures appeared out of the mist. Both sides saw each other at the same time but the GPMG gunner fired first and two adoo dropped. The third and another SAS man fired together. The third adoo spun round and fell, but two of his bullets had found their mark, hitting Lance Corporal Geordie Small in the thigh and severing his femoral artery. Small was not a large man and seemed to be in no great pain while he was bandaged and carried up to the high ground, where he sat smoking and chatting whilst they waited for help. Here the radio worked well and, despite a skirmish on the way, the patrol were able to call forward an armoured car to evacuate the wounded man to Defa. Tragically, however, Small's internal haemorrhage was worse than he or anyone else had realised and, by the time the helicopter arrived to fly him back to the FST, he was dead.

Meanwhile down in the wadi, Walker heard the shooting and heard, too, over the radio that Small had been hit. All chance of surprise was now gone and he decided to move north to join the protection group. The route up the western side of the wadi was obviously out, and Bell had reported the eastern ridge as being bare of cover, but he had noticed a small finger-wadi which began just opposite their position and ran off from the main wadi in a north-easterly direction. It would almost certainly lead them straight up to the protection group. Walker passed the word to be ready to move and told the two firqat to stay at the rear as he did not want them mistaken for adoo by Delius's group in the mist. Both men refused point-blank. Safety lay uphill and they wanted to be towards the front.

There was no time to argue and the patrol moved down into the wadi and up to the junction with the finger-wadi. Walker stopped for a few seconds to check his compass bearing, when a sudden burst of fire from the rear crackled amongst them and sent them all diving for cover on either side of the wadi, Walker scrambling up one bank, Bell up the other. The rear two men began to return fire and one shouted out, 'Tony's hit.'

Bell scrambled up the slope as fast as he could to gain height, but the bullets that cracked about him and tore branches off the bushes forced him back down towards the wadi. He had almost run into a bush before he saw the smoke rising from it and he told me that for a second he could not believe the adoo could be so close. Then he fired a burst into the bush and threw himself flat. Every man in the patrol was firing now and to add to the racket the battle had started again up at the protection group. Bell wriggled forward on his stomach into a more or less straight line with the others facing south. The firing was at close range and furious, the wadi resounding with the crackle and whine of bullets breaking up and ricocheting off the rocks. Walker decided to try to bluff the adoo into thinking there were more of them and began to shout instructions to Bell to translate into Arabic.

'Platoon, we are going forward to get our casualties. Number one section right, number two section left, number three section with me. Fix bayonets, Rapiiiiiiid FIRE!'

Each man fired two full magazines non-stop into the bushes in front. Whether as a result of the bluff, the fusillade or both, the adoo fire slackened and Walker and two others were able to scramble forward to where the wounded man lay.

Lance Corporal Tony Fleming was a sergeant major in his parent unit, the Army Physical Training Corps. He was a big muscular man, but now he lay on his back with his eyes closed. From the colour of his face Walker at first thought he was dead, but when he tapped him on the forehead Fleming opened his eyes and smiled weakly. He had been hit in the back, he said, and he could not feel his legs. Still keeping as low as they could, two men began to drag him up the wadi while Walker fired at anything that moved and the GPMGs sent long bursts less than three feet above their heads. An adoo jumped to his feet only ten yards away. Walker dropped him. Movement behind another bush caught his eye, so close that he had to shout out to Bell on his left, who was once again trying to worm forward up on the high ground, to ask whether the man was adoo or BATT.

'How should I know?' shouted Bell. 'Get up and see.'

Walker gingerly stood up and dived flat immediately as the adoo's rounds fanned his face. Bell's Armalite gave an answering burst, and a leg appeared from behind the bush, twitched once or twice and then lay still. The GPMG gunner had also managed to get up higher on the right, and Fleming was, by now, 15 yards up the wadi in the safety of some low rocks. Walker shouted to the others to move back in line. As Bell turned to do so, he spotted movement ten yards away up the hill. He let fly a burst and the man screamed.

Walker crawled back amongst the flying bullets and took another look at Fleming. The medic had already applied a field dressing and he was not bleeding much, but his face was the colour of putty. He lay very still, still as death, thought Walker, with his eyes shut, occasionally opening them to give a weak smile or a feeble thumbs-up. It would kill him to move him and, in any case, it would take four men to carry his fifteen stone. Walker picked up the radio and explained the situation to Delius: they would stay in their present position and fight to the end or until SAF could rescue them, whichever came first.

Delius had not been wasting time and mortar bombs and 5.5-inch shells had already begun to land up the western ridge and in the wadi to the south. Walker could not see where they were landing because of the mist, but they did not seem to be having much effect on the adoo's fire. 'Drop five hundred,' he radioed.

Suddenly, one of the patrol shouted and pointed to the crest. Walker followed with his eyes. He told me he felt a great surge of relief. Coming down the hill towards them from the west, in extended order like a scene from an instructional film, a line of troops was advancing. They wore the SAF's olive green, with canvas webbing equipment and green shamags on their heads. In the centre and from his gesticulations obviously the leader, strode a fair-skinned man wearing a peaked cap, apparently a British officer. Walker scrambled to his feet and began to wave his arm over his head. At the same time, one of the adoo hit by Bell earlier started to scream again from behind his bush, and to Walker's horror he saw the remaining firqatman aim at the approaching men. Bell leapt at him and grabbed his rifle, shouting at him to stop firing.

It was not until he saw the adoo raise their weapons to return the fire that Walker realized his mistake. The firqatman had been right. The enemy's fire began to pour into the wadi.

A great hammer seemed to strike Walker an almighty blow on the head. He felt suddenly numb and his knees buckled. He knew he was hit, but something told him he must stay upright at all costs; he must not give way. He pushed himself up to a kneeling position. Another hammer blow knocked him silly. As his wits cleared again, he struggled back up on to his knees once more. The third blow seemed to hit him right in the middle of the chest, and he was thrown flat. He lay for some seconds, staring at the sky, surprised, he told me, to find that he was still alive and listening to the shouts of the others as they, too, reported that they were hit.

The adoo worked their way skilfully forward to within 20 yards. It seemed to Bell that the screaming adoo was directing them, so this time he fired an M79 grenade at him. The bush shivered as the grenade splinters cut through it and the man behind became silent. An arm appeared from behind another bush and a grenade came curving towards him. Bell pressed himself as close to the ground as he could and tensed his body for the pain to come, but although the explosion left his ears ringing, by some miracle he was unhurt. He fired a long burst into the bush.

Men react strangely in battle. I defy anyone to say that his heart does not leap when that first burst rattles out close to him, but thereafter people vary. Some begin to shake with a rage to destroy the enemy: 'battle rage' some call it. Others become unnaturally cool, while some I have seen hunching up their shoulders as they charge as if against the rain. Others lose all fear in a feeling of total invulnerability. No one is really sane in battle. Bell was concerned now that he was using up too much ammunition, so he moved his change lever to single shots. He fired again, but another burst rang out. Disconcerted, he looked at his change lever. It was still on automatic; he had moved his sights instead. Walker, before he was hit, had a stoppage in his rifle. He carried out the right drill, magazine off, cock gun ... but then he threw the still full magazine at the enemy. Trooper Barrow put a tube of morphine into Walker's leg, and when he took it out, the needle was bent. Although the syrette was empty and there was nowhere else the morphine could possibly have gone but into Walker's leg, Barrow was sure that it had not worked, and gave Walker a second dose. Each man found his actions inexplicable afterwards.

The effects of their wounds and the shortage of ammunition caused the volume of the SAS fire to become much weaker now. Conversely, the adoo gained encouragement and theirs increased in intensity. The morphine had begun to have its effect on Walker, and he was feeling supremely confident. He was again hit, this time in the arm, but found that he felt no pain, only a detachment as if he were an impartial observer. He called to Bell to take over command as the drug was making him silly.

He had in fact been shot in the neck, not in the chest as he thought. The bullet had passed right through his neck missing nerves, bone and blood vessels in a thousand-to-one chance, and he was to make a complete recovery.

If their position was serious before, it was now critical and every man in the patrol admitted to me later that he thought they would be over-run, but they had underestimated the casualties the enemy had taken. The increase in the adoo's fire had been to allow them to extricate their wounded and now the adoo began to withdraw. They made a half-hearted attempt to stop the armoured cars moving down the eastern ridge with an RPG 7, and then pulled back. The SAF platoon and the cars put down heavy fire across the wadi into the mist on the western ridge, and moved to where they looked down into Walker's wadi. It was 0845 hours.

Delius's heart was in his mouth as he ran down the hillside into the wadi, and his relief at finding everyone still alive made him shout aloud with delight. Every single man needed medical attention, but it was Walker and Fleming who concerned him most; both lay with their eyes closed. He shook Walker gently.

'Rover, Rover, how do you feel?' he asked anxiously. One eye opened and then closed again. A lazy grin spread over Walker's face.

'It took the cavalry long enough to get here' he said.

Fleming was much worse. He was still conscious, but lay deathly quiet in a severe state of shock. Gentle hands then laid the two seriously injured on to the engine deck of an armoured car and, as carefully as the driver could manage, they were driven back to Defa. Bell sat on the engine deck, cradling Fleming's head in his arms. The wounded man whispered something and the big Scot dropped his head to try to catch what he was saving. He could only just make out the words.

'Danny, I'm going off,' Fleming murmured.

'Tony, you mustn't.' Bell spoke desperately. 'Try to hang on. Think of someone you love or something.'

A faint smile played on the wounded man's lips and his head moved slightly. 'No, not that,' he murmured 'I mean I'm falling off the car.'

FOURTEEN

THE END OF THE BEGINNING

October 1975

As an operation designed to provide a base from which the firqats could patrol into the Western Area, the Defa operation was a flop. The adoo were far too strong and any movement at all out of base was contested fiercely. The only chance of success lay in sallying forth in company strength. The firqats went out occasionally in ones and twos to visit their families but they achieved very little success overall. As a deception operation, however, it was very successful indeed. It would be fair to call both the advance on the Shershitti caves and Walker's patrol defeats for the Government forces, for neither achieved its aim. But the adoo did not see it that way at all and made no attempt to claim them as victories. They had lost many good men in the fighting and the fact that SAF could penetrate so deeply into the Western Area was proof enough to any, who cared to see it, that the Front in Dhofar had very little time left. The Front were worried men and, for the first time, regular PDRY troops were posted into the Western Area. It may well have been these who Walker mistook for SAF.

The build-up of SAF at Defa during the monsoon, following the two battles just mentioned and the Iranian strength in the Demavend Line, was enough to convince the Front that it was from the north-east that the last major SAF operation must come. Even the name of the Defa operation 'Operation *Badree*' meaning 'early', suggested that it was the opening of the big push. Nor could the Front believe that SAF would not make another attempt at the Shershitti caves.

The Front were, in any case, faced with a quandary by the great Wadi Sayq, which bisected their last jebel stronghold. It was far too wide and deep for troops to be able to move rapidly from one side to the other.

226

The adoo north of the wadi could take no part in the battle, should SAF strike south of the wadi, and vice versa. If however, the adoo concentrated all their troops upon one side of the wadi it would mean handing over the ground on the other side – half the Front's remaining terrain – to SAF without a fight. They decided to compromise and split their forces, half on each side of the wadi.

Besides confusing the adoo and deceiving them over the next SAF move, the Defa operation produced two further spin-off advantages. First was the ordnance expended upon it. The adoo were not short of ammunition in the Western Area by any means, but every round, shell and bomb fired at Defa was one less for the final operation. Second, it provoked the adoo into using the Soviet SAM 7 for the first time, and so lost them the strategic surprise its use might have achieved post-monsoon.

Akehurst's plan was quite different from what the adoo supposed. He intended to establish yet another line, the final one, from the *gatn* down to Dhalqut. While the adoo were concentrating about Defa, he intended to fly a battalion by helicopter on to the ridge south of the Wadi Sayq, and then patrol out in all directions from there. As a diversion, the battalion on Simba, the Muscat Regiment, would seize Capstan two days before D-Day.

It was certainly a bold plan and would undoubtedly achieve surprise, but whether it could succeed without heavy losses, I was not so sure. I had unpleasant visions of helicopters being shot down by SAMs into the Wadi Sayq, or troops stranded on the Darra Ridge and unable to walk back because of the adoo or fly back because of the SAMs. After ruminating over the plan for a couple of days, I mentioned my misgivings to Akehurst and to him alone, since it would not do to encourage doubt in the Commander's plan, but he seemed entirely confident that he had enough firepower lined up to hammer any opposition into the ground. The chances of achieving surprise were good. Apart from the move off Simba, deception would be achieved by a small operation east of the Demavend Line, by rumours about an operation to stretch from Simba to the sea, and by confusing leaflet drops.

Lieutenant-Colonel Ian Christie, Commanding Officer of the Muscat Regiment on Simba, was a man of great drive and energy, and he had no stomach for being bottled up on Simba for several months. From the day he arrived, he had been determined to get off the jebel.

Fortunately, he had a number of soldiers from the Beni Riyam tribe, mountain men from the Jebel Akhdar in Northern Oman and adept at creating steps and paths in a country not dissimilar to the Simba Ridge. Christie set them to making a path down the front of the position. It was slow, careful work, both because of the terrain and because of adoo mines, but each day it extended just a little further. Its gradual but steady progress served to attract the adoo's attention as Christie hoped, and frequent RPG attacks were made upon it. Meanwhile, operating only by night, the real route was being prepared down the back of the position along the Wadi Sarfait. He had intended to use this route to mount aggressive patrols down below the Capstan scarp, but now that he knew his part in the final plan, Christie reserved this secret route until he was ready.

The diversionary operation from Simba began on the night of 14th October. The adoo were caught completely on the wrong foot. There was almost no resistance, and Christie decided to reinforce success by pushing more companies through Capstan down to the sea. Almost before anybody realized it, he had created a new line of positions, not yet linked by wire and mines, it was true, but capable of making it a very bloody affair for the adoo to try to move through the line in either direction. The move down had been more successful than anyone had dreamt possible or had the right to dream. In effect, it had made the operation planned for two days later superfluous. There seemed little point in withdrawing the positions Christie had achieved, simply to establish another line further east, which might or might not work. The following day the new CSAF, Major General Ken Perkins, Akehurst and Christie, met on the Simba position. The three conferred together for some minutes, then Perkins and Akehurst broke away and talked alone for a further minute or two. Finally Akehurst strode over to where I was standing.

'Meet your flexible brigadier,' he said with a smile. I made no secret of my pleasure.

The one disadvantage of adopting the Simba Line, as against the one Akehurst had envisaged running down to Dhalqut, was that the PDRY guns at Hauf could range onto it. These now began to be felt as the Front made a frantic effort to dislodge the new positions by artillery. Whereas in July and August less than 30 shells had been fired at Simba, now in October the figure went up to over a thousand and by 16th October there appeared to be a real danger that the adoo would achieve success.

The newly built positions were being pounded heavily, and I saw a number of men running back into dead ground to get away from the shells. SAF had been forbidden to fire back across the border, although there were two 5.5-inch guns on Simba, because of the fear that they would invite retaliation from the huge Soviet 130-mm artillery pieces known to be in the Hauf area, but which had not yet been used. These guns could outrange the 5.5s and it was felt that if PDRY were driven to using them they might simply stand out of range and shell into Dhofar with impunity. The situation on 16th October, nonetheless, was critical. Another day or two like this and the Simba Line would be unlikely to survive. That afternoon, the Sultan ordered a retaliation air strike across the border at selected targets: the artillery positions, the PFLOAG headquarters and the PDRY police post.

The attack went in at dawn. The two headquarters were badly damaged and all but one of the 85-mm guns was destroyed. The morale effect upon the SAF and BATT troops was enormous, and they crowded the forward edge of the ridge to watch with delight as Hauf disappeared in a pall of smoke. At last we were hitting back. But it was a temporary respite and, as it was feared, the 130-mm guns began at last to lob their great shells on to the Simba plateau and the new positions below. Despite retaliation by the 5.5s and again by the Hunters, the Front continued to shell into Dhofar in increasing numbers until December, when almost 1500 incomers were counted.

On 17th October, and timed to coincide with Akehurst's original plan, the Iranians moved forward from the Demavend Line and carried out a helicopter-borne assault on to a ridge west of the line. The ridge looked up into the Shershitti Wadi and the adoo were convinced that this was the beginning of another assault on the caves. They resisted strongly and the Iranians suffered regular bombardment from Katyushas and recoilless artillery. But, just as the adoo's attention had been firmly distracted by the Iranian moves, SAF's Frontier Force, the battalion who were to have carried out the helicopter assault on to the Darra Ridge, began to move forward from Defa along the gatn, down into the tree line and out along the spurs that looked down into the Wadi Sayq, and across to the Darra Ridge, clearing the spurs of adoo as they went.

Confusion now swept through the Front's leadership. Within days, the SAF had advanced upon them from the west, east, and now the north. The adoo were rapidly becoming boxed in. Already the Sultan's Forces held the western flank with the Simba Line, the eastern flank with the Demavend Line and the southern flank with the Sultan's Navy. Now the SAF had begun to move inexorably westwards along the northern flank. The feeling increased amongst the Front leaders that they must get out before the lid closed, and the PDRY leadership became anxious about the international effect of PDRY troops being taken prisoner. First, they ordered the immediate return of all regular PDRY soldiers, and then PFLO, as it had now become, ordered all fighters to withdraw on to the Darra feature south of the Wadi Sayq. These moves achieved only temporary respite: a few more days proved that with their re-supply throttled and with continuous Government operations on all sides, the position was hopeless. A general withdrawal was ordered and, abandoning all their heavy equipment, the remaining adoo made their way out by night through the closing gap between Simba and the approaching Frontier Force, across the top of the Wadi Sayq, around the north of Simba and back into PDRY. Little attempt was made to stop them. A blood-bath would have been in nobody's interest.

Cautiously, scarcely believing that the adoo had gone, the Government forces moved down into the areas in which a short time ago it would have been death to venture. Huge finds of weapons and ammunition, shells, mines and bombs were recovered from Shershitti, 750,000 rounds in one cave alone. Dhalqut was entered on 1st December, and the following day patrols from the Muscat Regiment and the Frontier Force linked up on the Darra Ridge. There could no longer be any doubt about the adoo's total defeat. On 11th December 1975 the Sultan announced publicly that the war was over.

★   ★   ★

Unfortunately, revolutionary wars have a habit of ending less tidily than that, and this one was no exception. In the west it was now possible to walk anywhere you liked with merely a couple of firqatmen for guides, an eerie experience at first, but in the east you did so at your peril. West of the Hornbeam Line not a single adoo remained, but east of it was a different matter altogether. The adoo were down, but by no means out. Despite their lack of re-supply money, and of medical facilities, sizeable gangs of adoo still roamed about the Eastern Area, living as fugitives much of the time, but still with a sting when they wished. Months after the war was officially over, the adoo were still able to lob ten mortar bombs into Tawi Atair to celebrate the 9th June.

The BATT plan had always been to move ever westwards until the war was won and then to fall out and go home, but it gradually became apparent that it was not going to be as easy as that. Two separate problems remained to be solved.

In the west many civilians were in a sad plight. Their natural economy had been ruined by the war and they were living in remote caves where they had fled to seek shelter from the fighting. CAD's facilities were at full stretch and although every effort was being made to bring food and relief stores into the Western Area, the Department needed all the help it could get, particularly medical help. During the final two months of the war, the firqats and BATT had, metaphorically, to take a step back and leave the SAF to get on with it. It had become less a counter-revolutionary war than a straightforward limited war, army against army. SAF had an identifiable enemy and they could set about defeating the adoo by military means; this was what they were best at. Now that the fighting was over, however, it was SAF who had to take the step backward while the firqats and BATT came into their own, patrolling down into the wadis to meet the people and bring the Government's help to them, work which they in their turn were best at.

Second, for the previous six months or more, Akehurst's mind had been mainly occupied, like everyone else's, with operations in the Western Area. The BATT had moved out of the Eastern Area a year before and it was now controlled by a Baluch battalion of SAF. All the Eastern Area's firqats had been handed over to Firqat Forces. In theory, the remaining adoo bands in the east should have found it impossible to survive under the non-stop pursuit of SAF and firqat, and should have withered away, but this had not happened. Information seemed to have dried up altogether in the Eastern Area. The battalion had carried out an energetic policy of searches and sweeps, but it had not produced much in the way of results.

For some time, BATT had also been secretly concerned at some of the stories reaching them from their various sources about the progress of the campaign in the East. An SAF officer had talked casually over a drink about '*bait*-bashing', a term that immediately rang warning bells in SAS minds. He described an operation where his company surrounded a village, threw all the contents of the *baits* outside and then searched them with mine detectors. After they found nothing, they gave the children some sweets, did a little medical work and departed. It was not an experience that can have endeared the Government to the villagers or added to their respect for SAF. The battalion did not use firqat at all if it could be helped, and there seemed to be a dangerous rift developing between the two. On one occasion, the Firqat Al Umri and the SAF troops had faced each other with loaded and cocked weapons. Fortunately, wiser and cooler counsel had prevailed, but it was a sign, nonetheless, of the deterioration in relations.

I went to see the battalion commander in his headquarters on the plain not far from Mamurah. He was a short, dark man, and I took an immediate liking to him. In expression and mannerism, even in his physical build, he reminded me of Watts. He had the same restless energy about him, but it soon became clear that he did not share either Watts's ability to analyse a problem or his deep understanding of counter-revolutionary warfare.

He rose from his desk and walked to the wall opposite covered with a large-scale map of the Eastern Area, and for a good half hour he described to me in detail the operations his battalion had carried out. He had covered his area thoroughly, but still he had not been able to catch the adoo, he said. Partly, he knew, it was because the standard of his Baluch soldiers prevented them from patrolling in less than platoon strength and more often in company strength; the adoo saw and heard them coming from miles away and had no desire to take on the SAF in those sort of numbers. Even so, he conceded, the battalion should not always hit thin air. By the law of averages they should sometimes make contact. He walked back to his chair and sat down at his desk. Suddenly, he banged his fist on the table in anger.

'Intelligence. I'm just not getting intelligence,' he declared.

'Do you use the firqats?' I asked.

'Them!' He looked at me sideways. 'Don't talk to me about *them!*'I wouldn't trust 'em as far as I could throw 'em.'

It all came out: they were untrustworthy, they were in league with the adoo, they were undisciplined, they were cowards ... all the prejudice one had heard in the bad old days of 1971. The attitude of British SAF officers still covered the spectrum; at one end, those like Akehurst and Christie, who fully understood the firqats' limitations, but who fully realized too, in Akehurst's words, 'They are what this war is about. They are the future of Dhofar'; to the other extreme, like this man in front of me. He was, I knew, a superb leader of men, an aggressive and dynamic commander whom his officers and men worshipped – and without a doubt they would reflect his attitude. He was the sort of man who, in a major war, would come back with a chestful of medals. I felt a pang of despair. Did one still have to spell it out, after six years, again, in words of one syllable? Had he not learned a thing?

In February 1976 BATT returned to the Eastern Area and Akehurst issued a flat order to SAF units that all operations would be accompanied by firqat. There was resentment, of course, both from the battalion and curiously, at first, from some of the firqat, who had come to feel that they were being used for SAF's ends. But again Akehurst's phrase, 'Put a BATT with a firqat and you triple their output,' was proved true. It took diplomacy and patience. The BATTs lived right among the firqats once again. Their trust was rekindled, they became more co-operative, intelligence started to flow again, and the SAF started to get results. One by one, the last adoo leaders, mostly from the Bait Gatun tribe, the tribe that had suffered most at the hands of Said Bin Taimur's forces, began to surrender. The last of the four positions to form a square based upon Zeak was put in: Ashenhaib, Shair and now, lastly, Medinat Al San. But, ironically, the last Phase One firqat position of the entire campaign was the most eastern of them all, on the rocky soil between Tawi Atair and Eagle's Nest, where BATT and the firqats had carried out that first operation on to the jebel. This area really was the last refuge of the harassed adoo. It had been passed by and left almost untouched by SAF and Government aid as operations spread gradually westward. Here, even in 1976, the firqat were stoned by village women in a scene more like one from Northern Ireland than Dhofar.

These isolated bands, however, could no longer interfere with the civil development of the province. In the Western Area, the guns of the PDRY regular army ceased their shelling on 5th March and PFLO stopped its own bombardment with recoilless weapons on 30th April. The last obstacle to true peace had been removed. Civil development went on over the following months as fast as funds would allow, with emphasis rightly on the west. 600,000 lb of building materials were lifted by sea and air into Dhalqut alone. By September 29 schools had been erected in Dhofar, nine new Government Centres had been created and 54 boreholes sunk. The firqats now numbered 2500 men and were, at last, handed over to the civil government of Wali Baraik. It is said that the sigh of relief from SAF Headquarters in Muscat could be heard for a mile around.

BATT's job was done. In September 1976 the last SAS squadron left Dhofar for good, after an uninterrupted SAS presence in the theatre of exactly six years.

★ ★ ★

No two campaigns are ever the same; each has its own problems and requires its own way of resolving them. Only one wholly new lesson, I think, came out of the Dhofar War, but perhaps it is worth making observations on some of the principles used and how they were applied to this particular campaign. First of all, and probably most important of all, after Watts's 'fronts' had been accepted, the Government had a clear aim, a clear plan of strategy. The aim was to defeat the Communist rebels in Dhofar so that civil development could take place, and that aim was maintained unswervingly throughout. There was no vacillating, no change of policy with a change of minister, no 'special case', no question of trying to appease PFLO by ceding territory or coming to some form of compromise solution. Similarly, the strategy or plan of campaign was maintained by successive CSAFs and Commanders of the Dhofar Brigade according to the well-proven method of starting in the soft areas and gradually expanding government control into the harder ones.

The lines, Leopard, Hornbeam, Hammer, Demavend and finally even Simba, were created to provide protection for this process of expanding government control. They were patrol bases, from which SAF could extend its influence, and care had to be taken that the troops moved regularly out on patrol from them, for it is always a temptation to sit snugly behind one's wire and fortifications controlling, as T.E. Lawrence said, only the area within range of one's weapons. The lines proved to be extremely successful but the Dhofar campaign cannot claim to be the first to use the idea by any means. Fortified lines were used most effectively in the Boer War.

Next, the system of unified command made the strategy so much easier to maintain its unswerving aim. Whatever the disadvantages of autocratic rule may be, there is much to be said for having one man at the helm in war, particularly if he is a strong man. Sultan Qaboos is a charming man to meet, an impeccable host with a most attractive modest, even gentle, manner, but a man who overthrows his father in a *coup d'état* can be no milksop. The fact remains that when a decision was needed, like the one to carry out a retaliatory strike at Hauf, it was made firmly and quickly.

It was an enormous advantage also to have one commander of all the Sultan's Armed Forces – land, sea and air. It meant that there was one man to decide the allocation of resources and priorities without regard to inter-service bickerings and prejudices.

I have made frequent mention of the magnificent support given to the campaign in general by SOAF and a special relationship seemed to develop between the pilots and BATT. It went without saying that if an SAS patrol was in trouble, SOAF would come and get them out of it if it was humanly possible, and quite often when it appeared not to be.

This account contains very little about the Sultan's Navy, not because they did not play an important part in the campaign, but because, in comparison with the Air Force, their operations had little immediate effect on BATT. Nonetheless, their regular patrolling of the Dhofar coast prevented the adoo from using the sea flank to re-supply their fighters, and the *As Sultana* played an important logistics role in the final operation. She arrived in Dhofar as a general cargo ship, was transformed overnight into a floating airhead and then provided the base from which over a thousand helicopter lifts were flown into the Simba positions.

Bearing in mind the length of the Dhofar coast, it may seem surprising that more use was not made of amphibious operations. There were three reasons for it, I think. Firstly, most of the jebel lies some distance from the sea and is easier to reach across country from the north; it is only most of the Western Area and part of the Eastern Area which have a seaboard; the Central Area has none. Secondly, the surf, which occurs for much of the year, and the lack of suitable landing beaches, discouraged anything other than small patrol operations. And thirdly, and most important of all, the lie of the land is against it. In jebel warfare it is essential to hold the high ground, and any landing at sea level was therefore immediately at a disadvantage. Far better to start from the high ground and work downhill towards the sea.

Counter-revolutionary wars are first and last about people, and, throughout the campaign, the need to gain the support of the people was continually stressed to the soldiers. The seizure of ground was important only if it allowed Government forces to make contact with the people. Without their support guerillas cannot exist, and it was their belief that they had lost this support and the consequent fear of betrayal, rather than the pressure of Government military operations, that caused the adoo to move their heavy weapons out of the Eastern Area as soon as they did. It was this fear, similarly, which caused the remaining bands of adoo in 1976 to move every day to a new position, sometimes two or three times a day. They knew they had lost the support of the people. It was, of course, for this reason that the creation of the firqats was so important.

The SAS have had much experience of dealing with irregular forces, from the Senoi Praak of the Malayan Emergency in the 1950s through to the Border Scouts of the Confrontation with Indonesia in the 1960s, and various irregular and paramilitary forces throughout the world. It is a task for which only a certain sort of soldier is suited and, even within the SAS itself, some are more suited to it than others. The average regular officer or soldier finds dealing with irregulars a frustrating experience because they are anathema to all his military upbringing. He is taught to honour the military virtues of discipline, smartness and self-sacrifice. Irregulars are, for the most part, undisciplined, untidy and selfish.

Firqat Forces recruited a number of firqat liaison officers to run the firqats after BATT had handed them over. Some of these were ex-regular British officers, many of whom had served with British-officered Arab units before. By far and away the best, however, were those firqat liaison officers who had been non-commissioned officers in the SAS. These men joined Firqat Forces not only for the high rates of pay (a captain received the equivalent of a major-general's pay in the British Army), but because they loved the work. There were exceptions, but the firqat liaison officers one met on the jebel with their firqats, as against those propping up a bar in the Mess in Salalah, were almost always ex-SAS.

It takes a great deal of patience, understanding and tolerance to deal with irregulars. Given those qualities, and treated with fair and reasonable firmness, irregulars can become an invaluable adjunct to a regular army. The firqats provided information on the ground, the people and the enemy which could not have been obtained in any other way. Mistakes were made, of course. They could be very good guides and their eyesight was sometimes almost incredible – they could often tell whether a man was adoo, firqat or civilian from thousands of yards away – but they could also lead you astray, either by pretending to know ground they did not, or by misunderstanding where you wanted to go. The Shershitti operation was a case in point. That operation was an example, too, of another misuse of firqats by using them as a screen in advance to contact; they were not good at that sort of conventional tactic. Firqats were best used on operations of their own or with their BATTs within an overall SAF/BATT/firqat plan. The wadi searches of late 1974 and early 1975 were very good examples of this, when SAF provided the fire support and covering parties on the high ground, whilst the firqat and BATT did the actual searching.

The firqats' understanding of ground and their speed of manoeuvre were both superior to SAF troops', but when it came to straight military tactics, the SAF's discipline told every time. The two forces were complementary; neither could have won the war alone.

If the firqats were the most important Government department to be created to win the war, Civil Aid must run them a close second. The Civil Aid Department was, I believe, the one new lesson the Dhofar campaign provided in the study of counter-revolutionary war, yet it came about almost by default. The Dhofar Development Department could not provide aid fast enough to follow in the wake of the rapid SAF successes of 1973–75. The Department was, in any case, undermanned, but civil development is a long-term business. Roads cannot be built nor wells drilled overnight. It takes time. But time was something the Government did not have. If the people were to come across to the Government and give information about the adoo, that information was needed immediately, not six months later. The Government had to be able to demonstrate immediate bounty. So the CAD was created initially to fill a gap. It seldom had an executive staff of more than three or four, but its impact on the war was enormous. CAD's fingers reached into practically every wadi on the jebel before the war was over.

The other Government weapon which played such a major part in gaining the support of the people was information services, and although it was initially set up by BATT before being handed over to the Omani authorities, Arab advisers were used from the very beginning. The BATT might have the technical knowledge and know what needed to be said, but only Arabs knew how to say it in such a way that it would appeal to the Dhofari mind. The literal translations of some of the leaflets seemed unco-ordinated and crude to Western eyes, but leaflets written by Westerners were seen through immediately.

Leaflets were used a great deal. On the one side, a picture or a number of pictures showed simply and graphically what the leaflet was about, and the other side contained an exhortation of some sort for those who could read and write. Sometimes these leaflets were purely vehicles for information about new development projects, showing pictures of people in a new hospital, children at a new school or cattle at a new experimental farm; sometimes they were instructional with, for example, pictures showing the danger to children's eyes from allowing flies to crawl on them, but the purely military leaflets worked on the carrot and stick philosophy, threat and reward, the two basic stimuli of man. The difficulty was to get the proportions of the two correct. Too much threat could harden the resolve of the person being threatened, while too much promise of reward would be despised as Government weakness. The proportions had to vary according to the progress of the campaign, and broadly speaking, the more obviously victorious the Government appeared, the more magnanimous it could afford to be towards the enemy.

Only the Arab mind could interpret for the Western how Dhofaris might think. For example, the incongruous disparity between, say, the luxury of the Sultan's Palace in Salalah with its huge air-conditioned garages and riding stables in comparison with the one-room hovels – euphemistically called 'low-cost housing' – built for firqat families in Salalah, would appear to a Westerner as an immediate cause for disgruntled bitterness amongst the firqat. It was not so. The Arab mind tended to see quite a different picture. The Sultan was a great man and great men should have great palaces. He would be despised if he lived in a modest building. The Dhofaris had not yet succumbed to Western jealousy and desire to bring others down to their own level; their aim was to become rich and powerful themselves. Similarly many Westerners, including myself, were concerned at the danger of a firqat turning against the Government. Some even foresaw a union of all the firqats against the Government. As far as I know, no Arab was worried: *Wali* Baraik was certainly not. It was, again, a case of the Western mind looking at a situation in terms of Western logic, whereas the Arab mind has a wisdom of its own. In retrospect, my paper on the future of the firqats was too neat, too logical. Whatever the final outcome may be, the firqats' future will come about in Arab terms. It will probably not be neat or tidy, but it will be what best suits the Dhofari, and it will work where a Western solution would not.

Because it was a war about people, a counter-revolutionary campaign could not afford to go in for booby-traps designed to kill or maim the enemy. Very little private enterprise was shown and no official support at all given for the sort of thing which goes on in most wars: leaving behind bullets which explode in the breech for the enemy to find and use, poisoning his water supply, booby-trapping dead bodies, etcetera. These are, in any case, measures troops tend to take when they are losing and when they cannot get to grips with the enemy in any other way. Booby-trapping is a recognized form of warfare, but it should have no place in a counter-revolutionary campaign like the Dhofar War. First, there was always the danger that a civilian may suffer instead; blowing up Grandma is not a very good way of gaining the support of most families. Second, the aim was to persuade the adoo to come across to the Government. Blowing one man to pieces, or worse, blowing pieces off one man, may remove an adoo soldier from the enemy's order of battle, but it would harden the resolve of several more. Booby-trapping, in short, was counter-productive. A government cannot use all the means open to the enemy.

Perhaps this partly explains, but only partly, why the Front were able to unite men from different tribes, whilst the Government could not. For the first three years, it was the Front's practice, like the Romans or, for that matter, the British, to post men from one tribal area into another; although towards the end, when they depended upon the support of the people just to survive, they tended to revert to ensuring that the adoo leader came from the area in which he was operating. Our efforts to raise a multi-tribal firqat dissolved with the death of Salim Mubarak. How, then, did the Front manage to overcome tribalism and we did not? Certainly, coercion played a major part. The Front had sanctions open to it that were denied to the Government. If someone refused to go where he was sent, he was shot. When the mutineers from the Firqat Salahadin appeared before *Wali* Baraik for punishment, all he could was to discharge them from the firqat and relieve them of their weapons. But that does not explain it all. It does seem that the Front's teaching that tribalism was reactionary and a brake on progress, struck a chord of sympathy in the minds of many Dhofaris. Yet when the chips were down, these same men returned instinctively to the security of their tribes and their tribal firqats to fight for the Sultan against the very creed so many of them had been attracted towards.

One wonders how many of them ever really were Communists. One thinks of Qartoob's political commissar, Salim Said Dherdhir who surrendered at Sudh, one of the bravest men I have ever met, and who died fighting gallantly for the Sultan. He made that strange remark to Birrell, 'You are a Communist', because Birrell was talking about democracy and the impossibility of establishing it unless people like Dherdhir came across to help to do so, about the rights of man, and the need for the people to have a say in their own future. One thinks again of the political commissar of the adoo firqat defending Shershitti who surrendered during Operation Badree. He walked up on to the road being driven from Manston to Defa by Pakistani civilian contractors and was found sitting patiently alongside it at dawn one day, fully equipped for battle. His appearance had an electric effect on the contractors who reasoned, fairly, that if this man could pass through the geysh protective screen so easily, others might do so for less peaceful purposes, and only the promise of double pay could assuage their terror. He was a fine-looking man. Before becoming commissar of this unit, he had taught political affairs at the Lenin School at Al Ghayda and before that he had been in charge of political broadcasting on Radio Aden. If ever a man was a Communist, it was surely he, but when asked why he had come across to the Government he replied, 'Because you are here – and you could not be here in the West unless the loyal firqats were with you. You would not have any firqats unless the people supported them and you would only have that support if the rumours of progress and development I have heard are true. If they are true, then the Front has told me lies. If they lied on that, they have probably lied on other things. Therefore I have surrendered to you.' It was a brave little speech, but nowhere was there talk of dialectical materialism, the inevitable victory of the proletariat or any other Communist doctrine. He had fought for progress and, since progress seemed to have arrived, he could see no point in continuing to fight.

Even amongst those whose faith in Islam, or their outward profession of it at any rate had been eroded by Communism, tribalism still remained a dominating force and with it the rivalry and feuding between tribes and sub-tribes. A number of old scores were settled, like the murder of the firqat sergeant major at Jibjat, particularly after the adoo had been defeated. An order from Sultan Qaboos as religious head of the nation that feuding was to stop may have had some effect, but still about ten murders were committed between mid-1975 and mid-1976. It was the old men who instigated them. They would 'needle' a young man by reminding him of some murder committed against their family years before and, whenever he passed, they would stroke their chins, the sign for 'shame'. Eventually the young man would become so distraught that he would go out and kill someone from the offending family, and then spend the rest of his life waiting in turn for the retribution that must come.

Said Salim Baraikan, the lieutenant of the picket that carried out the Jibjat murder, explained to me two years later that he was still held responsible by the dead man's family. The murderer fled to the adoo who disarmed him and declared him insane before sending him off to Aden and out of reach. Said Salim, as the senior man, would never be able to return to Jibjat, and his picket eventually set themselves up much further west along the gatn as a separate firqat. Nonetheless, Said told me that he often met the man from the dead man's family, in Salalah or elsewhere, who was tasked to kill him. The man was always friendly and they shook hands whenever they met, but both knew that one day, when the time was ripe, he would try to kill Said.

Tribalism has rightly been called the curse of Arabia, but it is by no means all bad. There is no need for special homes for the weak or elderly in a tribal society. Decisions are reached by consensus and leaders are usually selected democratically. But the problem facing any Arab government in trying to become a modern society must be to preserve the best qualities of tribal society whilst allowing social development to progress across tribal boundaries.

In 1991 I returned to Dhofar together with some 20 other SAS men, as guests of HM Sultan Qaboos. We were looked after royally by the Sultan's Special Forces and travelled the length and breadth of the jebel, visiting old haunts and battlefields, meeting old friends, attending feasts and exchanging news.

The tribal firqats still existed, but the shining example of multi-tribal intergration was our hosts, the Sultan's Special Forces. This was, and is, a highly trained and effective unit of regular soldiers, trained to SAS standards and skills, and drawn from all tribes in Dhofar. The Special Forces' attitudes and discipline are far removed in every way from the caprices of the firqats.

A young Dhofari officer in his immaculately turned-out camouflaged uniform accompanied me on my visit to the *Wali* of Dhofar. The officer spoke perfect English. He was educated, humorous and urbane and would have been at ease in any society. As we passed through the ante-rooms of the *Wali*'s luxurious offices in Salalah, crowded with people waiting for an audience, I noticed a gnarled old sheikh sitting there in working clothes and carrying a camel stick. A look of recognition and delight crossed the officer's face, and he knelt to kiss the old man's hand. The old sheikh in turn, his face wreathed in smiles, took the officer's head in his hands and returned his kiss. I suddenly realised that my companion was as tribally minded as any of the firqatmen I had known, but he had moved beyond tribalism in a way that would have been thought impossible in the 1970s. He was enjoying the best of both worlds.

As we travelled throughout the country, the progress in every respect was plain at every turn. Material progress was manifest in the magnificent highway stretching into the western highlands, the hard-topped roads throughout the jebel and the modern towns. It was strange to find that places I remembered as being bare pieces of jebel, important only for their positions of tactical advantage, and as bases for the firqats, were now flourishing towns of white-walled houses with perimeter roads and street lighting. Where towns existed before, like Mirbat or Rakyut, the old towns have been left and new towns of the same name have been built nearby.

The coastline in the west, before the road runs up into the hills, has become a corniche. The road runs beside an unblemished beach with the magnificent cliffs of the western jebel rising sheer a few hundred metres inland. Along the beach small pavilions have been built at intervals for picnicking families. When I drove along it there was not another person or vehicle in sight. It was a developer's dream, but I was told that the Sultan had forbidden its development because of the effect it would have upon the people and upon the environment. Oh wise ruler!

Education is there for all. Schoolgirls clutching their satchels fled from me as I drove up to their school on the jebel. In fact, I was going to visit the *Wali* of the town, one of the original Firqat Salahadin. He was now a man of substance and I recognised him immediately even though he stood with his back towards me. He faced a group of Jebelis protesting about something or other. I smiled as I heard the word 'ureed...', and reflected that now the boot was on the other foot.

From behind I said 'Peace be with you. How are you, O Mustahail?' He turned round and, just for a split second, his face showed his feelings. 'Oh God, not him as well!', before he recovered and the normal Arab courtesy reasserted itself. I was shown into his office to wait, whilst he dealt with his recalcitrant townsmen.

To pass the time, another SAS man pulled out a battered copy of this book. A young firqatman opened it and looked at the photographs. Slowly, he read out the captions in English and where a name was mentioned he excitedly gave a potted history of the man. This is so-and-so: he was killed on the Jebel Aram. This is such-and-such: he took part in the raid on the Wadi Darbat, and was killed at Tawi Atair. Ah, Salim

Mubarak; he was the first leader of the Firqat Salahadin and died in Mirbat. At length the young firqatman apologised to us for his English. 'Our teachers are Egytian,' he said disparagingly.

I listened amazed, and expressed my astonishment to my escort. This young man spoke and read English, having been only educated at his jebel school, and I told him it spoke worlds for his teachers. He recognised the names of people he was far too young ever to have met.

My escort smiled. 'Our television is still rudimentary,' he said. 'It's not like yours. The tribesman still meet of an evening around the fire and tell stories of the war. You are all part of our history now. These people and the battles they fought; we know of them. They live on.'

Today, the Sultan's Armed Forces are almost entirely Omani and are probably the best-trained and equipped forces in Arabia. The only Europeans remaining, still mostly British, provide the technical and specialist knowledge not yet available in Oman. Problems no doubt there will be. For example, many of the jebel pastures have been eaten out by the number of cattle purchased with the increased wealth of the Dhofaris. The jebel is still green after the khareef but the colour comes from a weed, so fodder has to be grown on the plain and carried up the jebel to the cattle. The population, too, is expanding and employment will have to be found for the young people who are now reaching maturity. But these and their like are problems of success.

★   ★   ★

For the SAS, their return to Dhorar was both a consummation of Operation Storm and a cartharsis. Throughout the visit, the names of friends and comrades, British and Dhofari, who had been killed or maimed during six years of warfare were continually in their minds or on their lips. From time to time I would see someone break away to be on his own for a while and to sit quietly on some rock or hillside with his memories.

It was in a reflective yet contented mood that the little party finally left Oman, expressing their satisfaction at what they had seen and at all that had been achieved. The Secret War had not been fought in vain.

GLOSSARY

Abadan	Never. Much used word of disagreement
adoo	enemy
Ahlan	Welcome
Andover	Two-engined short range transport aircraft
argal	rope worn about the head or head-dress. Originally used to hobble one's camel, it has become a status symbol throughout Arabia
Armalite	The US Army's M16 5.56 mm rifle. Very light, it fires both fully and semi-automatic.
askars	armed tribesmen
ATLO	Air Transport Liaison Officer
bait	house
BATT	British Army Training Team. The name given to the SAS Squadron and its attached personnel. The term was used widely to describe the whole or part of a squadron, particularly for the SAS patrol attached to a firqat, e.g., the Firqat Al Nasr's BATT
boom	dhow. Arab small coaster
CAD	Civil Aid Department
Caribou	Two-engined short range transport aircraft
CAT	Civil Action Team
dead ground	ground out of sight from the viewer's position
firqat	literally 'company' but used to describe the Dhofari irregulars. Like BATT, it became a generic term used to describe all or part of an irregular unit
FOO	Forward Observation Officer. An artillery officer or NCO attached to an infantry or armoured unit to direct artillery fire

245

FST	Field Surgical Team
futa	long kilt
Gemini	Large rubber boat
geysh	army
GPMG	General Purpose Machine Gun. The British version of the FN MAG 7.62 mm machine gun, fully automatic with an adjustable rate of fire. Fired either from a bipod or for greater accuracy from a tripod
Jebel	mountain or hill
Jimpy	British Army slang for the GPMG
Jinn	Ghost, genie
kaid	commander
LZ	Landing Zone
naib wali	assistant governor of a town or district
National	Small, cheap, simple walkie-talkie radio
Point Five	Browning M2 0.50 inch (12.7 mm) heavy machine gun
RCL	Recoilless gun. 75 mm or 82 mm
RPG 7	Soviet recoilless anti tank rocket. Shoulder fired
SAM 7	Soviet shoulder-fired surface-to-air missile
sangar	a circle of rocks built for protection when it is not possible to dig a trench
Sarbe	Surface to Air Rescue Beacon. Small radio used to talk to aircraft from the ground
shaiba	greybeard
Siasi	Sultan's Intelligence Service
SEP	Surrendered Enemy Personnel
shamag	square cloth worn to keep the sun's rays off one's head
SOAF	Sultan of Oman's Air Force
souk	market
Strikemaster	Single-engined jet fighter ground-attack aircraft
tell	Archaeological mound. Remains of a settlement
Ureed	I want
Wali	Governor of a province or district

APPENDIX

Text of leaflet dropped in the Wadi Darbat in 1971.

★ ★ ★

In the name of God, the compassionate, the merciful. From the faithful men who are true in what they undertake for God. Some have died; the others are still waiting without deviating. God is true in what he has said.

★ ★ ★

Brothers in the mountains, in the plains, in the villages, in the towns and everywhere in this beloved country, you have been the sword to protect your country, to keep your dignity and to swear your faith. Do not be a hammer to knock down the fence of your spirit and belongings which is the Religion. The Religion has the key of your life and of the other life. The communists are waiting to trap you; do not allow them to oppress you; do not lose hope of rescue. The strong in faith is he who builds up the Religion and protects it. Be this faithful one; be this strong fortress to enable the lost to find his home. Protect your country, your brother and keep your family in righteousness by joining your national and faithful Government which carries out things for you. You cannot perform your duties unless among your relatives and with your Government. WE AWAIT YOU!

The communists do not serve your rights, do not fit with your beliefs. The communists are your worst enemies; do not let them deceive you. Listen my brother to what the communists have said and done. Listen that you may distinguish right and wrong. The communists said, 'THERE IS NO GOD WHO CREATES EVERYTHING'. The communists do not recognise the prophet MUHAMMED (blessing be upon his name) and others of God's prophets. There is no place for right amongst the communists. The communists, my brother, allow illegal things and the removal of the rights of man. These things are known to you. They kill fathers and leave the children as orphans. All these things have been done by the communists and carried out within sight and hearing of YOU. You are their protectors in an indirect way. You are their fuel and their slaves and later on you will be their target. Be careful for yourselves before it is too late. Start to join God's party. God's party will be the winners. The victory is yours for eternity my Muslim brothers. The death is for God's enemies, for those who are also your enemies and against freedom, dignity and Holy Islam. The Muslim fighters from all DHOFAR have joined Islam's party which is under Qabus' leadership. Start working hard and honestly to finish the communists in order to satisfy God and to purify this country which has been stained with the blood of criminals. Start my brothers, to link up with your brothers and to take your natural place in the service of your Government and country, which is your service because you have the most to benefit from this. Your Government welcomes you, looks after you, protects you, assures you of your rights and watches out for all your rights.

Come freely to the holy fight and enjoy all that your Government has ensured and done for you during these few months.

You are your own masters; do not try to suffer for others. God will ensure the victory whenever you fight for him.

Islam is our way. Freedom is our aim.

INDEX

249